EXPERIENCING TRANSLATIONALITY

This innovative book takes the concept of translation beyond its traditional boundaries, adding to the growing body of literature which challenges the idea of translation as a primarily linguistic transfer.

To gain a fresh perspective on the work of translation in the complex processes of meaning-making across physical, social and cultural domains (conceptualized as translationality), Piotr Blumczynski revisits one of the earliest and most fundamental senses of translation: corporeal transfer. His study of translated religious officials and translated relics reframes our understanding of translation as a process creating a sense of connection with another time, place, object or person. He argues that a promise of translationality animates a broad spectrum of cultural, artistic and commercial endeavours: it is invoked, for example, in museum exhibitions, art galleries, celebrity endorsements, and the manufacturing of musical instruments. Translationality offers a way to reimagine the dynamic entanglements of matter and meaning, space and time, past and present.

This book will be of interest to students and scholars in translation studies as well as related disciplines such as the history of religion, anthropology of art, and material culture.

Piotr Blumczynski is Senior Lecturer in Translation and Interpreting at Queen's University Belfast. He is the author of *Ubiquitous Translation* (2016), co-editor of *The Languages of COVID-19* (2023) and editor-in-chief of the journal *Translation Studies*.

EXPERIENCING TRANSLATIONALITY

Material and Metaphorical Journeys

Piotr Blumczynski

NEW YORK AND LONDON

EXPERIENCING TRANSLATIONALITY

Material and Metaphorical Journeys

Piotr Blumczynski

NEW YORK AND LONDON

Designed cover image: © Getty Images

First published 2023
by Routledge
605 Third Avenue, New York, NY 10158

and by Routledge
4 Park Square, Milton Park, Abingdon, Oxon OX14 4RN

Routledge is an imprint of the Taylor & Francis Group, an informa business

© 2023 Piotr Blumczynski

The right of Piotr Blumczynski to be identified as author of this work has been asserted in accordance with sections 77 and 78 of the Copyright, Designs and Patents Act 1988.

All rights reserved. No part of this book may be reprinted or reproduced or utilised in any form or by any electronic, mechanical, or other means, now known or hereafter invented, including photocopying and recording, or in any information storage or retrieval system, without permission in writing from the publishers.

Trademark notice: Product or corporate names may be trademarks or registered trademarks, and are used only for identification and explanation without intent to infringe.

ISBN: 978-1-032-45987-5 (hbk)
ISBN: 978-1-032-46545-6 (pbk)
ISBN: 978-1-003-38220-1 (ebk)

DOI: 10.4324/9781003382201

Typeset in Bembo
by Taylor & Francis Books

For Lauren

CONTENTS

List of figures		*viii*
Acknowledgements		*x*
	Introduction	1
1	What does translation do?	7
2	Squaring the circle: Episcopal translations	45
3	Holy bones: Translations of relics	83
4	From gift shops to the Custom Shop: Translationality for sale	144
5	The experience of translationality	174
	References	*195*
	Index	*206*

FIGURES

1.1	A group of mountaineers carrying their gear	11
1.2	Concentric shock waves on water "moving" outward from the point of impact	25
2.1	The First Council of Nicaea. Detail of a fresco from the church of St. Nicholas, Demre, southern Turkey	54
2.2	The Reformation Wall in Genewa, Switzerland, with statues of the four main proponents of Calvinism: William Farel, John Calvin, Theodore Beza, and John Knox	69
3.1	The Basilica of St Ambrose, Milan, Italy	86
3.2	The silver reliquary of St Adalbert (Wojciech) of Prague in the Gniezno Cathedral, Poland	89
3.3	Damaged sarcophagus in the church of St Nicholas in Demre (ancient Myra), Turkey	95
3.4	Seventeenth-century icon of the translation of the relics of St Nicholas of Myra	97
3.5	The Holy Shroud of Turin, Italy	104
3.6	A golden reliquary containing the relics of merchant and martyr Saint Cugat in the Basilica de Santa Maria Del Mar in Barcelona, Spain	110
3.7	"Shrine of St Patrick's hand". A silver gilt arm-reliquary on display in the Ulster Museum, Belfast, Northern Ireland	124
3.8	The heart of St Laurence O'Toole. Christ Church Cathedral, Dublin, Ireland	124
3.9	Queen Elizabeth II's funeral procession on 19 September 2022	134

3.10	The Chairman Mao Memorial Hall on Tiananmen Square in Beijing, China	141
4.1	Palaeolithic rock painting in the Altamira cave, Santillana del Mar, Cantabria, Spain	147
4.2	A variety of electric guitar models	150
4.3	Eric Clapton's Fender Stratocaster "Blackie" on display in the Guitar Center in New York City, USA	152
4.4	A close-up view of a vintage heavy relic electric guitar	162
5.1	A printer's tray	181
5.2	A collection of guitars	190

ACKNOWLEDGEMENTS

This book was conceived and largely written during an unprecedented global pandemic that shook the world as we knew it, transforming many of the established forms of social interaction, patterns of work and leisure, and countless other aspects of life.

Given the strong material focus of this book and its central theme of movement, it is somewhat ironic that my research and writing coincided with extended periods of involuntary immobility during national and local lockdowns. This had a dual effect. For one thing, being unable to (re)visit many of the sites I wrote about, I was forced to rely on my memory and imagination, which made me realize and appreciate the power of translationality even more. Meanwhile, I was able to consult a broad range of excellent materials available remotely. I owe an outstanding debt of gratitude to an army of people who compile and develop digital archives, enable the sharing of academic resources, manage and maintain the digital infrastructure, and make it possible for researchers like me to carry on with their work from behind computer screens. Your service may be discreet and invisible but it should never be taken for granted.

I am immensely grateful to an extended circle of scholars who have been willing to listen to my ideas, share their reactions, and offer valuable insights. Starting closest to home, I am indebted to my wonderfully supportive friends and colleagues from the Centre for Translation and Interpreting at Queen's University Belfast: Sue-Ann Harding (who inspired me to include images in this book), Chen-En (Ted) Ho, and Kathleen Kaess. Early conversations with David Johnston and Stephen Kelly helped me find a more robust conceptual fabric for my intuitions. As the manuscript was taking shape, Susan Bassnett, Adam Głaz, Maciej Litwin, Marek Kuźniak, Neil Sadler, Elżbieta Skibińska, Ye Tian, África Vidal Claramonte, and Yuan (Gabby) Zou kindly agreed to be critical readers for selected parts and offered a fantastic mix of supportive comments, corrections, and recommendations. Matt Valler's perspective on materiality was exceptionally helpful, as was his advice on various aspects of this book, including the title.

Special thanks go to Kobus Marais for providing both generous encouragement and much-needed challenge; in fact, it was a question (he may not even remember) he asked me at a conference in Hong Kong back in 2018 that kept pushing me deeper into translationality. This is complexity and emergence at work as raindrops combine into torrents.

Over the last few years, I have benefitted from opportunities to share my provisional findings with several academic communities. I am very grateful to Sergey Tyulenev and Binghan Zheng for the invitation to speak at Durham University, to Saihong Li for having me at the University of Stirling, and to the audiences at both seminars for their meaningful engagement.

The Nida Centre for Advanced Research on Translation in Rimini, Italy, has provided an essential forum for exchange and collaboration. Our monthly zoom meetings—bringing together Stefano Arduini, Brian James Baer, Paul F. Bandia, Salah Basalamah, Anna Chiara Bassan, Susan Bassnett, Bella Brodzki, Antonia Carcelén-Estrada, Kobus Marais, Salvatore Mele, Christi A. Merrill, Babli Moitra Saraf, Siri Nergaard, Vicente L. Rafael, Carolyn Shread, Sherry Simon, Giuliana Schiavi, and Michelle Woods—have been precious moments of togetherness in the otherwise grim reality of lockdowns and restrictions. The 2022 summer school "Exploring Translational Modes: Practices, Objects, Life Forms", that most of us were able to attend in person in Rimini, was an unforgettable reunion.

Elysse Preposi, Louisa Semlyen, and Harry Dixon from Routledge, have been, as always, excellent and made the publication process exceptionally smooth. I am also indebted to the two anonymous reviewers for backing my proposal with remarkable enthusiasm.

Some time has passed since I had a chance to acknowledge the vital support of my loved ones. In those few years, Ms MacKenzie has become Ms Blumczynski, and the number of child seats in my car has grown from one to two. My Lauren, my Senan, and my Alex—I love you more than you know. Thank you for your energy, patience, good humour, understanding, and endless help. Without you, I would not know the first thing about experiencing translationality.

INTRODUCTION

There is much discussion and little agreement within translation studies these days about its central concept. The ground is shifting, and considerably so. These tectonic shifts are causing tensions, ruptures and general upheaval as some territories recede and others emerge and become elevated. The meta-translational movements are not always clearly or immediately visible but can often be sensed or experienced. To many of us researching, teaching, studying, practicing, and otherwise dealing with translation, something feels different. Translation is not quite what it used to be.

Here is one dimension of this change, as I see it. Much of the traditional and dominant discourse in translation studies has been unapologetically concerned with human agency. We are used to discussing translational acts, decisions, strategies, approaches, purposes, agendas, processes and so on. We like to think of translation as *something we do*. That is in no small measure because the dominant view of translation focuses on messages, texts, languages and cultures—but largely ignores or glosses over the greater, more profound entanglements of matter and meaning, space and time, past and future. Yet it is quickly becoming clear that this limited and limiting view cannot dominate for much longer. As the Anthropocene continues to set in, translation cannot remain locked "into a defunct discourse of human exceptionalism that ignores the multiple signifying capacities of the species and objects with which we share an increasingly beleaguered planet" (Cronin 2020: 373). No one can doubt that the human species has unleashed forces it cannot control. We had better get accustomed to being on the receiving end of the influence we have proudly asserted over global ecosystems. Having translated our world, we are coming to realize that the world is translating us, whether we like it or not. Translating in a variety of ways, including the most basic, near-etymological sense (which is the main focus of this book): causing our bodies to move along, pushing us out of places that are becoming

2 Introduction

inhospitable and soon likely inhabitable, into new locations, configurations, and entanglements. Translation is upon us.

This material translational movement should hardly come as a surprise. After all, one of the oldest and most widespread conceptualizations of translation is transfer. It is so deeply entrenched in many languages that bypassing it in discourse seems virtually impossible. To translate is to move (meaningful) things around, even if only on etymological grounds. The precise images vary slightly—objects may be carried across a divide (*transfero* in Latin; *translate* in English), lifted over a barrier (*przekładać* in Polish; *übersetzen* in German), repositioned or turned over (*fānyì* in Chinese); subjects may be led from one place to another (*traduire* in French; *traducir* in Spanish; *perevodit'* in Russian)—but in every case, meanings are viewed as mobile enough to travel and concrete enough to be traced.

This concreteness, paired with the commonsensical ontological assumption that whatever is transferred does not cease being itself in the process, may be interpreted as supporting invariance. It is on this point that the idea of translation as transfer is usually challenged. Over the last several decades, considerable scholarly effort has gone into demonstrating that meanings *do* change in translation; that linguistic and cultural frameworks differ substantially, making comparisons problematic (hence the crisis of the idea of equivalence); and that the interpretive nature of the translation process makes it impossible to isolate the content (WHAT) from its context (WHO, WHEN, WHERE, WHY, and HOW). These are all good reasons to be suspicious of the concept of translation as simply moving stuff around—especially once we consider that linguistic translations involve imagined rather than material transfer. Translated texts do not disappear from their original location so that they can reappear elsewhere, in another language (rather, they multiply as new versions); the trajectory of their "movement" cannot be traced in strictly spatial terms. The underlying conduit model of communication has repeatedly been exposed as unable to account for the complex work of translation. Meanings are not shipped around like parcels from the sender to the addressee.

However, it is worth pointing out that even material transfers do not imply or guarantee invariance. Parcels do not always arrive at their destination intact. Objects subjected to transfer usually have to be wrapped in protective material, handled with care, kept at a certain temperature, and insured to mitigate against the undesirable change we call damage or decay. It seems, therefore, that some degree of change is presupposed in all transfer, be it physical or figurative, and attributing an expectation of invariance to all transfer-based models is an unhelpful simplification. Still, it makes more sense to speak about meaning-making as well as meaning-taking, negotiating and constructing—rather than merely conveying it, passing it along. A whole new vocabulary has emerged to describe translational phenomena from various angles (transcreation, transposition, transmediation, translaboration, resemiotization, cinematization, trans-editing, translanguaging, are only a few examples), though it is striking how many of them continue to rely on the prefix *trans-*, thereby evoking the idea of movement.

Introduction 3

At the same time, there is a growing recognition in the discipline that in liberating translation from its etymological shackles, we have likely lost sight of its material dimension and may have effectively thrown the baby out with the bathwater. After all, even the imagined "textual transfers" are mediated materially, whether your tablet is made out of clay or from electronic components, and whether the inscribed page you are holding is velum or cellulose. One way of addressing this perceived loss has been through the so-called material turn emphasizing the strong links between the medium and the message, though the focus continues to be on texts, whose "movement" is predominantly metaphorical—hence the inverted commas. More often than not, texts are "transferred" (metaphorically) rather than transferred (materially), and this trend will only increase as our communication moves even deeper into electronic channels. Pushing this argument to its logical conclusion, we need to accept that linguistic and textual "translations" are metaphorically modelled on material translations, whatever they might be.

This insight is quite clearly at odds with much of the conventional wisdom of the discipline. The legacy of Roman Jakobson's (1959) view about the central place of "translation proper" in the broader translational taxonomy lingers. Upon closer scrutiny, Jakobson's taxonomy is anything but broad: it presupposes that translation of any kind involves language. Consequently, it is often argued that non-textual translations (for example, of people, objects or places) are somehow extended, enlarged, or metaphorical—implying that the core, basic, fundamental concept and practice is interlingual translation. I find this opinion both intellectually and experientially unconvincing. First, following Kobus Marais's (2019) argument, from a semiotic perspective, (inter)lingual translation is but one instance of a fantastically wide spectrum of translational phenomena, and there is no reason to grant it a conceptually privileged position. In short, there is nothing inherently proper about "translation proper". The concept of translation as a fundamentally material transfer highlights a richer and more complex network of relationships and influences between various parties and objects involved in it than could be gleaned from textual "transfers". Material translations stress not just the start and end points of the journey (in lingual translations conceptualized metaphorically as "source" and "target" texts and contexts) but also the trajectory of the movement, the distance covered, the required energy and resources, issues of ownership, responsibility, and many other relevant questions. Textual "movement" may be (partially) understood by studying actual, non-metaphorical, material movement—but not the other way around. In short, to understand translation—including the most basic, fundamental terms used to refer to this phenomenon—we need to look beyond the traditional remit of translation studies.

This, to me, is both a humbling and a troubling realization. Humbling, because important things are to be learned in areas which have long been ignored or deemed irrelevant. Troubling, because the development of much of translation studies theorization seems, so to speak, unnecessarily convoluted—not historically

4 Introduction

but conceptually. Perhaps we should have known better than to settle, as a discipline, for a narrow, linguistic view on translation and allow it to be gradually expanded. As I will demonstrate in the following pages, that "initially narrow" concept was not quite the initial one. And the really initial one was not at all narrow.

This book responds to and engages with the recent research programme spearheaded by Kobus Marais, that seeks to overcome that "unhealthy bias toward language" (2019: 10) while attempting to formulate a (more) "comprehensive theory of translation that explains not only translational phenomena of all kinds, but also pragmatic, social embeddedness, and creative power of translation" (2019: 4). My contribution lies in demonstrating that some uses of the words *to translate* and *translation* not only challenge the central place assigned by Jakobson (and many other scholars after him) to "translation proper"—but are also, strictly speaking, non-metaphorical and in this sense primary. I suggest that a number of conceptions, both popular and scholarly, about what it means to translate can be traced to two related senses of this word, nearly forgotten but still attested in dictionaries of English: (a) "To transfer or move (a bishop, minister, etc.) from one ecclesiastical post to another" and (b) "To transfer or move (the dead body or relics of a saint, ruler, or other significant person) from one place to another" (*Oxford English Dictionary* 2022). A study of translations involving human bodies, both living and dead, allows us to gain a fresh understanding of a range of ideas often invoked in relation to translation, such as authority, power, patronage, authenticity, reception, fitness for purpose, functionality, and so on. It also opens up new perspectives on the "dark side" of translation: fraud, deceit, theft, hoax, violence, coercion, subjugation, and so on. In addition to these specific insights, arguably the most important theoretical contribution of this book is the claim that translationality—in short, "what makes translation a translation"—is a profoundly experiential category. Ancient and medieval translations could be seen, heard, smelled and felt as genuine (or not), and this sensory experience is still at the core of translationality.

Back in 1991, in *The Translator's Turn*, Douglas Robinson set out, in his own words, "to displace the *entire* rhetoric and ideology of mainstream translation theory, which … is medieval and ecclesiastical in origin, authoritarian in intent, and denaturing and mystificatory in effect" (1991: 260). Thirty years on—acknowledging my indebtedness to many of Robinson's (2017) insights concerning translationality itself—I propose to revisit much of this ancient, medieval and ecclesiastical terminology, rhetoric and ideology from a hitherto neglected, non-textual angle, and demonstrate that it is not at all incompatible with a holistic, embodied, somatic view of translation; indeed, that it encourages understanding translation as experience. Drawing on insights from the history of religion and focusing specifically on the reassignment of church officials (called translation) and the tradition known as translation of relics (*translatio reliquiarum*), I argue that translation as a cultural phenomenon and social practice involves a holistic, psychosomatic engagement traceable to corporeal transfer. Despite my focus on historical material and traditions possibly unfamiliar to many modern readers, I make links to a range of contemporary practices. Museums are profoundly translational sites; celebrity endorsement of merchandise invokes translationality; by recreating iconic instruments, guitar manufacturers offer a translational, multi-sensory (visual, tonal, and haptic) link to famous artists. In all cases, a powerful, visceral sense of connection with another time, place, or person is created, demonstrating a key aspect of translationality.

Tempting as it might be, I do not propose yet another turn to highlight the "expansion" of the concept of translation, its "liberation" from earlier restraining shackles, "redemption" from the looming threat of irrelevance brought about by "the relentless tunnel vision of the interlingual in the digital age" (Cronin 2020: 363) or even "return" to some mythical origins shrouded in mystery. Rather, recognizing that the evolution of the concept of translation does not follow a linear trajectory or even spatial expansion but has been existing in parallel realities, so to speak, I suggest approaching it through a higher dimensionality (see Blumczynski and Hassani 2019). In short, *Experiencing Translationality* offers a peek into a parallel universe of translation in which the "linguistic bias" never came to prevail.

Below is a brief summary of the subsequent parts of this book.

Chapter 1, "What does translation do?" sets the conceptual, theoretical, and methodological framework for the inquiry into translationality as an experiential category. After outlining onomasiology and semasiology as two main methods of conceptual mapping, it follows a semasiological approach, exploring the various—historical and contemporary—meanings of the words *to translate* and *translation*, and tracing the relationships between them. It argues that the basic, etymological sense of *transfero* in Latin and *translate* in English, invoking corporeal transfers and material journeys, offers a more historically accurate and theoretically robust centre of gravity for the concept of TRANSLATION than "translation proper", conventionally held as the conceptual core of the discipline. Exposing the conceptual dependence of textual "transfers" on material transfers helps counter the lingering linguistic bias, and dovetails with the main tenets of Kobus Marais's biosemiotic theory of translation. The linchpin of this theorizing effort is translationality understood as a predominantly experiential category. The chapter ends by outlining key theoretical inspirations and methodological commitments: semiotic experience, entanglement of matter and meaning, distributed agency, and ethics of representation.

Chapter 2, "Squaring the circle", considers the origins of episcopal translations (drawing on the canons of the early Ecumenical Councils), and traces the salient examples of this practice from antiquity and the Middle Ages, to Reformation and Counter-Reformation, all the way to the present day, including translations in the time of the global COVID-19 pandemic. The recurrent theme is an irreconcilable tension between doctrine and custom, authority and resistance, gain and loss, centre and periphery, reward and punishment, opportunities and threats, individuals and communities, all interlocking in the translation of bishops—a highly contentious practice: officially condemned and yet persistently carried out.

6   Introduction

Chapter 3, "Holy bones", explores the ancient and medieval tradition of translating the bodies of venerated individuals, or their relics, to places of physical and symbolic elevation. The first part of this chapter follows several notable ancient and medieval translations, exposing some salient themes—completeness and partiality, authenticity and effectiveness, the kairotic quality of translational ceremonies, the benefits and risks of relic translation—as it unravels translation's complex socio-political entanglements. The second part argues that a range of contemporary practices, both religious and secular, still reverberate with the ideas that fuelled the imagination and excitement around the translation of relics in late antiquity and the Middle Ages. The solemn translation of relics—both religious and secular—is one of the best examples of the entanglement of the material and the textual, of memories and dreams, of mourning and hope, of the past, present and future.

Chapter 4, "From gift shops to the Custom Shop: translationality for sale", builds on the key elements of translational movements of living and dead bodies, as well as religious and secular relics, consolidating them into a theoretical and experiential framework within which a range of contemporary cultural phenomena may be better understood. Animated by insights coming from Walter Benjamin, John Berger and Alfred Gell, and engaging critically with the distinction between replicas and relics, the first part of the chapter traces a spectrum of translational experiences deployed for (mostly) commercial reasons in present-day secular shrines such as museums and art galleries. The second part shows translationality as a formidable marketing mechanism employed in the production and sale of custom-made guitars—maximally corporeal instruments—holding the promise of mediating a metaphysical connection with admired artists or historical periods. The chapter closes with an in-depth inquiry into the fascinating history of Eric Clapton's Fender Stratocaster "Blackie" which blurs the distinction between replicas and relics, and between sacrum and profanum, cutting to the core of translational experience.

Chapter 5, "The experience of translationality", having synthesized the findings presented in the previous chapters, extrapolates them beyond their historical contexts as the focus shifts from the public and collective to the private and personal. It argues that the experience of connecting with another reality across temporal and spatial distance through material, sensory mediation, may be a distinctly individual matter. This is supported by an extended reflection on concrete examples of intimately personal translationality, involving a printer's tray and a collection of guitars. The chapter concludes with a call for further research, conducted from various disciplinary and methodological perspectives, into a broad spectrum of translations and translationalities.

1
WHAT DOES TRANSLATION DO?

Regardless of its deceptively abstract title, this book seeks to address a rather simple question, namely: *What does translation do?* The simplicity of this question is, of course, no less deceptive, given that it calls for a book-length response that despite my best efforts remains manifestly incomplete. But before we move on to the response, let us focus on the question itself.

"What does it do?" is a kind of question prompted by curiosity when encountering something intriguing. A complex device, mechanism or contraption. An extra button on an upgraded gaming console. A new app, plug-in or piece of software. A reactive substance. An unfamiliar life form. Anything that can make a change, however large or small, to our world (however broadly or narrowly construed). "What does it do?" is an ambivalent question that can signal fascination as well as anxiety. It may touch on matters of structure, design and operation ("how does it work?") but looks beyond them. "What does it do"—to me, to others, to the world around us? At its core, it is a question about experience.

This is the point of departure for *Experiencing Translationality*. I hope that you will be intrigued by this likely unfamiliar notion and want to think and feel your way into it. This initial emphasis on experience and its ambivalence is absolutely essential in that it pre-defines the main theme of this book. Before we get to translationality itself—to capturing, testing and exploring this concept and phenomenon—we need to be prepared to approach it experientially. This means first of all, being open to evidence coming to us through any and all of the channels of sensory perception—visual, auditory, olfactory, gustatory and tactile—mediated materially, processed mentally and shared socially. Given the limited range of material formats available to research monographs, my argument will necessarily be confined to the visual domain—words and images on the page—but will draw on and appeal to the full experiential spectrum.

DOI: 10.4324/9781003382201-2

In asking "what does translation do?", we make it a subject, and not just in purely syntactic terms. We afford it agency and power to influence its surroundings—and by doing so we decentre the role of human agents, their intentionality and volition. "What does translation do?" is an emphatically different question than "What do we do when we translate?" By making translation the subject, we accept the role of its objects.

Speaking and writing about translation in such terms is often prefaced or accompanied by some qualifications and hedging statements. It's not the *usual* or *typical* use of translation, you know. Not quite the kind of translation taught at universities or practiced as a profession. What we mean here is translation in a *broad* sense, not limited to linguistic operations or literary transcreations. Our concept of translation is *expanded* beyond its *initially narrow* linguistic and textual uses to include various social and cultural practices. It's a *new* and *innovative* view of translation. Perhaps it's a bit of a *metaphor* but that's okay—translation is an *enlarging* category, after all.

I am not going to offer any such pre-emptions. In fact, I intend to challenge the assumptions behind them in the pages of this book because I believe that many of these opinions are confusing, misleading, and in some cases simply untrue. Our current view of translation may or may not be expanding, but what is the framework for comparison? My contention is that early views of translation were not necessarily narrow, or focused mostly on language, or somehow conceptually poorer than later or modern developments. The history of translation theory is not a neat narrative of how chaos became order and simplicity gave way to sophistication. Rather, translation studies has been turning (and tossing, too) for quite some time now, with increasing realization that its object of study is growing, morphing, and slipping out of grasp of the earlier conceptual and theoretical frameworks. In a call to one of the most recent reorientations, labelled the "outward turn", Susan Bassnett and David Johnston stress the need "to expand our ideas about translation beyond the linguistic and to seek a redefinition of what translation actually is. We also need to understand how translation has functioned in the past" (2019: 187). Their call sketches a useful road map for this introductory chapter and indeed the entire project of *Experiencing Translationality*, especially if we reshuffle the sequence they suggest and start from the last stage. Throughout this discussion, my emphasis will be on *what translation does*—because that is how I understand translationality. However, before we start drafting the map, we need to specify its coordinates.

Coordinates: onomasiology and semasiology

In his collection of essays carrying the reassuring title "Science and Sanity", the philosopher Alfred Korzybski (paraphrasing an epigram by the mathematician Eric Temple Bell) famously states: "A map is not the territory it represents, but, if correct, it has a similar structure to the territory, which accounts for its usefulness"

(1933: 58). The importance of this observation for translation will be fleshed out a little later; what matters here is the basic cartographic principle of representation. Now, the territory of translation is rather complicated: it covers some objects, phenomena and processes that are called translations but also others that may not be explicitly given this designation yet are still felt to be in some sense translational. If conceptual explorations—including this one that ventures into translationality—are indeed mappings, then conceptual territories may be charted using two main methods: onomasiology and semasiology.

Onomasiology (from the Greek *onoma*, name) is an approach to studying meanings which starts with a concept—in our case, TRANSLATION (concepts are often rendered in small capitals to distinguish them from words)—and asks how it is expressed. An onomasiological analysis takes different, seemingly unrelated words or expressions and tries to establish links, overlaps and relationships between them, tracing them to a common overarching idea. A key concept in onomasiology is synonymy: a conviction that different words somehow describe more or less the same thing, though from slightly different perspectives. Onomasiological research involves a fair amount of speculation, experimentation and hypothesizing—but also allows a bit of creative license. The challenge is to ensure that the various *what ifs* and *how abouts* are convincing, plausible, and have explanatory power, rather than being mere impressions. Still, onomasiological pursuits are ultimately interpretative, discursive and persuasive: they postulate links between ideas but can seldom claim to have discovered "evidence" or "data" independent from the researcher's gaze. My earlier book, *Ubiquitous Translation* (Blumczynski 2016a), followed such an onomasiological approach. Its purpose was to survey translational phenomena occurring in other disciplines and typically referred to using other names, to demonstrate that the subject matter of translation studies extends far beyond what is usually called translation, and may potentially be found everywhere and anywhere (which is not the same as to say that "everything is translation", as my main premise is sometimes caricaturized). More specifically, I argued that translation has philosophical, theological, linguistic, anthropological, political, historical, social, and ethical dimensions (as well as many others) that are constitutive of it rather than auxiliary.

An opposite method to discussing meanings is semasiology (from the Greek *sēmasia*, signification), and this is the main approach followed in the present book. Here, the point of departure is a word, a specific lexical unit—in our case, the noun *translation* or the verb *to translate*—and the aim is to establish its various senses, sometimes only loosely related to one another. In semasiology, a key concept is polysemy: the recognition that one word may evoke different senses, and the challenge is to trace the links between them. The question is this: when thinkers or practitioners in various fields—and, even more interestingly, across centuries—refer to translating or translation, what exactly are they describing, and why do they choose this word rather than another? In short, what does the word *translation* mean, and why? Of course, this is a question that can meaningfully be asked in only one language at a time—or, with some caution, within a group of related languages. That is why my focus in the following pages is mainly on English and, to a lesser extent, Latin and Greek (for etymological reasons).

Both approaches complement one another (cf. Bartmiński 2009) and address similar questions but do so from different angles. Both my books take as their main premise the ubiquity of translation (though understood a little differently in each instance). Both look beyond the traditional boundaries of translation studies and are uncomfortable with the privileged status of "translation proper". Somewhat paradoxically, despite their titles, *Ubiquitous Translation* is thoroughly concerned with translationality (as the common conceptual element of various phenomena called by different names), and *Experiencing Translationality* firmly draws on certain specific uses of the word *translation*. Underpinning both projects is the fundamental question: What is translation?

In semasiological research, such preliminary definitional queries are not usually seen as a problem. They are not particularly controversial and require little intellectual effort. That is because they are mostly dictated by data. Translation is simply whatever carries this designation. The relevant information can be drawn from dictionaries, corpora, literature reviews, and so on—and merely collecting it is arguably the easy part. The challenge begins when one starts to wonder why a certain practice, process or object is called translation, and how it is related to other things called translations. For example, what does it mean to translate theory into practice (the common ambition of policy-making) or translate anger into votes (as a slogan of a political campaign)? What is translational medicine, and where does this term come from? What is translational lift in aviation? What is a translating sleeve in a jet engine?[1] Are these non-textual translations somehow modelled on the idea of translating a verbal message from one language into another—which translation studies has traditionally held as its conceptual base—or are they independent from it? Which senses are more central, and which more peripheral? Which can be considered primary, and which are derivative? Which are earlier and which developed with time? Which are essential and which accidental? Which are widespread and which idiosyncratic? What do the various kinds of translation have in common, if anything at all? And what is the significance of all these factors in building our understanding of what translation is, and experiencing what it does? These are some of the wider mapping questions that guide the present project.

Carrying things over, moving people around

Having outlined the two main dimensions of conceptual mapping, we can start charting the translational territory following the lines of enquiry suggested by Bassnett and Johnston. Part of understanding "how translation has functioned in the past" involves at least two things: examining the origins of the term and its historical uses. In our case, the first, etymological question is quite straightforward. It is common knowledge that the English words *to translate* and *translation* are derived from the Latin verb *transfero*, meaning "transfer" or "carry across".

Now, translation studies scholars are usually very quick to take this idea and apply it to languages, texts, and works of literature, before even more quickly debunking it as metaphorical, inadequate, limited, and so on. Therefore it is important to stress what should be obvious but often is not: namely, that on etymological grounds, translation and transfer (which semantically are the same word, despite using different stems, *fero* and *latum*), either in English or in Latin, do not in any way privilege linguistic or textual "transfers". In fact, I immediately stress the figurative use of this term by putting it in inverted commas. The conceptual basis behind the word *translation* is maximally concrete: it is an image of someone carrying something—prototypically using their hands, but just as well using baskets, bags, backpacks or any other containers (see Figure 1.1)—from one place to another.

The implications of this observation are immense. Contrary to objections against transfer as a mechanistic or automatic activity (which comes from metaphorizing it in the first place), it is a very human act. Carrying things from one place to another means feeling their size, shape, texture and weight—sometimes also their smell and taste. It means choosing the most adequate path (not necessarily the shortest one), avoiding obstacles, overcoming the physical force of gravity and the psychosomatic sense of exhaustion. Carrying things across takes effort and requires planning. It implies a sense of value (hence an ideology) and a purpose (why would anyone carry something useless or irrelevant?). Fragile objects must be carried with care. Carrying objects too heavy for one person

FIGURE 1.1 A group of mountaineers carrying their gear.
© Media Whalestock | Dreamstime.com

requires collaboration and coordination, pooling and sharing resources, and entering into a complex dynamic of obligations, concessions, favours and debts. Relocating things immediately throws up questions of ownership, power, and control. Translation is work in the strict physical sense: it is "the energy transferred to or from an object via the application of force along a displacement".[2] Seeing translation as material transfer directly highlights a range of insights that translation theory only reached after a long time of sustained reflection, and only after some unhelpful illusions and simplifications had been abandoned. Carrying things across is a profoundly material, purposeful and contextual process with psychosomatic, social, economic, ideological and countless other corollaries. Thus defined translation is implicated in a myriad of forces, influences, experiences, allowances and constraints. And that is before we even started considering anything spoken, signed or written down.

This brings us to the second element of the brief historical overview of translation from a semasiological perspective. What did the verb *to translate* come to mean across centuries? In its extensive entry, *Oxford English Dictionary* (2022) having first discussed a group of various meanings developed around figurative or metaphorical transfer ("to convert from one language to another and related senses"), moves on to the second main group of uses describing material transfer ("to convey from one place, position, etc., to another"). In this section, the first transitive usage is defined as follows: "To convey or move (a person or thing) from one place to another; to transfer or transport (a person or thing); to exile or deport (a person or people)". What is striking is that in every instance of this movement people are mentioned before things! Translation, in one of its basic historical uses, is about moving people—in the most literal, material, physical sense. At the same time, this physical movement invokes a broad spectrum of possible inflections: it may be neutral, voluntary or forced, friendly or hostile, as evidenced by the various synonyms. Translation transports, but also exiles and deports.

Importantly, translating as moving people and things is not attested as being in any way later or earlier than translating as converting meanings between languages. Both senses stretch back to the beginnings of Modern English in the late 14th century. Traces of textual translation are found in Chaucer ("Thow hast translatid the romauns of the rose", c. 1395) and bodily translation in Wycliffe ("þou settedest þi woordis. þat translatid … shulde ben þe bones of oure kingis & þe bones of oure faders fro þis place", c. 1382). With time, the former sense started to dominate and the latter waned—so much so that some specific usages are now considered "chiefly historical" or "obsolete". Among these are the following: (a) "To transfer or move (a bishop, minister, etc.) from one ecclesiastical post to another" and (b) "To transfer or move (the dead body or relics of a saint, ruler, or other significant person) from one place to another" (*Oxford English Dictionary* 2022). Each of these will be considered in detail in the subsequent parts of this book, exploring episcopal translations (Chapter 2) and translations of relics

(Chapter 3), respectively, but for now it is important to stress that the linguistic and corporeal senses of translation—as well as a number of their various conceptual hybrids[3]—have historically co-existed and illuminated one another. But that does not suggest any conceptual parity or equilibrium. In fact, given that they both draw on the idea of carrying objects across, it is only reasonable to propose that linguistic (metaphorical) transfer draws on material (actual) transfer.

This means that the material practices of bodily translations can help us understand some aspects of textual practices, rather than vice versa. Translating people is a more basic practice—in all conceivable respects: experiential, cognitive, and civilizational—than translating texts. (If you are unsure about it, consider that, from an evolutionary perspective, people carried their babies—and other human bodies unable or unwilling to move on their own—for a very long time before any writing systems were invented.) Still, my main argument is not a chronological one. Establishing the chronological primacy of a certain word sense over another would be notoriously difficult, and I have neither the skills nor resources necessary for such a venture. Consequently, I do not claim that references to translated bodies necessarily *predate* mentions of translated texts—but that both draw on a common concept which is (mostly) literally applied to the former phenomenon and (mostly) metaphorically to the latter. As we will see, this insight runs counter to the conventional wisdom of translation studies.

Today, living and dead bodies are unlikely to spring to mind as the most obvious objects of translation but the notion of corporeal transfer, with its rich material and symbolic significance, is arguably still behind a number of conceptions—including preconceptions and misconceptions—both popular and scholarly, about what it means to translate. That valid, valuable and relevant scholarly insights can be drawn from corporeal translation is demonstrated by the fact that some of its rather obvious aspects are now being picked up, in a somewhat roundabout way, in various innovative strands of research in translation studies which focus on performance, materiality, energy, and so on.

Still, among the translation studies community, the awareness of non-textual translations is very limited. Despite his admirable erudition in offering what is possibly the most extensive hermeneutic account of translation in his classic *After Babel* (1998), George Steiner does not mention translated bodies, whether dead or living, once! Could the approach signalled in the subtitle ("aspects of language and translation") have such blind-siding effects? Likely so, considering that the rare mentions of corporeal transfers are made on the margins of "properly textual" studies and are usually presented as curiosities or pieces of trivia not really deserving of serious attention. Here are several recent examples.

On the first page of his preface to *Translationality: Essays in the Translational-Medical Humanities* (2017), Douglas Robinson mentions

> various kinds of transfer or conveyance from place to place: of a human body to heaven without dying (Elijah was 'translated' to heaven in a chariot of

fire), of a bishop from one diocese to another, or a holy relic from one shrine to another, or of a disease from one part of a body to another.

(2017: viii)

—but gives them no further thought in the nearly three hundred pages that follow, which is hardly surprising given that bodily translations in his account involve heaven-bound chariots of fire.

At the other end, in the concluding paragraph of her chapter in the volume *Hybrid Englishes and the Challenges of/for Translation*, Karen Bennett observes that, "[i]n the medieval period, translation was a far-reaching concept, with a vertical as well as a horizontal dimension" (2019: 209), and in the final endnote, she quotes an encyclopaedia entry which notes that in Middle English, "flowers, bishops, captured peoples and the relics of saints are all translat[ed] from garden to garden, see to see, kingdom to kingdom, shrine to shrine" (Watson 2008: 76 cited in Bennett 2019: 2011). One cannot help but wonder when and how we lost this rich, multidimensional view of translation as bodily movement? Over centuries, it seems to have been relegated to the fringes of dominant accounts of textual translation.

I mean this quite literally: in an endnote under her article "Translation and Religion: Issues of Materiality", Anne O'Connor comments that in the Christian tradition, "the word 'translate' has been used not just for the movement of words, but also the movement of relics and people" (2021: 15). This sequence speaks for itself: the figurative "movement of words" takes precedence over the material movement of dead and living bodies. The scope of what translation does appears to have narrowed quite radically, pushing corporeal transfers to a peripheral position. But it is important to remember that it once was centre stage, defining key aspects of translationality. It is there that its traces still remain: translationality can only be fully appreciated, understood and indeed experienced if one bears in mind (by the way, another reference to metaphorical "carrying") its corporeal origins.

Linguistic fixation: translation proper—appropriation—property

This discussion of shifting emphases between the central and peripheral senses of the word *translation* brings us straight to one of the main challenges faced by semasiological research. *Oxford English Dictionary* (2022) or similar resources can help us identify various uses of the word *translation* or *to translate* reflecting its different shades of meaning, but it will not establish clear structures of relationships between them. Dictionaries and corpora offer lists (arranged according to certain logical criteria, I grant that) but not maps or genealogies. Yet it does not take long to realize that many semasiological questions concern issues of importance, expressed in various ways: chronological (primacy), geographical (spread), quantitative (volume or coverage), qualitative (significance), frequential (popularity), and so on. However understood or measured, importance is influence, and influence is power. It is only natural to expect that in asking questions about central and peripheral instances, primary and secondary senses, literal and metaphorical applications, and trying to find answers, one will stumble upon tensions, disagreements and controversies. Egos are hurt, toes are stepped on, concerns are voiced about trespassing and hogging. Fears are expressed that translation risks dilution, losing its flavour and becoming too vague to be a meaningful or useful concept anymore. It is not rare to come across opinions—though more often implied than expressly stated—that something "is not *really* [a] translation" or "not a *real* translation" or that it constitutes only an unusual, weird, marginal, imprecise or otherwise negligible use of the concept. That of course implies some benchmark, yardstick or prototype against which various uses of the term are gauged. Much as "we need to expand our ideas about translation beyond the linguistic" (Bassnett and Johnston 2019: 187), it is worth asking how this linguistic fixation came about in the first place.

The elephant in the room is of course the tripartite definition proposed by Roman Jakobson in his 1959 essay "On Linguistic Aspects of Translation". The clue is already in the title. Despite many later attempts to broaden the scope of his categories (especially the last one), Jakobson's view of translation of any kind involves language: "We distinguish three ways of interpreting a verbal sign: it may be translated into other signs of the same language, into another language, or into other, nonverbal system of symbols" (1959: 233). The first process is "interlingual translation or *rewording*", the second "interlingual translation or *translation proper*", and the third one "intersemiotic translation or *transmutation*"—but all three kinds of translations begin (and two of them also end) with "verbal signs" (233; original emphases). Jakobson's insights are both nuanced and commonsensical, as you would expect of a polyglot, but they proceed from an unshakable assumption that translation is fundamentally and exclusively a matter of language.

To a linguist, what could be better than a language? Two languages, of course! Given Jakobson's fascination with language in general and his fluent command of several languages, it is not at all surprising that translation employing two verbal "codes" or "systems", as he calls them, holds the central, dominant place in his classification. Rewording and transmutation are kinds of translation because they both involve a language, but only an operation between two languages is the prototypical, ideal, "proper" model. There can be little doubt that this designation is evaluative and delimiting.

Calling one category in a taxonomy "proper" automatically creates a conceptual hierarchy that renders all remaining categories somehow "less proper". The structure of Jakobson's own argument proves that: having defined the three kinds of translation, he devotes only one short paragraph to its intralingual variety (a rather uninspiring discussion of the partial synonymy between "bachelor", "celibate" and "unmarried man") and pays no further attention to intersemiotic translation. From then on, clearly all translation worth discussing and analysing is interlingual. This "properization" of interlingual translation effectively amounts to "selective appropriation"—a standard framing procedure "realized in patterns of omission and addition designed to supress, accentuate or elaborate particular aspects of a narrative" (Baker 2019: 114). In this case, rather than relying on omission or addition, framing involves the amount of attention given to the preferred category. "Translation *proper*", having *appropriated* the broader concept, delimits the *properties* of translation (what it is and what it is not), and thus becomes a *property*. It is now *owned* by linguists and other gatekeepers of textual processes. It must be guarded, watched over and policed. If this sounds like an overly dramatic and exaggerated allegation, here is Jakobson again: "Widespread practice of interlingual communication, particularly translating activities, must be kept under constant scrutiny by linguistic science" (1959: 234). This scrutiny should include, in his view, production of "bilingual dictionaries with careful comparative definition of all the corresponding units in their intention and extension" as well as "differential bilingual grammars [which] should define what unites and what differentiates the two languages in the selection and delimitation of grammatical concepts" (234).

It is worth noting that the vocabulary used to describe this "properly translational" reality is unashamedly agentive: *compare, analyse, differentiate, define, select* and *delimit*. Divide and conquer! The scientific scrutiny imposed over translation activities proceeds from a position of asserted authority, knowledge and control. There are no traces of conceptual uncertainty or experiential anxiety of what translation is capable of doing. Appropriated translation, "translation proper", is a thoroughly domesticated beast at the service of its masters: it does as it is told.

Those stubborn metaphors

This sense of ownership of "translation proper" and full control over it organically dovetails with the suspicion of any potentially metaphorical use of the translation concept. Such use tends to be viewed as rebellious and subversive. Objections against some deployments of translation as "metaphorical", meant to strip such uses of any explanatory or scholarly value, are not infrequent and crop up in unexpected places. Let us consider some prominent examples.

In her introduction to the special issue of *Translation Studies* devoted to "the translational turn", Doris Bachmann-Medick (in Kate Sturge's translation) starts from stating the crucial role of "the processes of cultural translation" for the globalizing world society. She notes that "[t]ranslation is opened up to a transnational cultural practice that in no way remains restricted to binary relationships between national languages, national literatures or national cultures" (2009: 2). As "the horizon of translation is expanding and differentiating", she argues that

> Certainly it is not enough to disengage the category of translation from a linguistic and textual paradigm and locate it, as a cultural practice, in the sphere of social action, where it plays an ever more vital role for a world of

mutual dependences and networks. In this respect, important studies within translation studies have long been moving the category far beyond its traditional contexts .... But a "translational turn" goes further because it is born specifically out of the translation category's migration from translation studies into other disciplinary discursive fields in the humanities.

(2009: 3)

This augurs very well for a thorough exploration into translational discourse found across the humanities (and possibly beyond). The success of the translational turn, claims Bachmann-Medick, "depends on the translation category undergoing methodological specification as it moves through the disciplines. Only then will translation fully develop its potential for the study of culture" (3). Her intention is "to open up the agenda for more far-reaching experiments, in a very wide range of disciplines, that attempt to develop the translation category into a more general translational category of investigation and to apply it concretely in more comprehensive cultural analyses" (3).

Welcoming the ever-growing reflection on all things translational across the humanities and social sciences, Bachmann-Medick is keen to see "a translational thinking" widely applied "more than just metaphorically" but at the same time expresses her worry: "will the translation category, as it moves beyond the textual and linguistic level, stubbornly stick to the path of purely metaphorical uses of the translation concept?" (4).

Setting aside their annoying persistence ("stubbornly", "stick to"), what exactly are these "purely metaphorical uses" (note the emphatic adverb)? What are they implicitly contrasted with? It would follow that a meaningful translation of the translation concept worthy of a translational turn would be in some ways non-metaphorical—or at least not *purely* or *just* metaphorical. But, once again, what practice or phenomenon are we talking about? A key to understanding this position lies in Bachmann-Medick's three-stage model of "when a turn becomes a 'turn'" (2007: 25–27). "Metaphorization" is the middle step which comes after "expansion of the object or thematic field" and is itself followed by "methodological refinement, provoking a conceptual leap and transdisciplinary application" (2009: 4). Metaphorization, in this view, signifies a largely intuitive, non-reflective, half-baked, crude grasp that only becomes adequately developed through methodological fine-tuning and a conceptual leap. What I find unclear in this model is whether—and if so, how exactly—a transition from stage two to three incurs a loss of metaphoricity. Are not conceptual leaps (characterizing stage three) metaphorical by definition? Are methodologically refined concepts non-metaphorical? Still, my present purpose is not to question this pattern of "turnification" but to demonstrate that it associates metaphorical uses with earlier stages of conceptual development and thus downplays their usefulness. But is not textual translation a metaphorical construct drawing on material transfer?

Confusing as they are, similar sentiments are echoed elsewhere. In her recent critical examination of various "turns and fashions in translation studies and beyond", Cornelia Zwischenberger (2023) draws on Bachmann-Medick's model and shares its suspicion of metaphorical uses of the concept of translation. Zwischenberger argues that "[i]n order for the concepts behind a turn to become analytical categories and go beyond loose metaphors, considerable conceptual work is necessary" (2023: 7). She notes that

> In fact, the translation concept in cultural studies is applied in a highly (superficially) metaphorical way, for example, when people have to "translate" new experiences, behavioural patterns, values etc. for themselves but there is no explanation of this translation process, for example, in terms of what concretely changes and/or who is affected by this change.
>
> *(2023: 7)*

In this account, metaphors are "loose" and a metaphorical deployment of translation in cultural studies is "superficial" (regardless of the obviously metaphorical sense of both these designations, evoking concepts of density and depth, respectively). Casting the non-textual use of translation in inverted commas openly foregrounds this suspicion: translating experiences, behavioural patterns and values is not "translation proper"—so it is probably not *proper translation*. And definitely not *properly developed* to merit serious examination.

If this approach sounds delimiting, that is not accidental. Bachmann-Medick admits that the aim of the special issue on the translational turn is "to provide an impetus for the expansion of the translation category into the most varied of areas, while also critically scrutinizing and delimiting that category" (2009: 13). She goes on to add:

> For not everything that is called translation generates a "translational turn". In individual cases we must ask very carefully what insights are really gained, what empirical research is furthered by working with the category of translation, and whether we might not merely be witnessing the start of a new metaphor's triumphal march.
>
> *(13–14)*

There is the pesky, obstinate, triumphant metaphor sneaking back in as soon as we let down our critical guard! What I find puzzling is that this undeniably rich, insightful, and thought-provoking article—so wary of the dangers of stubborn metaphorical deployments of translation—in its final lines postulates a multilayered metaphorical construct: "the move" from "an ivory tower of theory and research" onto "hard ground of social and political relationships" (Bachmann-Medick 2009: 14). Are metaphorical arguments fine, after all, but only as long as they do not destabilize our own central concept?

This is a revealing realization. For all the breadth and depth of the translational turn, its admirable scope of ambition and unquestionable insightfulness, Bachmann-Medick insists that "[i]n all these moves outward to wider horizons, clearly the role of language, and with it 'translation proper', cannot be ignored" (2009: 6) and all "efforts of cultural contextualization still need the procedures and positions of textual translation to gain important correctives to a critique of representation that risks sweeping generalizations" (2009: 9). Does all this turning bring us back to the initial position that we apparently never left behind: the underlying conviction that *real, proper, non-metaphorical* translation is linguistic and textual?

An even more conservative position on what constitutes translation and a still more vociferous attack on what is perceived a metaphorical use of this concept are found in Lawrence Venuti's recent book *Contra Instrumentalism. A Translation Polemic* (2019). Here is its opening paragraph:

> Translation is and always has been ubiquitous. Today it figures significantly in the practices housed in many cultural and social institutions—economic and political, legal and military, religious and scientific. The arts and human sciences depend on translation for their invention, accumulation, and dissemination of forms and ideas. Nonetheless, translation remains grossly misunderstood, ruthlessly exploited, and blindly stigmatized. Now is the time to abandon the simplistic, clichéd thinking that has limited our understanding of it for millennia.
>
> *(Venuti 2019: ix)*

One would hope that abandoning this simplistic and clichéd thinking about translation would surely involve opposition to conceptualizing it as a predominantly "linguistic and cultural" operation; that it would leave behind ideas such as "equivalence to the source text" (however "variable") and demands for "writerly and intellectual sophistication"; finally, that it would go beyond trivialities such as "every text is translatable because every text can be interpreted" (Venuti 2019: ix–x). On the contrary—each one of these positions is presented as constituting Venuti's initial "provocations". The first pair is particularly worth noting:

> STOP treating translation as a metaphor.
> START considering it a material practice that is indivisibly linguistic *and* cultural.
>
> *(Venuti 2019: ix; original emphasis)*

There is no doubt that, according to Venuti, it is not only advisable but possible *not* to treat linguistic-cultural translation as a metaphor. In other words, it should be possible to point to some phenomenon or practice that is in some way primary, fundamental, and explanatory of any potential metaphorical extensions (much of Venuti's book is devoted to deconstructing various metaphors of translation that he deems inaccurate, misleading, mechanistic and otherwise supportive of what he calls "instrumentalism"). Moving on to the affirmative elements of his "provocations", we discover what he posits as such fundamental, non-metaphorical notion of translation: "a material practice that is indivisibly linguistic *and* cultural" and involves "the establishment of a variable equivalence to the source text" (ix); at this point, it is also worth noting that Venuti's exclusive focus is on literary and cinematic texts. The mention of a "material [practice]" promises an account of translation that goes beyond a narrow linguistic/literary domain—but it soon becomes clear that Venuti uses the adjective *material* metaphorically (!) to refer to certain linguistic, cultural, and literary imponderables (in what other sense can language be a "material medium" [25] or "materiality of the translated text [risk] vanishing amid philosophical abstraction" [74]?). If this is a provocative view of translation, that is because it dogmatically constrains its (allegedly non-metaphorical) scope to the process of giving texts written in one linguistic, cultural and historical context an expression in another complex context. What is shocking is its conservatism, not innovation.

It is ironic that insisting on a privileged conceptual status of "translation proper" both within and beyond the traditional domain of translation studies brings about exactly those effects that "proper translationalism" is so keen to avoid. Consider this example. The edited volume *Rethinking Medieval Translation: Ethics, Politics, Theory* (Campbell and Mills 2012a) presents a rich account of translation understood beyond a strictly textual and linguistic focus—a welcome and important contribution, no doubt. At the same time, one may wonder to what extent this project (and others like it) achieves what it promises to do, that is *rethink translation*, and how radical this rethinking really is. Following the all-too-familiar narrative, the editors claim that the use of the term *translation* has in recent decades been extended "from primarily linguistic uses to other areas of cultural production, enabling it to function as an explanatory metaphor for practices through which the transformation of cultural forms takes place" (Campbell and Mills 2012b: 13). Is this not exactly the kind of argument that Venuti finds upsetting when he commands: "STOP treating translation as a metaphor" (2019: ix)? Do insights from textual translation really temper metaphorical explanations of culturally transformational practices or offer them any helpful correctives?

I seriously doubt it—and why should they? It is illogical to expect that a metaphorical explanation will somehow reverse its trajectory and recede to its source domain; that would make it counterproductive and nonsensical. Its explanatory power comes precisely from the movement away from its initial base into a new territory. When we say that "theory needs be translated into practice" do we really mean that the nature of this abstract transformation may be elucidated by examining textual operations? Can the complex process of spreading the culture, knowledge and political power from one civilization to another—*translatio studii et imperii*—be explained by restricting the spectrum of all colonizing activities to the rewriting of texts between languages, however "indivisibly linguistic and cultural" (Venuti 2019: ix) we take that practice to be? Once again, I doubt it. "Metaphoric thought creates an excess of meaning that can neither be fully retranslated to the literal meaning nor drained by literal paraphrase" (Guldin 2010: 182). A meaningful and valuable application of the concept of translation across other fields and disciplines depends on the ability to look above and beyond what is covered by the narrow construct of "translation proper". The irony is that by moving towards corporeal translation we arrive at a *less* metaphorical concept!

By now, the tensions and sensitivities involved in semasiological explorations of translation begin to be exposed, accompanied by less-than-enthusiastic acknowledgement of various kinds of anxieties—disciplinary, territorial, reputational, and so on. Ironically, holding on to the dominance of "translation proper" as a fundamental, central, and emphatically non-metaphorical concept, capable of providing "scrutiny" or "correctives" to broader translational enquiries, renders it a rather cumbersome property if not dead weight. Despite its undeniable gravitational pull, it is conceptually incapable of providing a main point of reference for the perpetually expanding universe of translation studies. That is because it is internally conflicted: wrapped around a thoroughly metaphorical concept (of transfer) and yet openly uncomfortable with its own inevitably metaphorical extensions. This self-defeating sense of identity is hardly promising material for our discipline's master concept.

Troublesome transfer

One could object to my argument by saying that it is possible to conceive of "translation proper" apart from the idea of transfer. Perhaps so—after all, other models are possible (rebirth, repetition, contagion, refraction, and so on) but they are so rare that collecting these several examples has required some intellectual effort: they do not immediately jump to mind. More importantly, the problem of metaphorical conceptualization is not solved by swapping one underlying metaphor for another. Meanwhile, the transfer metaphor continues to be one of the most common, instinctively used tropes of theoretical discourse in translation studies in English and a range of other languages. In trying to salvage some shreds of its alleged literalness, it could perhaps be argued that translation of technical texts, especially when accompanied by the introduction of new technologies (both hardware and software) into new physical locations, would lend itself most readily to the image of transfer. Far from it. In fact, the opposite tendency is true: the less tangible the phenomenon under consideration, the more likely metaphorical accounts are. Consequently, transfer discourse is typically found in discussions of abstract ideas, literary compositions or at least texts viewed as having concrete authors and readers—that is, in contexts where it arguably makes little sense to postulate any kind of physical movement. There is no getting away from the image of translation as carrying non-material objects across. Here are a few examples, collected in a rather random fashion from my desk(top) and the nearest bookshelf:

> As texts travel across time, space and different orders of indexicality in translation, they must be re-contextualised.
>
> *(House 2014: 5)*

> [T]exts travel, especially in today's world of continual movement of people and of accelerated and expanded communication.
>
> *(Mason 2014: 44)*

> ... theoretical texts and ideas also travel across and through languages ...; the role that translation has played in the way concepts travel.
>
> *(Harding 2020: 611)*

> ... translation should be taken seriously as one of the major elements in the transmission of ideas, texts and cultural practices.
>
> *(Bassnett and Johnston 2019: 181)*

> ... a fuller picture of the complex material conditions through which ideas and values circulate across languages.
>
> *(Marinetti 2022: 272)*

To be sure, I am not implying that any of these scholars would for a second entertain the notion of ideas or texts traveling through languages and cultures in any other than strictly figurative terms. Even though we know that meanings, ideas and messages do not really change physical location, we still continue to rely on this metaphor as a convenient, near-instinctive way of speaking. Jakobson is well aware of this point: he notes that referring to sunrise and sunset, "we still use this Ptolemaic imagery without implying a rejection of Copernican doctrine, and we can easily transform our customary talk about the rising and setting sun into a picture of the earth's rotation" (1959: 234). Perhaps so—although in our case, transforming the customary talk about translation as transfer into a more insightful, non-metaphorical description is proving anything but easy.

One reason is that in developing any alternative account one would have to break out of a firmly entrenched conceptualization framework. We routinely speak about getting ideas across, spreading information, conveying opinions, putting thoughts into words, etc. That IDEAS ARE OBJECTS and WORDS ARE CONTAINERS for meaning is Cognitive Linguistics 101 (going back over four decades, at least to Lakoff and Johnson's *Metaphors We Live by* [1980], if not all the way to Aristotle's substance metaphysics). This way of speaking and thinking is not only common; it may also be theoretically productive and insightful, as demonstrated by Mieke Bal's *Travelling Concepts in the Humanities* (2002)—a book and its central image which has garnered a lot of excitement in various disciplines (e.g. Berns 2009; Cooke 2009; Neumann and Nünning 2012; Peng-Keller 2019), including translation studies (e.g. Federici 2011; Bachmann-Medick 2012; Blumczynski 2016a; Underhill and Gianninoto 2019; Hsiung 2022; Vidal Claramonte 2022; Zwischenberger 2023). Indeed, translation is often instinctively linked with this idea of traveling ideas—and the link is the image of transfer itself. Zwischenberger explains how

> The translation model developed in organisation studies by Czarniawska and Joerges (1996) and Czarniawska and Sevón (2005) departs from the question of how new ideas can travel in an organisation or institution. Firstly, ideas need to be materialised in order to travel – they need to be turned into objects such as pictures or sounds. They must be written down, spoken out loud or recorded before they can travel. Similarly, Czarniawska and Joerges (1996, 32) note that "the simplest way of objectifying ideas is turning them into linguistic artifacts" … The translation process is completed when the idea ultimately arrives at a new place and is translated into action …. Ideas are kept in motion by the energy produced by each translation.
> *(Zwischenberger 2023: 12)*

The link between translation and energy, signalled here, will resurface throughout this book. For the time being, it is important to register two observations which by now likely start to sound familiar. First, that linguistic transfer, once again, despite some nods to its material aspects, appears to be construed as largely metaphorical (how else can things "written down, spoken out loud or recorded" be said to travel?; what are "linguistic artefacts"?). Second, that this exclusively metaphorical deployment of translation is felt to be somehow unsatisfactory. The comment that "[e]ven if a reference to lingual translation seems to impose itself here, there is no mention of lingual translation, let alone of translation studies" (Zwischenberger 2023: 12) betrays unpleasant surprise, if not disappointment.

It is here that things become complicated further. Enthusiastically embraced in some areas of translation studies as worthy of focused study (e.g. Gonne et al. 2020), in others transfer is no longer viewed as a useful theoretical concept at all. For example, it is not even indexed in the 800+ pages of the third edition of the *Routledge Encyclopedia of Translation Studies* (Baker and Saldanha 2020). Coming from a clearly critical angle, Andrew Chesterman, in his recent essay "Transfer Troubles" (2020), highlights several problematic aspects of this notion, including (a) the hidden assumption of movement; and (b) the hidden assumption of invariance. It seems that the major conceptual effort in translation studies at large has gone into challenging the second assumption. The gradual fading away of the concept of equivalence (no longer deserving an entry in the third edition of the *Routledge*

Encyclopedia of Translation Studies, either) can partially be attributed to a widespread suspicion of invariance. There is no shortage of research underscoring the transformational, creative, epistemological, political and other dimensions of translation, all highlighting change. (As I signalled in the Introduction, attributing an assumption of invariance to all transfer is misguided. We routinely prevent change, identified with damage, from occurring during material transfer, which demonstrates that it is a norm rather than exception. Things tend to change in transfer, usually for the worse).

Meanwhile, the assumption of movement—one would argue, the more fundamental of the two—is often glossed over. It seems nearly impossible to remain in the primary, material domain for long, despite the best efforts. For example, Anthony Pym, in his book *Translation and Text Transfer* (2010[1992]), suggests a conceptual geometry accounting for "the simple moving of inscribed material from one place and time to another place and time" (2010[1992]: 13), and develops this idea thus:

> To the extent that they require material supports, texts move in time and space. Sitting on library shelves, they move through time …; manually, mechanically or electronically reproduced, the can be moved through space; translated, they can move from culture to culture.
>
> *(Pym 2010[1992]: 134)*

It soon becomes clear, though, that the movement described here is already far from literal. Most obviously, the idea of moving "in time" or "from one time to another" metaphorically draws on the material experience of space and distance to conceptualize an entirely different, temporal dimension (cf. Ricoeur 1990). After all, books sitting on library shelves are manifestly inert in physical terms; their "movement through time" is imagined or at the very least *of a different kind* than their relocation to another shelf. Similarly, their reproduction—manual, mechanical or electronic—does not involve any material movement apart from taking the volume off the shelf so that it can be copied, scanned or digitized (which is probably not the kind of movement Pym has in mind anyway). Reproduction is not movement—it is generating more/new material elsewhere. The image of translated texts as moving from culture to culture is almost entirely metaphorical. Consequently, Pym's proposition that "if there were no material transfer, if texts were not moved across time and space, there would be no translation" (2010[1990]: 16), does not concern *material transfer* in the fundamental, non-figurative sense: it has little to do with relocating matter.

In his discussion of some problems created by what he openly calls "the transfer metaphor" (2020: 209), Chesterman points out that in contrast to the transfer of material objects which produces an absence in the original location, "the source text does not automatically disappear when it has been translated"

FIGURE 1.2 Concentric shock waves on water "moving" outward from the point of impact.
© Galló Gusztáv | Dreamstime.com

(210). Translated texts do not move—instead, their new versions, iterations or incarnations emerge in other languages, places, and times. However, having made this clear, Chesterman admits that, "in some sense texts do move, carried by postmen or optical fibers or sound waves or whatever" (210).

Again, it is ironic that even this short list of examples of purportedly actual and material movement of texts cannot avoid slipping onto the metaphorical plane almost immediately. Yes, letters are literally carried by postal workers and printed books are delivered from warehouses to our doorsteps—but optical fibres or sound waves (or other physical media) surely do not "carry texts" in a remotely material sense! Carrying implies a change of position and relies on classical (Newtonian) mechanics that deals with macroscopic objects. But sound waves involve vibrations rather than movement of air molecules across space (even if they did, that still would not make these molecules "texts"), and photons ("particles" of light) have no mass but are rather excitations of the electromagnetic field. In both cases, it is more accurate to speak about propagation of energy than about movement (see Figure 1.2). Summing up, the extent of real, actual, material—one would be tempted to say "proper"—movement attributed to "translation proper" is so marginal that it can be ignored for all intents and purposes. The materiality of translation cannot credibly depend on an imagined movement of texts and meanings.

A double bind

Here is the crux of the issue. The stronger the insistence on the conceptual centrality of "translation proper", the clearer it becomes that it is construed metaphorically. The two tenets of the translational turn—(1) expansion of the concept of translation into other areas (2) while being subjected to the correctives of textual translation viewed as a conceptual anchor—are logically incompatible. "Translation proper" cannot be the ultimate benchmark of all translational phenomena as long as it is founded on the metaphor of transfer (or, for that matter, any other metaphor) because metaphors offer only partial mappings. Ideas are not *really* objects. Meanings do not *really* travel. Communication is not *really* transfer. These are merely conceptual metaphors which allow us to get some grip of the complex, abstract, intangible and mysterious experience of thinking, speaking, and communicating with others.

At this point, a brief terminological comment is in order. In contradistinction to its predominantly evaluative deployment in the arguments discussed above ("metaphorical" as imprecise, loose, crude, underdeveloped, etc.), I refer to metaphor in a strictly descriptive sense as a basic cognitive procedure of understanding one thing (usually something abstract) in terms of another (usually something concrete). This mapping of one domain onto another is always partial: while highlighting some aspects of convergence, metaphors conceal other, divergent aspects. Positing this partiality as a fundamental flaw of metaphorical arguments (which seems to be the ambition of some of their critics who often happen to advocate a privileged position of "translation proper") is a moot point. Of course metaphors offer partial mappings; otherwise they would not be metaphors. Paraphrasing Venuti's (2019: 3) statement about translation, no metaphor "can be understood as providing direct or unmediated access to its source" domain. Its epistemological and hermeneutic power comes from its ability to offer insights that are not universally "true" but immediately relevant and instinctively accessible, often drawing on embodied experience. (Indeed, body and experience are key elements of the argument presented in this book). But the explanatory power of any metaphor comes to a grinding halt as soon as we lose sight of its figurative nature and start treating it as a literal description. For example, how insightful is it to conceptualize translation as "the replacement of a text in a source language by a semantically and pragmatically equivalent text in a target language" (House 2006: 345), and re-contextualization as "taking a text out of its original frame and context and placing it within a new set of relationships and culturally conditioned expectations" (356). Let me guess—it is not *real* "replacement" or "placing within", is it? We lock ourselves into a double bind if we demand that *real* translation must be linguistic/textual while recognizing that linguistic/textual transfers are not *real*.

I would suggest that there are only two ways out of this definitional and conceptual conundrum. One is to drop the assumption that textual translation is somehow conceptually privileged and therefore uniquely capable of illuminating other translational phenomena; the other is to drop the metaphor of transfer (or any other metaphor) and look for a literal, non-metaphorical account of translation (despite the risk that such an account will necessarily be abstract). Ideally, we should be able to take both these steps.

Most theoretical attempts to unravel this knot consist of abandoning one metaphorical framework and replacing it with another conception. Let us have a closer look at what has been proposed. Chesterman, having identified the shortcomings of the transfer concept, suggests memetics as a viable alternative (1997; 2020). Drawing on Richard Dawkins's concept of memes, cultural analogues of genes, he argues that "[g]enes propagate via (mostly) exact duplication, with occasional mutations; but memes, being cultural elements, are less constrained by sameness, and spread via imitation which can be much less constrained" (Chesterman 2020: 211). The same melody can be played on different instruments and with certain variations, or the same joke may be told in different ways, situations and languages, but "it can still remain essentially the same joke" or "the same theme" (212). Chesterman proposes that

> Translations can be seen as ways of propagating memes. Seeing translation through the lens of a memetic metaphor does not need the idea of transfer. The underlying notion here is that of sharing, spreading, propagating, duplication-with-variation … In Darwinian terms, ideas (etc.) can be thus said to spread from one population to another, and also to evolve via inevitable mutations. According to this metaphor, the process of translation is not an equative one of replacement or substitutions, such that there is a target text that somehow equates to a source one. Nor is it a transfer movement involving the transport of something from one place to another. Nor does it imply invariance. Rather, translating is seen as an additive operation: alongside (not instead of) one text, another is created that is relevantly similar to the first one … We might call this a similarity condition (or even … an equivalence condition …). …
>
> After the translation process, the source text A continues to exist (usually) but now alongside a variant of it (A^1), e.g. in another language or medium. …
>
> The memetic metaphor … anchored in a theory of similarity … highlights aspects of translation that are not highlighted by the transfer metaphor: that translation is an additive process, that source texts do not normally disappear after translation, and that mutations are normal.
>
> *(Chesterman 2020: 212–213)*

These are all valid and insightful observations. Highlighting that translation is an additive rather than equative process allows us to go beyond crude comparisons, and chimes rather well with several of Venuti's calls: "STOP assuming that translation is mechanical substitution … STOP evaluating translations merely by comparing them to the source text" (2019: ix–x). But this alignment also signals a weakness if one hopes for a truly semasiological account: like Venuti, Chesterman is clearly working with "translation proper" as his prototypical category (note the repeated references to source texts, etc.). He offers a brief discussion of various non-textual uses of translation, from Shakespeare ("Thou are translated!" in *A Midsummer's Night Dream*) and Salman

28 What does translation do?

Rushdie ("we are translated men") to biosemiotics (translation as semiosic change) and chemistry (genetic information), to mathematics (geometric movement), sociology (translation of ideas), to healthcare (translation of knowledge into clinical practice), but voices his suspicion that "translation scholars will … see all these usages as metaphorical ones" (2020: 218). His conclusion that "[t]he concept itself, or at least the term 'translation' is becoming a meme, like a fashion, as it spreads and mutates" (218) signals a coalescence of onomasiological and semasiological perspectives (are we talking about the concept or the term?) and little interest in explaining the patterns of this spread and mutation.

In the end, by swapping transfer for memetics as the master metaphor for translation, Chesterman is able to expose certain entrenched misconceptions and suggest conceptual correctives, but arguably brings us no closer to understanding what translation is and what it does. Having taken us on a fascinating walk through wonderfully diverse phenomena called translation, Chesterman safely brings us back to where we started: to firmly textual ground. This decision seems to be motivated by a delimiting impulse: "If one can see anything as translation or the result of translation—parks, churches, government organizations etc.—does the concept retain any meaning?" (Chesterman 2020: 219). If this is a genuine question, it demands a serious response, not a dismissal using absolute quantifiers (does he *really* mean "anything"?) and an effective reduction to an absurdity. Who knows: perhaps parks, churches, government organizations and other things do have something in common that allows them to be translated in some sense? What is that sense? How do we make sense of it? How is it related to other senses? Chesterman stresses the value of holding in mind various, even mutually incompatible metaphors for translation, and recommends a critical attitude against their rhetorical power, but is satisfied with a metaphorical account. Yet his final line, "As the map is not the territory, the metaphor is not the thing itself" (2020: 221), offers some ontological hope for the existence of "the thing itself". What is that thing called translation, then, and what does it do?

Another attempt to surpass the limitations of translation conceptualized as transfer is offered by Matthew Reynolds and the contributors to his edited volume *Prismatic Translation* (2019a). Reynolds's initial observation about "translational multiplicity", that "translation breeds more translation" (2019b: 1), announced a radical rupture with the concept of transfer. One facet of this break is pluralizing the traditional definitions,

> so that 'translation' becomes the process of turning from one language into others, *da una lingua in altre*, producing chains of signifiers in target languages, creating multiple equivalent, authentic texts, while 'a translation' correspondingly figures as just one of many actual and/or possible linguistic realisations? Translation's dominant metaphor would change: it would no longer be a 'channel' between one language and another but rather a 'prism'. It would be seen as opening up the plural signifying potential of the source text and spreading

it into multiple versions, each continuous with the source though different from it, and related to the other versions though different from all of them too.

(Reynolds 2019b: 2–3)

But this prismatic view—inspiring as it is—is also explicitly linguistic and textual: the plurality of translations "has its origin in the inherent fluidity of every source text, which in turn arises from the multiple textuality out of which, and into which, every text is woven" (2019b: 7). At first sight, translation appears to be an active force in this account; it is described as "doing" various things:

> It can be hyper-obedient to national standards of correctness and norms of usage: this is the regime of fluency so vigorously denounced by Lawrence Venuti. … Yet it can also push against the forces of regimentation and division, blurring the boundaries between languages, and re-creating an awareness of language as a continuum of variety and change.
>
> *(2019b: 8)*

Yet, despite all its entanglement in nation-state ideologies, in the projects of building empires and subverting them, in the service of "glossodiversity" and "semiodiversity", this "work" of translation is never considered much beyond textual terms. The limits of the prismatic approach come from its own position that "the work of translation is best described as co-creating meaning in both source-text and translation-text" (2019b: 10). The prisms, though "angled in both directions" (7), are thoroughly metaphorical—all they project is "prismatically translational textuality" (13). It would be unfair to criticize *Prismatic Translation* for failing to achieve what is not its purpose—after all, it is not a semasiological project—but it nevertheless needs to be stated that its dual commitment to textuality (effectively, "translation proper") and an explicitly metaphorical conception of it does not bring us closer to understanding what translation—in the broader, arguably more fundamental sense of this word—is and what it does.

Many other conceptual efforts in translation studies follow a similar pattern: brave excursions into new grounds in search of translational phenomena are usually found to be tethered to an assumption of real or imagined textuality. Once again, there is undeniable value in studying all sorts of social, cultural, artistic and material practices intertwined with and constitutive of translation—the problem is that the conceptual framework of "translation proper" tends to cast its long shadow over most such attempts. True, the concept of text is extended to encompass various, not only linguistic semiotic systems, but that is precisely the problem: all these meaningful resources are metaphorically locked into the domain of language and textuality. "[T]he textual turn taken in material culture in the 1980s … advocated approaching objects as texts that could be 'read' against shifting backgrounds and contexts" (Burkette 2016: 318). As a result, "[i]n today's world, images, sounds, sensory perceptions, nonverbal communication, spaces, linguistic spaces, cities, and even bodies are considered texts because they communicate" (Vidal Claramonte 2022: 2). But why does communication need to be textual (metaphorically or not)?

Even something as promising as a debate on the materialities of communication, held several years ago in the journal *Translation Studies*, for all its wealth of important insights (such as "[t]he text is fluid, the objects mobile, and the material of the medium meaningful" [Armstrong 2016: 104]), did not manage to break away from this overpowering textual emphasis. In her initial provocation, Karin Littau, while recognizing that "language, meaning and interpretation … have dominated the humanities, translation studies included" and setting to challenge this paradigm (2016: 83), chose to draw on book history and textual biography:

> Translation brings into focus the instability of language as much as it does that of the physical text. This is a reminder that 'translation is not in some ethereal state' … but is embedded, just like the source text, in a material object, which itself is subject to translation or, we might say, transmediation.
>
> *(Littau 2016: 89)*

The responses largely followed suit; while admitting and exploring the materiality of translation, they invariably conceptualized it in textual—and often also implicitly literary—terms:

> Translation, as a discrete set of interlingual and/or intermedial cultural practices is, and always has been, conducted in and by "things": written texts are produced (and reproduced) by various historically located agents, inscribed into physical or mnemonic storage devices, circulate within social networks, with relative (and mutable) symbolic values, with the discrete object travelling through time and space.
>
> *(Armstrong 2016: 103)*

> [E]ven when cultural context is emphasized over the texts themselves, neither is it possible for translation to ignore the text itself. The translated text is the material container for all the relations it stages as well as matter in itself, which always exceeds or resists being completely subsumed into its relations.
>
> *(Kosick 2016: 316)*

> A glance at common translation praxis immediately reveals how necessary transmediation processes are to translation, and how they involve both immaterial and material elements. The translator takes up meaning from a text in some medium or other (say, a printed book); she creates new meaning in her translation also using some medium, likely not the same one (perhaps first on pencil and paper, or with keyboard and screen).
>
> *(Coldiron 2016: 97)*

If "[c]ommunication happens on many levels, the gestural, the olfactory, the visual, the linguistic" (Campbell and Vidal 2019b: xxv), why does this latter level persistently continue to frame all others? If "*[l]inguistic landscapes* do not refer simply to language displayed in public spaces but also include images, smells, clothes, food and graffiti" (Vidal Claramonte 2022: 3; added emphasis), why are they still *linguistic* landscapes—rather than, for example, experiential or "sensory" (a term suggested by Cronin and Simon 2014: 120) ones? Why are urban translation spaces (Sywenky 2014), and even "the ideas and methods of writers and philosophers, of theorists and practitioners" across translation studies (Bassnett and Johnston 2019: 181), imagined as palimpsests—a doubly textual concept? Are not Chesterman's (2020: 219) reservations (about whether various elements of the urban landscape, such as parks or churches, may be meaningfully "translated") fuelled by precisely this propensity to textualize all translation?

My own work is not immune from this critique. *Ubiquitous Translation*, even though it programmatically refused to define translation in any specific terms, while tracing translational phenomena occurring across various disciplines, repeatedly related them to linguistic and textual practices. Still, I could not quite shake the conviction that translation "is not exclusively an object, but rather a phenomenon and experience … Translation is not just a question of the WHAT but also the HOW, the manner as well as the matter" (Blumczynski 2016a: 27); that "translation is not a lifeless, motionless, a-temporal form, but a complex, pulsating event" (70–71), and translations should not be conceptualized as abstract, objective facts, but rather as "experiences of the perceiving subject, spatiotemporal 'occasions'" (82). This was the beginning of a "eureka moment" which only came later.

A semiotic perspective

If translation must indeed be approached phenomenologically and experientially (for important reflections on translation experience, see e.g. Berman 1984, 2008; Massardier-Kenney 2010; Robinson 1991, 2001), there is no reason to conceptualize it primarily in relation to "translation proper" and within the (inter) linugual framework presupposed by it. Bassnett and Johnston's statement that "the practice of translation [is] broadly conceived as the outworking of translational processes" (2019: 186) is delightfully liberating in its definitional circularity. Their point is that translation can be recognized and experienced as it "operates in terrains beyond the textual—whether in translational medicine, processes of memorialization, or identity politics, to name but three instances in order to exemplify a wide range of professional, cultural, social, individual and political activities" (186). From this perspective, there is nothing "proper" about (inter)lingual translation. Not only that: if some prototype of truly proper translation (without inverted commas) were to be proposed—"the thing itself", in Chesterman's (2020: 221) words; "the territory, not the map", paraphrasing Korzybski (1933: 58)—it *could not* be lingual or textual because, as we demonstrated above, all such conceptualizations of translation draw on more fundamental notions which are material, embodied and experiential.

At this point, my argument dovetails with the position recently advanced by Kobus Marais who in his book *A Bio(semiotic) Theory of Translation* offers a much more extensive body of evidence for what he calls "a bias, in general, toward language, literature and culture in translation studies", concluding that "[a]pproaches such as the sociological and power turns do not change the conceptualization of translation itself. Scholars utilizing these approaches still study interlingual translation … [w]hat was DNA in Jakobson has, thus, developed in a limited way" (2019: 44). Against this narrow construal, Marais offers a much more complex, historically contextualized conceptualization based on the semiotic theory of Charles Sanders Peirce, which is worth quoting here at some length:

> Translation is a process that is being enacted on something, which thing is not itself a translation, but a thing that has been translated or that has come to be through translation. This is why one always conceptualizes translation as 'translation of': translation of language, translation of literature, translation of text, translation of specialist knowledge, translation of pictures, translation of plans.
>
> The various turns in translation studies have usually taken one of these concomitant categories, i.e. language, pragmatics, culture, power, ideology, or society, and turned it into 'the' stuff of translation. Inevitably, someone then came along later and pointed out that translation is more than the translation of language, or the translation of culture, or the translation of literature, or the translation of power. It is my contention that the most profound way of conceptualizing translation is to think of 'translation of meaning'. The 'stuff' of which translation is the process of meaning, meaning in all its myriad of forms, shapes, shapelessness, materialities, instances. A comprehensive theory of translation needs to be embedded in a comprehensive theory of meaning, i.e. semiotics.
>
> *(Marais 2019: 83–84)*

This broad semiotic position allows him to offer a theory of translation that could be used "to study all instances of translation process-phenomena"; consequently, his view of translation includes "semiotic processes in which language does not play a role at all" (Marais 2019: 121). If we are "to understand the full semiotic scope of translationality", he argues, "we need to be able to study the translationality of all and any phenomena"—meanwhile, he is very clear that "a theory limited to language will not provide that to us" because "[l]anguage is only one aspect of translationality" (43).

This is a momentous step; truly a watershed moment. No wonder that Michael Cronin, in his review of Marais's book calls it "discipline changing" for demonstrating that "translation studies has been almost fatally compromised by a misreading" (2020: 371). In fairness, it was not so much a misreading as an appropriation; the problem was not carelessness, incompetence or misapplication but rather a strictly disciplinary focus resulting in tunnel vision. In his essay "On Linguistic Aspects of Translation", Jakobson was explicitly concerned with linguistic signs when he declared that for both

> linguists and ordinary word-users, the meaning of any lingual sign is its translation into some further, alternative sign, especially a sign 'in which it is more fully developed', as Peirce, the deepest inquirer into the essence of signs, insistently stated.
>
> *(1959: 232–233)*

Jakobson as a (largely structuralist) linguist was surely within his rights to apply Peirce's pan-semiotic definition of meaning as "the translation of a sign into another system of signs" to language. Maciej Litwin makes a strong case that "Jakobson's argument is a method, not a ruling, in translation studies, a theoretical essay on aspects of translation, not a theory of translation properly speaking"—actually, an essay which he had filled "with paradoxes for translation scholarship to live by" (2023). Litwin is certainly right in pointing out that "linguistic aspects of translation are not translation" (2023). The problem is that translation studies scholars for decades chose to focus their vision on those aspects, which included looking at Peirce's semiotics through the lens of Jakobson's linguistics. Marais spectacularly breaks with this tradition of a linguistically mediated encounter and turns directly to Peirce for semiotic insights. Making a clean cut from a lingual conceptualization of translation, he instead provides the following definition:

> Translation is negentropic semiotic work (performed by an agent) in which any one or more of the components of a sign system or any one or more of the relationships between them are changed, or in which the relationship between the sign and its environment (time and/or space) is changed.
>
> *(Marais 2019: 141)*

An understanding of translation as "creation of new semiotic relationships by means of changes that are required" because of various factors (Marais 2019: 144), represents a ground-breaking theoretical advance. Jakobson's triad is no longer relevant because "all translation is intersemiotic, i.e. translation between (inter) semiotic systems" (144). Likewise, the use of categories such as "intra" or "inter" is called into question, because they are relative to the level of observation: all translation is between (inter) systems, inside (intra) larger systems and, yet outside (extra) smaller systems, depending on perspective (144–145). The crucial thing is that the Peircean conceptualization "makes it possible to explain the 'translationness,' or the translationality of all of the 'inter' and 'trans' process-phenomena, and even process-phenomena indicated by other terms, thereby expanding the power of translation studies" (Marais 2019: 7).

Translationality

Thus we have come to the second part of the title *Experiencing Translationality*. I imagine that by now some researchers, students and practitioners of translation—especially those more practically minded—may be stirring in their seats, shaking their heads, and staring at these pages with a growing sense of scepticism or at least apprehension. What is translationality anyway? What is wrong with good old translation and why do we need another abstract, ethereal concept on top of it? Does it not unnecessarily complicate matters and muddy the waters? These are all valid questions that demand a serious response.

I hope we all agree that theorization cannot go far without abstraction. Any attempt of going beyond a single instance, an isolated unit of experience (as much as anything in our experience can be "isolated", given the fundamental principle of entanglement, more of which soon), and comparing it with another element of reality, means picking up some salient features and detaching them mentally from their object. It is a fundamental cognitive process that quite simply allows us to think, to form ideas: mental groupings, relationships, and processes. It is through abstraction that we can call various four-legged, furry, barking creatures "dogs" even though they come in different colours, shapes and sizes. Abstraction is the prerequisite of categorization, which is how we organize our experience and deal with the complexity of the world. It is worth noting and bearing in mind that even this simplest example of near-instinctive categorization draws on multiple sensory channels: visual ("four-legged"), tactile ("furry") and auditory ("barking"). In this way, experience is often self-triangulating. Now, it could be argued that in processing our experience with dogs, we do perfectly well without an explicitly formulated concept of "dogness" or "doghood", and it is only in philosophical accounts that we come across such weird constructs. Perhaps so—but for all intents and purposes, the concept DOG is just as abstract in the sense that there is no "dog in general" that could be pointed out as existing in reality: only particular animals representing various breeds and, more often than not, their mixtures. While we are at this analogy, we should also ask, if someone declares their interest in exploring all things concerning dogs "in a broad sense" (a qualification often used in translation studies), can they really ignore wolves, coyotes, jackals, foxes, dingo, and so on? What do all these species have in common if not some idea of DOGHOOD, specified, for practical purposes, in taxonomies using traditionally Latin labels, such as *Caninae*? Let us not forget that translations carry one such Latin-based label, too.

So, what makes a translation translation? This is not a trivial question for an entire discipline wrapped around this concept. If we accept a broadly semiotic conceptualization of translation along the lines suggested by Peirce and developed by Marais, then we have to let go of any concrete translations as its definitive instantiations. "'A translation' process-phenomenon is never something that you can point to in order to distinguish it from some other thing. Thus, one would never be able to say, 'This is translation, and that is not translation'" (Marais 2019: 83). Meanwhile, as our sensitivity to various translational phenomena, practices and modes grows, we will begin to perceive translationality even in the absence of explicitly recognized translation. This is how "ubiquitous translation" manifests itself. Abandoning the idea of "translation proper" pushes us towards translationality.

Once again, this abstracting impulse is a standard, necessary element of any description that has explanatory aspirations. It is what allows us to see *canine* teeth in a *human* mouth. Certain kinds of human teeth are "canine" in a semiotic sense; we recognize their similarity to the kinds of teeth typical of dogs (of which we have some idea already), and on that basis draw various conclusions concerning our evolution, diet, and so on. Similarly, observing and experiencing various translational processes and their outworkings, we already entertain some idea of translationality. The next step in theorization is to give this translationality the attention it deserves, to explore it thoroughly and systematically, discern its prototypical and peripheral exemplifications, test its limits and links to other concepts. This is precisely the direction advocated by Marais who believes that "translation studies would, like literary studies, benefit from moving towards an interest in translationality, rather than translation or translators—although the former does not exclude the latter" (Marais 2019: 7). This is a helpful analogy. Literary studies does not confine itself to analysing novels, poems and plays, their various groupings or genres; it does not just focus on writers, poets and playwritings or even processes of composition and reception; rather, it deals with the enormous and fuzzy concept of LITERATURE which includes all these (and many other) elements but also transcends them. In a similar way, translation studies is concerned with TRANSLATION, with all things translational. Translationality is an attempt to capture all this complexity in one word.

Douglas Robinson, in his *Translationality: Essays in the Translational-Medical Humanities* (2017), makes a number of partially overlapping approximations of this concept, tracing it, on the one hand, to translational medicine (and other disciplines that eagerly picked up this adjective [see also Blumczynski 2016b]), and on the other hand, to "Anton Popovič's ... own English translation of his Slovak term *prekladovost*'" (Robinson 2017: ix). From a textual standpoint, paraphrasing Popovič, he defines translationality as "a relation holding between the proto-[source] and meta-[target] text and having a transformative semiotic or modeling character" (ix). "Performed translationality" is his shorthand for *"felt-becoming-mobilized-becoming-performed translationality"* (ix; original italics). Translationality means "change, force, impact, motion, energy" (ix). It can also be approached as "transformationality: the constant emergingness of everything, through embodied, situated, performative interactions" (x). It is performed as well as "periperformed": "If literary translationality is 'performed' by writers, translators, and adapters, it is 'periperformed' by audiences, including editors and critics" (x). Periperformed translationality is extremely elusive but also, for the same reason, often irresistible: "it is about cultural change as an almost imperceptible 'groundswell,' as a 'watershed' without inciting events, indeed as 'reality,' as 'human nature,' as 'the way things are'." (x). Robinson's use of translationality is undeniably rich but also angled towards his focus on translational-medical humanities; my interest in corporeal transfer as its conceptual basis gives it a slightly different inflection.

Back to translation(s)

At the same time, as Marais himself admits, "when one thinks about translation from a Peircean perspective, one has to conclude that anything in reality could have a translational aspect that could be studied" (2019: 140). Indeed—the claim of translation's ubiquity makes it difficult to isolate concrete phenomena, relatively discrete bits of reality, to be examined as specific instances of translation. Marais's (bio)semiotic conceptualization of translation is manifestly non-metaphorical but, for that very reason, also extremely abstract. When was the last time you, as an agent, performed

> negentropic semiotic work … in which any one or more of the components of a sign system or any one or more of the relationships between them [were] changed, or in which the relationship between the sign and its environment (time and/or space) [was] changed?
>
> *(Marais 2019: 141)*

When or where did you last see someone "periperforming translationality" (Robinson 2017)? The puzzlement I anticipate in response to these questions signals to me the need to combine Marais's deductive approach with an inductive perspective.

Much as we need to study the broad spectrum of translationality, we should not forget about a semasiological approach outlined earlier and study phenomena that are explicitly called translations. Assuming that they all have some translational aspect (if they did not, why would they be called translations in the first place?), we can explore how the various uses and senses are related, and how they can be mutually illuminating. This is an inductive, bottom-up method, so to speak: the data is pre-selected conceptually, linguistically, and historically—some things, at various times, have been called translation, others have not—but it is possible to keep a maximally descriptive baseline, avoiding the trap of conceptual elitism and protectionism reminiscent of "translation properism". Unless one use of a concept clearly builds on another (by demonstrable mechanisms of semantic evolution), there is no reason to view it as derivative, secondary, extended, and so on. In short, "metaphorical" and "material" uses have to be demonstrated, not assumed. All translation is fair game. Only by applying these two sets of coordinates can we peek beyond the map and catch a glimpse of the territory it represents.

I find it reassuring that a champion of a deductive approach and proponent of what he describes as a "meta theory or a philosophy of translation" (2019: 178), Kobus Marais, also shares the conviction that the notion of translationality and explicitly translational practices must speak to each other. In the volume *Translation beyond Translation Studies* (Marais 2022), he invites a group of scholars to reflect on what it means to translate in their disciplines, from mathematics to computer science, medical and biological sciences, organization studies, digital humanities, and so on. It is a fascinating, original and in many ways groundbreaking work, which offers a radical "reimagining of what we mean by translation" and "how translation is understood and practiced beyond the narrow perspectives of the field of translation studies itself" (publisher's blurb). However, one area missing from its purview is precisely the historical, specialized sense of translation as transfer of bodies: the living bodies of religious officials and the dead bodies of martyrs and saints (that is, relics). *Experiencing Translationality* seeks to fill this gap in building our understanding of what translation is and what it does. Since "[w]e need to think more about what it is that makes translation this 'transfer thing'" (Marais 2019: 45), why not go back to where it all started, when the transfer was physical and material before it became, by and large, imagined and metaphorical?

Key theoretical inspirations and methodological commitments

Given that the rest of this book is devoted to exploring translations of bodies, living and dead, from a semiotic and experiential perspective, it is appropriate to signal some theoretical inspirations and methodological commitments guiding this exploration. Readers less interested in this theoretical foundation can probably skip this part without much detriment (if you have read until this point, you have a fairly good idea where I am coming from anyway).

In my take on experience, I follow the semiotician John Deely (1994; 2009), who "specifically wants to avoid the initial worry over whether some experience is 'about' something inner or outer, subjective or objective" (Corrington 1996: 105). While we cannot entirely bypass a critical discussion of distinctions such as these and several others—internal/external, subjective/objective, material/mental, natural/cultural, and so on—a fundamental premise is that "reality as we experience it is neither purely objective nor purely subjective nor purely intersubjective, but rather a constantly shifting mixture and proportion of all three not at all easy (perhaps not even fully possible) to keep complete track of" (Deely 2009: 116).

The human semiotic experience encompasses the physical, the social and the cultural—with each of these domains containing the previous one but also going beyond it. Deely stresses that "[t]he cultural transcends the social even more than the social transcends the simply physical" (1994: 3). Physical objects—including our own bodies—have social functions inscribed in cultural practices; meanwhile, these functions and practices are dictated by the affordances and limitations of physical conditions (cf. Sinha and Jensen de López 2001; Zlatev et al. 2008). From this perspective, the concept of material culture sounds tautological; matter and culture presuppose each other and make little sense in isolation. We need to pay attention not only to "how cultures and societies shape translation process-phenomena, but also … how translation process-phenomena shape cultures and societies" (Marais 2019: 9). This shaping occurs within and via a multi-layered, messy web of experience that cannot be disentangled into discrete strands (Marais 2019: 38).

The mention of entanglement brings us to another key concept and important thinker. Karen Barad, in her book *Meeting the Universe Halfway* (2007), draws on her expertise in theoretical particle physics, philosophy, history of consciousness, and feminist studies, as she proposes entanglement—a term borrowed from Erwin Schrödinger—as a rudimentary principle of world-making, carrying profound ontological, epistemological and ethical implications. This is how she explains it:

> To be entangled is not simply to be intertwined with another, as in the joining of separate entities, but to lack an independent, self-contained existence. Existence is not an individual affair. Individuals do not preexist their interactions; rather, individuals emerge through and as part of their entangled intra-relating. Which is not to say that emergence happens once and for all, as an event or as a process that takes place according to some external measure of space and of time, but rather that time and space, like matter and meaning, come into existence, are iteratively reconfigured through each intra-action, thereby making it impossible to differentiate in any absolute sense between creation and renewal, beginning and returning, continuity and discontinuity, here and there, past and future.
>
> *(Barad 2007: ix)*

Once we accept an ontologically realist view that the world is made of objects "as diverse as mind, language, cultural and social entities, and objects independent of humans such as galaxies, stones, quarks, tardigrades and so on" (Bryant 2011: 18), there is no reason to view translation as an exclusive or even predominant prerogative of humans, let alone as a prototypically mental or linguistic process. In his thought-provoking book *The Democracy of Objects*, Levi Bryant claims that "all objects translate one another" (2011: 18) by stimulating changes through their interactions. Following Bruno Latour's critique of the Modernist bifurcation into the distinct domains of culture and nature, Bryant challenges the tendency to treat culture "as the world of freedom, meaning, signs, representations, language, power, and so on" and nature "as being composed of matter governed by mechanistic causality" (23). He points out that within this culturalist and modernist distinction, "[s]ignifiers, meanings, signs, discourses, norms, and narratives are made to do all the heavy lifting", while ignoring

> the role of the nonhuman and asignifying in the form of technologies, weather patterns, resources, diseases, animals, natural disasters, the presence or absence of roads, the availability of water, animals, microbes, the presence or absence of electricity and high speed internet connections, modes of transportation, and so on.
>
> *(23–24)*

In a post-COVID-19 world, the futility of distinguishing between the cultural and the natural, between meaning and matter, is more obvious than ever. The microscopic virions of SARS-CoV-2 whose collective mass within the global human populace has been estimated to fall between 0.1 and 10 kilograms (Sender et al. 2021)—somewhere between a handful and a small bag worth of matter—have not only claimed the lives of over six million people[4] but also have had literally incalculable impact on economies, international relations, urban development, social practices, languages, patterns of work, leisure, and countless other dimensions of human (and non-human) existence, both on individual and collective level. As Barad puts it,

> Matter and meaning are not separate elements. They are inextricably fused together, and no event, no matter how energetic, can tear them asunder. … [M]atter and meaning cannot be dissociated, not by chemical processing, or centrifuge, or nuclear blast. Mattering is simultaneously a matter of substance and significance [and] … the smallest parts of matter are found to be capable of exploding deeply entrenched ideas and large cities.
>
> *(Barad 2007: 3)*

It does not take long to realize the relevance of these insights to corporeal translations. Translation understood as physical transfer, as negentropic work involving kinetic energy, yields itself to a strongly materialist emphasis that problematizes the notions of spatial and temporal otherness:

> The very nature of materiality is an entanglement. Matter itself is always already open to, or rather entangled with, the "Other." The intra-actively emergent "parts" of phenomena are co-constituted. Not only subjects but also objects are permeated through and through with their entangled kin; the other is not just in one's skin, but in one's bones, in one's belly, in one's heart, in one's nucleus, in one's past and future. This is as true for electrons as it is for brittlestars as it is for the differentially constituted human.
>
> *(Barad 2007: 393)*

A very similar observation in relation to anthropology (of art) is made by Alfred Gell, another intellectual patron of the present quest. He advocates focusing "on the social context of art production, circulation, and reception, rather than the evaluation of particular works of art" and recognizing that "this production and circulation has to be sustained by certain processes of an objective kind, which are connected to other processes (exchange, politics, religion, kinship, etc.)" (1998: 3; cf. Chua and Elliott 2013). He does not use the word *entanglement*, but relies on this idea in his insistence that art is not so much a matter of meaning or communication but it is instead about "doing" (Thomas 1998: ix). This is how he outlines it:

> I place all the emphasis on *agency, intention, causation, result*, and *transformation*. I view art as a system of action, intended to change the world rather than encode symbolic propositions about it. The 'action'-centred approach to art is inherently more anthropological than the alternative semiotic approach because it is preoccupied with the practical mediatory role of art objects in the social process rather than with the interpretation of objects 'as if' they were texts.
>
> *(Gell 1998: 6; emphasis in original)*

This side-lining of a metaphorical "textuality" of material objects along with a quasi-linguistic method of interpretation strongly tallies with the view of translation proposed in this book. Gell's anthropological theory of art (which he roughly defines as the study of "social relations in the vicinity of objects mediating social agency") is particularly promising and relevant as an element of a conceptual and methodological framework in that it "merges seamlessly with the social anthropology of persons and their bodies" (1998: 7). Gell's key notions of "distributed person" (see also Strathern 1988), "fractal personhood" (see also Wagner 1991) and "efficacious agency" are not only readily applicable to the study of translations involving people and relics but are also profoundly insightful (after all, relics are "distributed persons" in the most literal, material sense!). Inasmuch as "doing" is theorized as agency, it is important to decouple this concept from a single person, be it an artist, a writer or a translator. In Gell's view, agency is distributed, extended and entangled. It is mediated by "material entities which motivate inferences, responses or interpretations" (Thomas 1998: ix). What works of art or objects of translation "do" to someone who is affected by them cannot be explained by a self-sufficient agency of the artist or translator; instead, it is the outcome of complex material, social, semiotic, aesthetic and countless other entanglements (at this point, Robinson's [2017] concept of "periperforming" comes to mind). While this distribution of agency can at times seem very abstract and intangible (as when one thinks of authorial intent or translational *skopos*), once we consider that soldiers distribute "elements of their own efficacy in the form of landmines" (Thomas 1998: ix), this abstraction suddenly gives way to concreteness that is rather chilling. Translations of bishops and relics, discussed in the subsequent chapters of this book, have this kind on immediate concreteness to them; they are embodied in the strictest, near-tautological sense.

Gell challenges the distinction between religious worship and aesthetic contemplation (a point particularly relevant to relic translation in Chapter 3), expressed in the opinion that "an image viewed as a source of religious power, salvation, exaltation, is not appreciated for its 'beauty', but for quite different reasons" (1998: 97). Pointing to Western "quasi-religious veneration of art objects as aesthetic talismans" (3), he argues that it is impossible "to tell between religious and aesthetic exaltation; art-lovers … actually do worship images in most of the relevant senses, and explain away their *de facto* idolatry by rationalizing it as aesthetic awe" (97). This brings a refreshing and liberating air of transdisciplinarity: theological and artistic arguments—especially when subjected to the scrutiny of semiotic, anthropological, sociological and historical perspectives—may be mutually illuminating. By Gell's own admission, broader social and religious frameworks provide a context in which the anthropology of art finds itself. If, in relevant theoretical respects, "art objects are the equivalent of persons, or more precisely, social agents" (7), then surely the same is true of relics, and to an even fuller extent. Relics are not just the equivalents of persons: they *are* persons. That is how they are treated, handled, spoken about, addressed and translated. Plus, given the religious dimension, the agency of relics is tied not just to a saint's presence, but to God's.

Recent developments in translation theory have sensitized us to questions of representation and its ethics, to ways of looking at others, ourselves and at the world. Much as this book argues that translationality is something to be experienced and not only performed—it is a way of *seeing* (and being seen), not just a way of *looking*—approaching translations embedded in an ancient and medieval world is a precarious translational act in itself. África Vidal Claramonte, in her *Translation and Contemporary Art*, writes:

> Throughout history, the artist's gaze has translated the world from different points of view—sometimes offering the perspective of a patron, and others, especially in the contemporary era, translating with various semiotic systems the look of the most vulnerable. The look that translates should do so from a position of respect, a word that literally means "to look back" …
>
> Translating from respect means looking again. Looking at the other from the pathos of distance, not as a spectacle. Distinguishing *respectare* from *spectare* is the key. Looking to translate, translate as a way of looking, is to become closer to the other, to know that the other also looks at us and that that look counts.
>
> *(2022: 56–57)*

This commitment to a respectful look, and the awareness of simultaneously looking and being looked at (even as a psychological projection), has several immediate, concrete implications. Throughout much of the discussion in the chapters that follow, "certain important concessions must be made to medieval ways of seeing the world" (Geary 1978: 4). Historians, anthropologists, and translation studies scholars drawing on accounts made long ago, in a very different cultural, religious and intellectual climate, must be sensitive to how the authors viewed reality and wrote about it. I am keen to follow the approach thus outlined by Patrick Geary in his *Furta Sacra: Thefts of Relics in the Central Middle Ages* (1978):

> [F]or the purpose of this study, certain phenomena will be accepted without question: the relics discussed herein are all genuine unless proven otherwise by contemporaries; these relics are miraculous, giving off pleasant odors when touched, healing the sick, and otherwise expressing the wills of the saints whose remains they are. Without the acceptance of these postulates, the entire phenomenon becomes incomprehensible and scholarly investigation remains at the level of antiquarian triviality or anachronistic skepticism.
>
> *(Geary 1978: 4)*

A similar approach is advocated by Gell: "To appreciate the art of a particular period we should try to recapture the 'way of seeing' which artists of the period implicitly assumed their public would bring to their work" (1998: 2). Yet, at the same time, one needs to be aware that such epistemic sympathy, sensitivity and respect—commendable and necessary as they are—carry the risk of a patronizing approach that may easily trivialize the studied practices, and idealize the more ephemeral elements such as beliefs and attitudes by taking them at face value. Geary argues that

> [S]ympathy for the contemporary view of these sacred objects must not be equated with accepting relic cults as pure manifestations of religious devotion devoid of any extraneous considerations. This view would be as naïve as, say, considering the contemporary interest in collecting art objects as the spontaneous expression of aesthetic appreciation, completely divorced from any interest in sound financial investments. ... The medieval problem is perhaps the more problematic since people's attitudes towards relics were seldom clearly articulated or differentiated in categories or human perception immediately recognizable today.
>
> *(Geary 1978: 4–5)*

This effort to maintain a delicate balance to avoid the dual danger of (a) uncritical acceptance of ancient and medieval statements, and (b) anachronistic cynicism towards them, is reflected in the discursive style I have adopted in this book. I do not deem it necessary to employ continual hedging to signal my own epistemic reservations towards some of the described phenomena (e.g. "these allegedly miraculous events"). At the same time, I have no qualms about situating spiritual and religious events in their historical and cultural circumstances through extensive, detailed, "thick" descriptions: the following pages will bring no shortage of names, places, dates and examples. Since the kinds of translations considered here will likely be unfamiliar to many readers, I wanted to offer them a sense of immersion, allowing them to encounter a wide spectrum of experiences and thus have a chance to form their own impressions and judgements. In an exploration of such a rich, multi-sensory, experiential phenomenon as the translation of living and dead bodies—and yet necessarily confined to the printed medium—this felt like the right approach.

Finally, a few words about both the limitations and affordances of language. It is all too easy to project our own sense of certain words and expressions—including some finer nuances of meaning, such as evaluation or connotation—into other times and places, and even across linguistic boundaries. The best example is the word *translation* itself. My discussion of translation practices involving bishops and relics usually quotes materials written in English but often based on Latin or Greek sources. Yet it is important to remember, as Zrinka Stahuljak points out, that

> Translation in the Middle Ages was a crossroads of multilingual and multicultural contacts and encounters … The medieval Latin term *translatio* stands for transfers of power (*translatio imperii*), knowledge (*translatio studii*), physical objects (such as relics in *translatio reliquiarum*) and linguistic translation. Medieval translation was thus a nexus of a will to knowledge and technologies of power; *translatio* theorized the original and the effect of their transmission, but not its medium, that is, human agency. Put differently, even when medieval translation refers specifically to linguistic translation, it does not highlight or theorize issues of linguistic difference and identity and it rarely gives us the privilege of seeing the human being behind translation.
>
> *(2012: 149)*

Translatio in Latin is not quite *translation* in English but it is not quite *transfer*, either. The fact that one Latin concept is split into two in English is no small challenge, especially when we are working our way back into the broader concept. In fact, it is not just "broader" but different in several respects. The verb *transfero* and the noun *translatio* (not to mention some participles suspended somewhere between the verbal and the nominal) are governed by slightly different grammatical conventions than their English counterparts, including patterns of transitivity that have semantic implications (how often can you simply "translate" in English, without specifying the object?). The passive voice in Latin is not quite the same device as in English. Even the language we call, with a sense of reassuring familiarity, "Modern English", has changed enormously over the last several hundred years, and it is impossible to establish conclusively what stylistic or connotative baggage certain references to translation carried with them in the past. Today, speaking about translated people or non-textual objects in English gives such descriptions an immediately metaphorical bend (according to the gravitational pull of "translation proper", discussed in detail earlier), but how exactly they sounded to an English ear in previous centuries is a matter of speculation. In approaching material coming to us across such a considerable linguistic and cultural distance, it is important to apply a certain way of both reading and writing. Some authors, like Stahuljak in the passage quoted above, opt to retain the original form and highlight it in italics. I decided not to follow this linguistically foreignizing strategy and instead allow the experience of unfamiliar practices to be mediated by a familiar word, hoping that this word, *translation*, will itself be transformed and have something important "done" to it, becoming a familiar-yet-new lens through which to view all things translational.

Notes

1 This is how the company ACS Aviation Industries defines it: "The translating sleeve forms the outer surface of each C-duct. In the forward thrust mode, the translating sleeve is held against the form of the C-duct. This gives an aerodynamically smooth surface to the engine nacelle. In reverse thrust mode, the translating sleeve moves aft on tracks near the top and bottom of the C-duct. As the translating sleeve moves aft it moves the blocker doors down and uncovers the cascade, which point the flow of fan air coming in to the duct outward and forward through the cascades." https://acsai.co.uk/translating-sleeve/ (Accessed 31 October 2022). This website contains some useful illustrations.
2 https://en.wikipedia.org/wiki/Work_(physics)
3 Consider the following examples (*Oxford English Dictionary* 2022):

   1. 1794 J. Hutton *Diss. Philos. Light* 47 Heat is translated among bodies in a certain manner, and electricity in another.
   2. 1917 E. M. Jamison et al. *Italy Mediaeval & Mod.* 87 The Papacy translated the Empire from the Greeks to the Germans.
   3. 1948 C. Wildman tr. B. Constant *Adolphe* vi. 51 The various vicissitudes we had experienced together, caused every word, almost every gesture, to arouse memories which translated us into the past and filled us with an involuntary emotion.

4 As of 1 November 2022, the global coronavirus death toll stood at 6,595,100 (https://www.worldometers.info/coronavirus/coronavirus-death-toll/).

2
SQUARING THE CIRCLE
Episcopal translations

In the year 325 CE, the Emperor Constantine—who only twelve years earlier issued the Edict of Milan whereby the Christian religion was legalized throughout the Roman Empire—summoned a council of all the Christian bishops in Nicaea, present-day Turkey. This gathering of church leaders was the first of its kind and scope; it has since become known as the First Ecumenical Council. "Ecumenical" meant that the broadest possible representation was sought: some 1,800 bishops were invited although only some three hundred or so were able to attend. The council was summoned to mark twenty years of the Emperor's rule and at the same time address several urgent challenges to church unity, of both doctrinal and organizational nature. What is important from our perspective is that translation—in various senses of the word—was critically involved in some of these matters as both a part of the problem and a part of the solution.

"As the Greeks say"

In the doctrinal aspect, the greatest threat was perceived as coming from Arianism, a view proposed by Arius of Alexandria not long before, according to which Christ did not share the same divine nature and thus eternal existence with God the Father but had been begotten out of nothing as his first creature. This constituted a denial of what had become the orthodox Trinitarian doctrine which clearly distinguished Christianity from Judaism, and an overwhelming majority of the bishops at Nicaea condemned the Arian ideas as radically heretical. Consequently, the most important outcome of the Council was the formulation of a joint profession of faith, hereinafter known as the Nicene Creed, which asserted that Jesus was *homoousion tō patri* ("of the same *ousia* as the Father"). The carefully crafted term *homoousios* was meant to contrast with the deceptively similar

DOI: 10.4324/9781003382201-3

homoiousios ("of a similar *ousia*") which was seen as promoting the heresy. Of course, at the heart of this controversy was the question of how to understand and translate *ousia*, a key ontological concept in Greek. This cornerstone of Aristotle's ontology, most fully developed in his *Metaphysics*, has long been a stumbling block for translation. Derived from *einai*, "to be", the present participle *ousia* behaves partially like a noun or an adjective (in that it can be inflected for gender, number and case), and partially like a verb (in having a tense and voice). What exactly does it mean, and how should it be translated into languages in which these grammatical categories are distributed differently or absent altogether? Writing about the Greek grammar, Daniel Wallace argues that "just because a particle is ... substantival, this does *not* mean that its verbal aspect is entirely diminished. Most substantival participles still retain *something* of their aspect" (1996: 620; original emphasis). In a bid to do some justice to this conceptual tension arguably involved in *ousia*, contemporary translators and commentators routinely reach for solutions from outside of the standard vocabulary set. For example, Joseph Owens (1963: 139) tentatively considers "Beingness" or even "a Beingness" (note the semantic role of the indefinite article) as the "nearest English equivalent morphologically" of *ousia*, which however "implies a different type of abstractiveness from that of the Greek term" (140). David Bostock demonstrates even greater creativity:

> One the one hand, he [Aristotle] uses it [*ousia*] as an abstract noun, speaking of the *ousia* of the thing, and often equating this with what being is for that thing. Here we could perhaps speak either of the "be-ence" of the "be-ity" of the thing. But he also uses it as a concrete noun, naturally taking a plural, and in this use he will claim that men, horses, and trees are all *ousiai*. Here, "be-ity" would seem a little less harsh. For example, the claim that "men are be-ities" could be construed on the model of "men are realities". Indeed, though it lacks the etymological connection with the verb "to be", the word "reality" would serve well as a translation. For it has both the grammatical uses just mentioned, and at the same time, reflects another facet of Aristotle's word: that *ousiai* are the things that really, genuinely, or fundamentally are.
>
> *(Bostock 1994: 43)*

Given that more than six centuries separate Aristotle from the First Ecumenical Council, any comparisons of their respective word usages must be made with extreme caution. Still, a translational perspective offers us important insights into how these ontological ideas were construed at the time. Even though a majority of the bishops attending the Nicene Council came from the Greek-speaking East, and the discussions were no doubt conducted predominantly in that language, Latin was also present (at least as the mother tongue of the Emperor who presided over the Council, and a group of Western bishops), which means that the nuanced doctrinal points were being immediately put to a translational test. A comparative analysis of the Greek and Latin versions of the Council documents brings evidence of palpable conceptual and doctrinal tension mediated in translation. The Latin text at several critical junctures inserts the phrase *quod Graeci dicunt* ("as the Greeks say") followed by a transliteration of the original word to signal a complex, fluid relationship between the established terms in Greek and those emerging in Latin. For example, the Latin declaration *unius substantiae cum patre* ("[of] the same substance as the Father") is firmly anchored to, "as the Greeks say", *homoousion* (Baron and Pietras 2001: 24). In the documents of Nicaea, *substantia* is not being offered as an unproblematic Latin equivalent of *ousia* but rather its tentative counterpart, tempered by the Greek usage. Unfortunately, this translational awareness in relation to the provisionality of *substantia*—and, consequently, substance-based metaphysics—was rather short-lived. There is evidence that "[b]eginning with the Nicene-Constantinopolitan Creed of 381, the Latin versions of the official documents produced by the subsequent Ecumenical Councils ... [were] no longer explicitly concerned with 'what the Greeks say'" (Blumczynski 2019: 173). *Ousia* was to be re-forged in Latin as *substantia, essentia, materia*, and later also as *forma* and *natura*, amounting to a major conceptual leap. As I argued elsewhere,

> The reinterpretation of a participle as a noun, far from being a minor grammatical adjustment, is a radical interpretative step. A nominalised *ousia* becomes reified: it is something one can *have* as well as *be*. This is a critical moment. ... [W]hen conceptualised as an object of possession rather than an aspect of being, *ousia*—understood as estate or property—can be completely abstracted from the entity it is predicated on, and denote something physical, material, and tangible: for example, land, house, money, personal belongings.
> *(Blumczynski 2019: 166–167)*

The history of the Western Church, with its unique doctrine of transubstantiation of the consecrated bread and wine into the real body and blood of Christ during the Eucharist, demonstrates how pervasive this reconceptualization turned out to be. The consecrated elements, far from being mere symbols or vehicles of remembrance, became sacraments, material means of salvation, whose administration was the exclusive prerogative of duly authorized priests of the Roman Catholic Church. It is hard to resist an impression that the conceptual and theological rift between the East and West—that several centuries later culminated in the Great Schism of 1054, and in many ways remains unbridged to this day—was first allowed to arise and develop because a delicate, fluid, context-sensitive translational balance attuned to "as the Greeks say" gave way to terminological surety within a largely monolingual framework.

Cheirotonia: haptic transfer of authority

At the time when the practice of interlingual translation was still keeping the avenues of doctrinal dialogue between the East and the West somewhat open, another kind of translation was scandalizing the Christian Church by upsetting its emerging administrative structure. The relatively young institution whose hierarchical organization was only just taking shape faced constant threats of disunity and fragmentation. The need for some form of leadership was never seriously contested—indeed, it was viewed as part of the natural order. Writing around mid-third century CE, Cyprian, a bishop of Carthage, in his *Letter LXVIII* points out that "[t]he bees have a king and the flocks keep their leader and their faith" (Cyprian 1964: 227); in fact, as he goes on to argue, even "mercenaries obey their legal purchaser with the full allegiance of humility … There the leader is known and feared, one whom Divine Decree has not appointed, but upon whom a wicked faction and a harmful band agree" (227). It was precisely the issues of divine appointment and communal support as well as obedience that were intertwined in the emerging structures of church governance. The process of selecting or appointing ecclesiastical officials—referred to in Greek as *presbyteroi* ("elders"), *episkopoi* ("overseers") and *diakonoi* ("helpers"), and in Latin (and a number of other languages) usually by terms derived from these designations—was not entirely straightforward or transparent and seems to have varied somewhat from one locality to another. The Acts of the Apostles, dating to the late first century CE, describe the governance actions of the early Christian leaders, Paul and Barnabas, as they toured a series of cities in Asia Minor:

> After they had proclaimed the good news to that city [Derbe] and had made many disciples, they returned to Lystra, then on to Iconium and Antioch. There they strengthened the souls of the disciples and encouraged them to continue in the faith, saying, "It is through many persecutions that we must enter the kingdom of God." And after they had appointed elders for them in each church, with prayer and fasting they entrusted them to the Lord in whom they had come to believe.
>
> *(Acts 14: 20–23;* New Revised Standard Version *2021)*

The verb *cheirotoneo*—translated here as "appoint[ed]"—merits a closer examination because of its various shades of meaning. As mentioned in a footnote to verse 23, the phrase "[Paul and Barnabas] appointed elders" could be alternatively translated as "had elders elected" or "ordained elders" (*New International Version* 2011)—each of these renditions carrying distinct but complementary emphases to be discussed in turn.

First, it is worth pointing out that there is no reason to assume any specialized Christian usage for *cheirotoneo*. Its literal sense, "to stretch out the hand", had arguably acquired political overtones as it came to denote voting or an expression of support by raising one's hand in both secular and ecclesiastical settings. This would suggest a practice of communal vote modelled on the tradition of municipal elections in the Greco-Roman world (Brown 2011). Edwin Hatch in his *Organization of Early Christian Churches* argues that the relation between church officers and ordinary members was not only "one of presidency and leadership" but also that "the presidency and leadership was the same in kind as that of non-Christian associations" (1881: xviii). It is likely in this sense that Paul in his Second Epistle to the Corinthians (8:19) mentions his fellow missionary Titus as one who had been "appointed by the churches to travel with us while we are administering this generous undertaking" (*New Revised Standard Version* 2021). The appointment in this case likely meant broad endorsement and popular support, without necessarily any electoral process involving multiple candidates.

Roughly a decade later, around 65–66 CE, Paul in his pastoral Epistles instructed his two closest disciples about the personal and social qualifications of aspiring church leaders (*episkopoi*)—which implies a process of scrutiny and selection on the basis of publicly available evidence. Both passages are worth quoting here because they highlight the emerging problems that some two centuries later were identified by the First Ecumenical Council as underlying the scandals of ecclesiastical translation. To Titus, Paul writes:

> I left you behind in Crete for this reason, that you should put in order what remained to be done, and should appoint elders in every town, as I directed you: someone who is blameless, married only once, whose children are believers, not accused of debauchery and not rebellious. For a bishop, as God's steward, must be blameless; he must not be arrogant or quick-tempered or addicted to wine or violent or greedy for gain; but he must be hospitable, a lover of goodness, prudent, upright, devout, and self-controlled. He must have a firm grasp of the word that is trustworthy in accordance with the teaching, so that he may be able both to preach with sound doctrine and to refute those who contradict it.
> (Titus 1:5–9, New Revised Standard Version *2021*)

These same expectations are articulated in Paul's *First Epistle to Timothy*:

> Whoever aspires to the office of bishop desires a noble task. Now a bishop must be above reproach, married only once, temperate, sensible, respectable, hospitable, an apt teacher, not a drunkard, not violent but gentle, not quarrelsome, and not a lover of money. He must manage his own household well, keeping his children submissive and respectful in every way—for if someone does not know how to manage his own household, how can he take care of God's church? He must not be a recent convert, or he may be puffed up with conceit and fall into the condemnation of the devil. Moreover, he must be well thought of by outsiders, so that he may not fall into disgrace and the snare of the devil.
> (1 Timothy 3:1–7, New Revised Standard Version *2021*)

In these and similar passages, *cheirotoneo* is used "in the sense of 'elect' or 'appoint' (by show of hands)" (Roberts, Donaldson and Coxe 1885: 381)—in fact, this communal choice is taken as an indication of the early date of the writings in question (ibid.). It is evident that the leaders of the emerging churches were not "parachuted in" from the outside but rather recognized within local faith communities after a prolonged formative period. This local emphasis, the bishop's identification with and responsibility for his local church, is of paramount importance for understanding the outrage caused by episcopal translations.

At the same time, in all instances mentioned above, the act of election was validated by authoritative figures, such as one of the apostles or their direct delegates—which brings us to the second possible sense of *cheirotoneo*, translated as "ordain". This act of ordination or authorization was enacted haptically, by laying on of hands (*cheirotonia*)—a practice taken over directly from the Jewish tradition (e.g. "Joshua son of Nun was full of the spirit of wisdom because Moses had laid his hands on him, and the Israelites obeyed him, doing as the Lord had commanded Moses", Deuteronomy 34: 9, *New Revised Standard Version* 2021). The laying on of hands involved conferral of authority and blessing via an unbroken chain of personal contact, and therefore may be described as transmissional and indeed translational. In the ceremony of *cheirotonia*, the line of spiritual succession could be traced back along an arborescent structure to one of the main apostolic branches sprouting from the single stem, Christ himself. (Writing at the time of global COVID-19 pandemic, I cannot help noting that the mechanism invoked here, despite the opposite evaluative charge, is analogous to that imagined for viral transmission in which all individual cases can be traced back to a singular point of contamination and contagion, and eventually to a "patient zero", creating a similar chain of personal contact.) This literally manual transfer of authority ensured its centralization and helped protect it against imposters. Since ordination required the physical presence of a duly authorized official in a public ceremony, it could not be performed by proxy, in private or *in absentia*.

Consequently, the two senses of *cheirotoneo* should not be viewed as mutually exclusive but rather as complementary, designating two stages of the process of appointment, and pointing to the two sources of election. A suitable candidate, having garnered the support of his local community, was subsequently installed in office by existing bishops from other, usually neighbouring congregations. The work called *The Apostolic Tradition*, attributed to Hippolytus of Rome and dated at early third century CE, contains the following instructions:

> Let the bishop be ordained after he has been chosen by all the people. When he has been named and shall please all, let him, with the presbytery and such bishops as may be present, assemble with the people on a Sunday. While all give their consent, the bishops shall lay their hands upon him, and the presbytery shall stand by in silence. All indeed shall keep silent, praying in their heart for the descent of the Spirit. Then one of the bishops who are present shall, at the request of all, lay his hand on him who is ordained bishop, and shall pray as follows …

(Easton 2020 [1934]: 33)

Around the same time, in his *Letter LXVII*, Cyprian writes:

> We see that this very fact also comes from divine authority, that a bishop be chosen in the presence of the people before the eyes of all and that he be approved as worthy and fit by public judgment and testimony; ... The Lord orders the bishop to be appointed before the whole synagogue, that is, He instructs and shows that priestly ordinations ought not to be performed except with the knowledge of the people present that, in the presence of the people, either the crimes of the evil doers may be revealed or the merits of the good may be proclaimed and that the ordination which has been examined by the suffrage and judgment of all may be just and lawful. ...
>
> Because of this, we must preserve diligently and keep of the divine traditions and apostolic observance what is kept among us also and through almost all of the provinces that, for the celebrations of ordinations with suitable ceremony for that people for whom a prelate is ordained, all the nearest bishops of the same province should assemble also and a bishop should be chosen in the presence of the people, who know most fully the life of each one and perceive the actions of each from his manner of living.
>
> *(Cyprian 1964: 234–235)*

This practice constituted a basic system of check and balances, in which the line of apostolic succession was not only vertical—linking the new bishop to Christ—but also horizontal and composed of multiple threads. "The newly elected bishop was installed in office and given his authority not by his predecessor, who was dead or deposed, but by the bishops who supervized the election and performed the ordination"—as a result, "[n]o bishop or Christian community ... was autonomous; each was necessarily a part of a broad network of bishops and their churches" (Burns 2001: 91).

At the same time, addressing matters of discipline and dealing with a non-conforming bishop required broad collective action. J. Patout Burns Jr. points out that prior to the coalescence of the power structures of the Roman Empire and the Roman Church,

> The church was not in a position ... to utilize the assistance of the government in removing a bishop who had been deposed. Successful action, therefore, might require extensive collaboration among a wide range of bishops, in order to render an obstinate bishop ineffectual. Thus Donatus of Carthage and Fabian of Rome were needed to endorse the deposition of Privatus of Lambaesis. The removal of Marcianus of Arles was beyond the power of the bishops of his province, so that the support of the bishops of Carthage and Rome was being sought. In extreme cases, the bishops had to urge the congregation to withdraw and abandon its deposed leader.
>
> *(Burns 2001: 91)*

At other times, the opposite was the case: it was the congregation, stirred by disgruntled contenders, that would occasionally remove its leaders, to the understandable discontent and concern of other bishops who might fear that a similar fate should one day befall them. One of the earliest Christian writings, the *First Epistle of Clement*, dated at late first century CE, addresses one such mutinous incident in the church in Corinth. The author admits the apostles had anticipated that "there would be contention for the title of overseer" (*tou onomatos tēs episkopēs*; 44: 1), which signals that the office—not just the performance of the role—had become as desirable as it was contentious. He goes on to say that should the bishops appointed by apostles "fall asleep" (an indication of permanent appointment, only terminating with death), "other approved men should succeed to their duties" (44: 2):

> Those therefore that were appointed by them, or afterward by other reputable men with the consent of the whole church, and have blamelessly served the flock of Christ, humbly, quietly, and disinterestedly, and for a long time have been universally approved—these men we consider are being unjustly removed from their ministry. For we shall be guilty of no small sin if we depose from the position of overseer [*episkopēs*] those who have blamelessly and piously made the offerings. Blessed are the elders [*presbyteroi*] who have gone before, who experienced a fruitful and perfect departure, for they have no need to fear that anyone will remove them from their appointed place. For we see that you have dislodged some men who were conducting themselves well from the ministry they had blamelessly respected.
>
> (First Clement 44: 3–6; [Goodspeed 1950: 70])

What is noteworthy in this passage and in the remainder of the letter is the careful mixture of reproach and persuasion. Recognizing the complementary role of apostolic succession and congregational support, Clement mobilizes a full range of arguments: from strictly theological ones, yet posed in the face-saving first person plural ("we shall be guilty of no small sin if we depose from the position of overseer those who..." [44: 4]), to pragmatic and emotional ones ("your division has perverted many, it has plunged many into despondency, many into doubt, all of us into grief" [46: 9]), to a blend of flattery, shaming for being impressionable, and reputational concerns ("It is disgraceful, dear friends, utterly disgraceful, and unworthy of Christian conduct to have it said that because of one or two people the old, established church of the Corinthians is in revolt against its elders" [47: 6]). The letter ends on a conciliatory note ("[W]e have been more glad to remind you of these things because we knew well that we were writing to men who were faithful and of high repute" [62: 3]), in full awareness that the Corinthian Christians can only be convinced but not coerced to restore their deposed leaders.

In the first several centuries, an appointment to a church office should probably be seen as involving a permanent shift in one's social and spiritual identity, with some important implications for one's social status. Mary Sommar points out that

> In the latter half of the third century the Christian bishop's role changed. He went from being simply a local spiritual leader to become an important functionary in civic as well as religious affairs. In the third century of the Common Era the secular society began to recognize bishops (and other clergy as well) as persons of status in the community. And, quite humanly, the bishops responded positively to that recognition and gradually the bishops changed their *personae*, their behaviors and their self-concept to fit the model that elicited the most positive social reward, that of a professional in the service of the secular as well as the ecclesiastical hierarchies.
>
> *(1998: 3–4)*

Some clues regarding the leaders' roles and functions may be gleaned from the terms used to refer to them. In the early Christian period, the designations *presbyteros, episkopos* and *diakonos* appear to be used interchangeably—as in *First Clement* quoted above—and in ways reflecting the primary sense of these terms: "elder", "overseer" and "helper", respectively. The church leaders are often referred to in the plural, as in the opening salutation of the Epistle to the Philippians, where Paul and Timothy address "all the saints in Christ Jesus who are in Philippi, with the bishops [*episkopois*] and deacons [*diakonois*]" (1: 1, *New Revised Standard Version* 2021). This suggests a collective structure of early church leadership, and the *New Revised Standard Version* in a footnote to this verse offers an alternative semantic rendition "overseers and helpers". Within the next century or two, however, there is a noticeable shift towards a hierarchy as bishops come to be strongly identified with their congregations in a one-to-one relationship. "The procedure for the succession of bishops was designed to establish a single bishop in each town or city and to secure his status through recognition by other bishops in an episcopal college of indefinite extension" (Burns 2001: 90). "Cyprian argued that once an election had been completed and the candidate installed by the attending bishops, no other bishop could be elected as a replacement" (Burns 2001: 91). As long as due procedures had been followed, primacy was the deciding criterion: "Any dispute over succession had only to establish which of the claimants had first completed the two stages of the process" (ibid.). "Whence you ought to know that the bishop is in the Church, and the Church in the bishop", writes Cyprian (1964: 229) in his *Letter LXVI*, at the same time stressing that there is no legitimate alternative to the ecclesiastical structure: "if there is anyone who is not with the bishop, he is not in the Church" while "the Church which is one, Catholic, is not divided nor rent, but is certainly united and joined, in turn, by the solder of the bishops adhering to one another" (ibid.). At Nicaea, this coherence in the ordination of bishops was officially mandated at

54 Squaring the circle

FIGURE 2.1 The First Council of Nicaea. Detail of a fresco from the church of St. Nicholas, Demre, southern Turkey.
© Neil Harrison | Dreamstime.com

a provincial level. Canon 4 of the First Ecumenical Council states that "It is by all means proper that a bishop should be appointed by all the bishops in the province" (Percival 1886: 11). In exceptional circumstances, such as urgent necessity or long distance, some bishops were allowed to send their suffrages in writing, but the actual presence of at least three bishops—a strong principle of episcopal triangulation—was still required for the ordination to take place.

Summing up, the procedures of appointing Church officials, especially bishops, ensured a delicate balance between a certain measure of self-government (necessary to secure goodwill and loyalty of the congregation), a hierarchical structure of ecclesiastical authority, and horizontal relationships among what came to be called, after Cyprian, "the college of bishops" or the episcopate (see Figure 2.1). Unconstrained ecclesiastical translations appeared to put each one of these three elements at risk.

The Nicene canons

It is against the background sketched above that the Nicene Council's canons can be properly appreciated and understood. As a separate "genre", they have a special place in the conciliar promulgations. Following creeds (that sought to precisely express and define important doctrinal issues) and anathemas (that rejected unorthodox positions and condemned their propagators), canons announced decisions on a range of disciplinary issues and were "the result of episcopal deliberations on canonical problems which the bishops probably encountered in their dioceses" (Weckwerth 2021: 158). They may therefore be legitimately read as a record of perceived serious threats, admission of widespread and persistent problems, and agreement of proposed remedies or sanctions. In this way, they are highly context-sensitive documents, capturing unique historical challenges.

The Council of Nicaea announced twenty disciplinary canons addressing a rather dizzying range of issues. It is difficult to ascertain whether their arrangement reflects an order of importance. Probably not; otherwise we would have to accept that the problem of self-castration among clergy—as distinguished from emasculation sustained through surgical operations or barbarian acts of violence—topped the list of concerns (Canon I). This is followed by warnings against appointing newly converted pagans as bishops or presbyters (Canon II), a strict prohibition for any members of the clergy against improper female companionship—excepting mothers, sisters and aunts (Canon III); the principle of collective appointment of bishops (Canon IV); and instructions for readmitting believers who were previously excommunicated (Canon V). Canons VI and VII establish the primacy of certain provincial capitals (Rome, Antioch, Alexandria, and Jerusalem). Then, detailed orders are given for dealing with a specific sect ("those who call themselves Cathari") and in particular its leaders to ensure that there is no duplication of bishops (Canon VIII). Further proclamations concern annulling illegitimate ordinations (Canons IX–X), adequate penance for remorseful sinners, apostates and ex-soldiers seeking reinstatement into military service (Canons XI–XII and XIV), and administration of communion to the dying (Canon XIII). The substance of canons XV and XVI will be discussed in detail below. Next, clergy is prohibited from practising usury and pursuing ignominious gain (Canon XVII), the observance of hierarchical structure in the administration of communion is re-emphasized (Canon XVIII), and conditions for re-baptizing the former followers of Paul of Samosata, the deposed bishop of Antioch, are specified (Canon XIX). Finally, Canon XX, in pursuit of a uniform practice across the Christian churches, decrees that prayer should be made standing rather than kneeling.

Ecclesiastical translations: the fourth century

This brief overview signals the diversity of problems facing the fourth-century church. Some of them may be attributed to underlying doctrinal controversies, others seem symptomatic of any large and ever-growing organization that seeks to reconcile its expansion with centralized governance and uniformity of operations. The vast majority, in one way or another, concern issues of leadership, and threats posed by certain practices in this area. Here, the following canon is of particular interest:

> Canon XV [of Nicaea]
> On account of the great disturbance and discords that occur, it is decreed that the custom prevailing in certain places contrary to the Canon, must wholly be done away; so that neither bishop, presbyter, nor deacon shall pass from city to city. And if any one, after this decree of the holy and great Synod, shall attempt any such thing, or continue in any such course, his proceedings shall be utterly void, and he shall be restored to the Church for which he was ordained bishop or presbyter.
> *(Percival 1886: 32)*

In the original Greek text, the linguistic linchpin is the verbal noun *metabainein* (aorist infinitive of *metabaino*, "depart", "leave", "move", "pass from place to place"). It is rendered into Latin as *transferatur*, which fully corresponds to the meaning of *translate* as "transfer or move (a bishop, minister, etc.) from one ecclesiastical post to another" (*Oxford English Dictionary* 2022)—the focus of this chapter. The English rendition given above, "shall pass" [from city to city], is somewhat misleading on grammatical grounds, as it suggests a sense of agency. This is one the first aspects of ecclesiastical translation that calls for closer attention. *Transferatur* is a passive form, and while it does not necessarily have to be translated as "shall be transferred" [from city to city] rather than "shall transfer", the explanation that follows ("if any one … shall attempt any such thing, or continue in any such course"), paired with what we know about the procedures of ecclesiastical appointments, indicates that the impetus for translations could originate with various agents, or indeed that several parties could be complicit. The Nicene canons were not sufficiently clear on who was to be held to account for the translations of church officials, which is confirmed by the fact that only several years later, in 341 CE, the Synod of Antioch, fine-tuning many of the laws given at Nicaea, announced the following:

> Canon XXI [of Antioch]
> A bishop may not be translated from one parish to the other, either intruding himself of his own suggestion, or under compulsions by the people, or by the constraint of the bishops; but he shall remain in the Church to which he was allotted by God from the beginning, and shall not be translated from it, according to the decree formally passed on the subject.
> *(Percival 1886: 118–119)*

The Antiochian formulation removes any doubt concerning the inspiration for translation: it could—and, in all likelihood, did—come from the bishops themselves, their fellow (or superior) bishops, or their congregations. However and by whomever instigated, all translations are condemned in equal measure. This is evident from the choice of vocabulary: communal initiative is described as "compulsion", episcopal pressure as "constraint", and a bishop's own translational urge as "intrusion". All these images imply a violation of the existing order and presuppose resistance against these acts of defiance.

At the same time, despite the clearly articulated prohibition, the conciliar bodies at Nicaea and Antioch make an implicit admission that translations will likely continue to be attempted. The church cannot prevent them; it can only reverse them or declare them void. The consequences are canonical, not material: "shall not be translated from it" (Antioch, Canon XXI) refers to blocking the legal effect, not the physical transfer. The Hefele-Clark rendition of the Nicene Canon XV is even more explicit in this regard: "the translation shall be null, and he shall return to the church to which he had been ordained bishop and priest" (Hefele 1883: 422). The canonical view of marriage comes to mind: the Roman Church does not grant divorces—but it may declare that a marital union was never properly entered into and is therefore null and void. The argument is largely practical and experiential, based on the conviction that "for the local spiritual leader to break with the group of which he is the spiritual symbol and to re-bond with another group … is nearly impossible" (Sommar 1998: 4).

Though condemned, translation is not morally disqualifying as long as it is promptly reversed or otherwise rendered ineffective. It is worth noting that in the context of the wider body of canons which specify conditions of penance and full or partial readmission for lapsed believers and leaders who renounce their unorthodoxy, there are no such provisions for bishops who attempt a (failed) translation. Episcopal translation is treated as an act of disobedience and insubordination, not heresy. Consequently, in remedial action the church simply seeks to restore the earlier status quo. Any nuptial analogies clearly do not apply here: there is no trace of a rhetoric of infidelity, betrayal or even breach of trust. "Back-translated" bishops are instructed to resume their original positions as if the translation never happened. This is likely a political strategy: there is less risk in pardoning unsuccessful mutineers than in confronting them openly, thus provoking further rebellion.

Indeed, the position of the Nicene Council on the issue of ecclesiastical translation is both surprisingly dogmatic (given the more moderate stance of both earlier and later canon-law) as well as thoroughly pragmatic in addressing its inevitable instances in strictly administrative terms. Conciliar documents, in order to secure the support of a majority if not all delegates, had to be politically balanced, non-inflammatory, and worded with the greatest precision. Individual bishops were under no such restrictions. Athanasius, who accompanied Bishop Alexander to Nicaea as his secretary, and within several years succeeded him as the patriarch of Alexandria, made translation a central point of his polemic against bishop Eusebius, lambasting him as someone who perhaps never received any appointment to his office at all; or if he did, has himself rendered it invalid. For he had first the See of Berytus, but leaving that he came to Nicomedia. He left the one contrary to the law, and contrary to the law invaded the other; having deserted his own without affection, and holding possession of another's without reason; he lost his love for the first in his lust for another, without even keeping to that which he obtained at the prompting of his lust. For, behold, withdrawing himself from the second, again he takes possession of another's, casting an evil eye all around him upon the cities of other men, and thinking that godliness consists in wealth and in the greatness of cities, and making light of the heritage of God to which he had been appointed; not considering the words of the Apostle, 'I will not boast in another man's labours;' not perceiving the charge which he has given, 'Are you bound unto a wife? Seek not to be loosed.' For if this expression applies to a wife, how much more does it apply to a Church, and to the same Episcopate; to which whosoever is bound ought not to seek another, lest he prove an adulterer according to holy Scripture.

(Athanasius 1892: 103–104)

Athanasius takes his argument against translation to full ethical, moral and emotional lengths. Leaving one's original church is not only illegal but also sinful and dishonourable: it is desertion and betrayal of one's first love. Likewise, taking charge of another congregation is nothing short of invasion and adultery prompted by uncontrolled sexual urge. Coming from a patriarch, Athanasius's statement is unapologetically patriarchal—a bishop's symbolic wife is reduced to the object of his possession, labour and pride—but for all its blatantly sexist rhetoric, it identifies two main motivations for episcopal translation: prosperity and prestige ("thinking that godliness consists in wealth and in the greatness of cities").

These were no doubt twinned concerns—yet, the pursuit of greed was probably seen as more serious than seeking self-importance. The early list of necessary qualifications of bishops, as outlined by Paul in his pastoral Epistles quoted earlier on, highlighted the following characteristics: "above reproach, married only once, temperate, sensible, respectable, hospitable, an apt teacher, not a drunkard, not violent but gentle, not quarrelsome, and not a lover of money" (1 Timothy 3: 1, *New Revised Standard Version*). The instructions found in the early Christian treatise *Didache*, dated at the late first or early second century, testify to an already shifting centre of gravity: "Elect, therefore, for yourselves bishops and deacons worthy of the Lord, humble men and not covetous, and faithful and well tested" (Glimm, Marique and Walsh 1947: 183). Comparing these two lists, one cannot fail to notice that being "covetous" (*aphilargyros*) moves from the final place in the inventory—almost an afterthought—to a much more prominent position, becoming a principal disqualifying feature.

Meanwhile, a pursuit of greater recognition and influence could easily be spun as following a heavenly call rather than merely one's own ambition. One of the greatest leaders of the Eastern Church, Gregory, first appointed as bishop of Sasima, had no qualms to describe his original ecclesiastical post as an "utterly dreadful, pokey little hole; a paltry horse-stop on the main road ... devoid of water, vegetation, or the company of gentlemen" (McGuckin 2001: 197); it is no wonder that in the course of his career he desperately sought a *de facto* translation to Constantinople. Yet, a translational stigma eventually did catch up with him, and years later frustrated an even greater aspiration: "there can be no doubt that the chief reason why St. Gregory Nazianzen resigned the Presidency of the First Council of Constantinople, was because he had been translated from his obscure see Sasima ... to the Imperial City" (Percival 1886: 33). Even when translations were officially allowed or rather tolerated, they could rarely become occasions for celebration and pride—likely because they were still seen as violating the spirit of Paul's insistence for bishops to be "married only once" and in this respect never quite lost their incriminating potential, as Gregory's example shows.

Coming back to the promulgations of Nicaea, the wording of canon XV ("it is decreed that the custom prevailing in certain places contrary to the Canon, must wholly be done away") leaves no doubt that the translations being prohibited were not isolated incidents but had become a pattern, at least in some regions. Fighting against an established tradition is never easy—but in this case it was additionally compounded by a history of concessions. In his comment on this canon, Charles Hefele points out that "[t]he translation of a bishop, priest, or deacon from one church to another, had already been forbidden in the primitive Church" (1883: 422), yet he immediately adds that, "[n]evertheless, several translations had taken place, and even at the Council of Nicaea several eminent men were present who had left their first bishoprics to take others" (ibid.). One would not expect that "eminent men" should be legislated against in their presence, and there is no record of debate or disagreement amongst the delegates on this point. Not only that—in fact, despite appearing to forbid translation under any circumstances, the bishops assembled at Nicaea, according to Sozomen's *Ecclesiastical History*, were "so sensible of the purity of the life and doctrines of Eustathius, that they adjudged him worthy to fill the apostolic see; although he was then bishop of the neighboring Berœa, they translated him to Antioch" (Hartranft 1890: 241). This apparent contradiction between theory and practice indicates that the prohibition was not absolute but carried an implicit clause for exemption in special cases. Pre-Nicene documents support this view. One of the earliest collections of canon-law, known as the *Apostolical Canons*, dated for around mid-fourth century CE but codifying a much older tradition, contain the following rule:

> [Apostolical] Canon XIV
> A bishop is not to be allowed to leave their own parish, and pass over into another, although he may be pressed by many to do so, unless there be some proper cause constraining him, as if he can confer some greater benefit upon

the persons of that place in the word of godliness. And this must be done not of his own accord, but by the judgement of many bishops, and at their earnest exhortation.

(Percival 1886: 594)

A "proper cause" could thus open a door for a legitimate translation—yet what constituted such a cause was established within a framework of rather complex ecclesiastical economy combining spiritual and earthly factors. It is not clear how the prospects of "greater benefits" were to be weighed or what exactly they should encompass but it stands to reason that the church—to put it in unapologetically contemporary, even corporate terms—wanted to safeguard the best use of talent (spiritual as much as administrative) and ensure optimal deployment of its human resources. At the same time, an open admission that the "benefits" brought about by translated bishops "in the word of godliness" were somehow measurable and open to comparison, must have raised understandable concerns about the robustness of church governance. Henry Percival (on whose comprehensive "Excursus on the Translation of Bishops" I draw extensively here) points out that, if these were to be tolerated,

> the result would be that smaller and less important sees would be despised, and that there would be a constant temptation to the bishops of such sees to make themselves popular with the important persons in other dioceses with the hope of promotion.
>
> *(1886: 33)*

In other words, it was recognized that translations created opportunities for corruption, opportunism, and fawning.

It was therefore crucial that translations be made in good faith, not for personal gain but with the interest of the wider church community in mind. Whether this was the case could only be decided collectively—hence the "judgment of many bishops", which in practical terms meant provincial councils or local synods. It was also recognized that a translation involved two communities—a "source" and a "target" one—and each of them had a role to play in preventing unauthorized transfers, either temporary or permanent. This is stressed in the canons that immediately follow the prohibitions of ecclesiastical translations in both the Nicene and Antiochian collection:

> Canon XVI [of Nicaea]
>
> Neither presbyters, nor deacons, nor any others enrolled among the clergy, who, not having the fear of God before their eyes, nor regarding the ecclesiastical Canon, shall recklessly remove from their own church, ought by any means to be received by another church; but every constraint should be applied to restore them to their own parishes; and, if they will not go,

they must be excommunicated. And if anyone shall dare surreptitiously to carry off and in his own Church ordain a man belonging to another, without the consent of his own proper bishop, from whom although he was enrolled in the clergy list he has seceded, let the ordination be void.

(Percival 1886: 35)

Canon XXII [of Antioch]
   Let not a bishop go to a strange city, which is not subject to himself, not into a district which does not belong to him, either to ordain any one, or to appoint presbyters or deacons to places within the jurisdiction of another bishop, unless with the concept of the proper bishop of the place. And if any one shall presume to do any such thing, the ordination shall be void, and he himself shall be punished by the synod.

(Percival 1886: 119)

These regulations, despite some brief references to "the fear of God", leave no doubt that the main concerns behind the ban on episcopal translations had to do with disruption to the governance structure by bishops undermining each other's authority. Churches are seen not so much as communities of faith but rather as sites of jurisdiction that must be protected at all costs—hence the more severe sanctions: cancellation of illicit ordinations and punishment for the insubordinate bishop, all the way up to excommunication.

An even stronger condemnation was issued by the Council of Serdica, convened within a few years of Nicaea (probably in 343 CE), in its first canon:

Hosius, bishop of the city of Corduba, said: A prevalent evil, or rather most mischievous corruption must be done away with from its very foundations. Let no bishop be allowed to remove from a small city to a different one: as there is an obvious reason for this fault, accounting for such attempts; since no bishop could ever yet be found who endeavoured to be translated from a larger city to a smaller one. It is therefore evident that such persons are inflamed with excessive covetousness and are only serving ambition in order to have the repute of possessing greater authority. Is it then the pleasure of all that so grave an abuse be punished with great severity? For I think that men of this sort should not be admitted even to lay communion. All the bishops said: It is the pleasure of all.

(Percival 1886: 415)

Hosius's astute observation about the inconceivable transfer "from a larger city to a smaller one" holds true for translation of any kind, whether textual or material, and across all epochs. Following a clear axiological trajectory, it always seeks to enhance the status of its object. In short, translation adds value. The popular perception of interlingual translation as a process involving loss in comparison to the original, as reduction of meaning, delivering "second best", and so on, finds an almost perfect opposition in the idea of ecclesiastical translation: a pursuit of higher honour, stronger prestige, more influence. Translational gratification is never in doubt—on the contrary, it is so precious that it must be strictly guarded and carefully mandated.

The austerity with which these rules were announced indicates that the threat of rampant translations was real and widespread. Though allowed only in special circumstances, "these exceptional cases increased almost immediately after the holding of the Council of Nicaea" (Hefele 1883: 423). Ironically, "the custom prevailing in certain places" not only had not been "wholly ... done away", as Nicene Canon XV would have expected, but with time became even more prevalent—so much so that "in 382, St. Gregory of Nazianzum considered this law among those which had long been abrogated by custom" (Hefele 1883: 423). The practice of translation, once unleashed, was not to be easily supressed.

This discrepancy between the conciliar prohibitions and the practice of the church was calling for further reflection and more detailed regulations. Later authors started to claim that "the Nicene Canon does not forbid Provincial Councils to translate bishops, but forbids bishops to translate themselves" (Percival 1886: 33–34). The author of the tract *De Translationibus* makes a finer terminological point by declaring that

> the thing prohibited is 'transmigration' (which arises from the bishop himself, from selfish motives) not 'translation' (wherein the will of God and the good of the Church is the ruling cause); the 'going,' not the 'being taken' to another see.
>
> *(Percival 1886: 34)*

Some modern commentators agree that the canonical prohibitions were likely "directed against irregular translations effected by invasions, subversion, or party politics" (Hess 2002: 166), admitting that the exact meaning of the injunction hinges on the interpretation given to the infinitive *methistasthai*:

> If this is rendered in the passive voice, following Hefele, translation seems to be prohibited in principle, affecting translation by conciliar enactment as well as by personal desire or factional intrigue. As expressive of the middle voice of the present infinitive this form of the verb may, on the other hand, be interpreted as meaning that it is the bishop in question who is himself the agent of the action. This interpretation is supported by the use of the active voice (*transeat, transire,* and *migret*) in the fifth- and sixth-century Latin translations of the canon ... and the recognized possibility of a bishop being regularly translated to a vacant see by the judgement and consent of a council.
>
> *(Hess 2002: 166)*

This takes us back to the precarious balance of autonomy and discipline, agency and submission, intention and interest, in the overarching framework of power play. The chord being struck here is worth registering because it will return in our later discussion. The emphasis on the divine will and the benefit of the church as the defining criteria of admissible translation regularly resurfaced in the debates concerning the translations of relics (see Chapter 3).

Episcopal translations in the Middle Ages

As centuries wore on, episcopal translations showed no signs of abating, both in the West and in the East—which, overall, seemed less concerned about their dangers. Theodore Balsamon, the principal Byzantine legal scholar of the medieval period and patriarch of Antioch in the second half of the twelfth century, distinguished three kinds of translations:

> *metathesis*—"when a bishop of marked learning and of equal piety is forced by a council to pass from a small diocese to one far greater where he will be able to do the Church the most important services, as was the case when St. Gregory of Nazianzum was transferred from Sasima to Constantinople"
>
> *(Percival 1886: 34)*

> *metabasis*—"when a bishop, whose see has been laid low by the barbarians, is transferred to another see which is vacant"
>
> *(ibid.)*

> *anabasis*—"when a bishop, either having or lacking a see, seizes on a bishopric which is vacant, on his own proper authority"
>
> *(ibid.)*

Among these three, it was apparently only translation of the last kind—arbitrary, reckless and self-serving—that was prohibited. Writing in the thirteenth century, the Byzantine bishop and judge Demetrios Chomatenos allows a situation in which

> a bishop, elected and confirmed, and even ready to be ordained for a diocese, may be forced to take the charge of another one which is more important, and where his services will be incomparably more useful to the public.
>
> *(Percival 1886: 34)*

Similarly, the *Book of Eastern Law* confirms that

> if a Metropolitan with his synod, moved by a praiseworthy cause and probable pretext, shall give his approbation to the translation of a bishop, this can,

without doubt, be done, for the good of souls and for the better administration of the church's affairs, etc.

(Percival 1886: 34)

In her study, "The Changing Role of the Bishop in Society: Episcopal Translation in the Middle Ages", Mary Sommar (1998) analysed theological and canonical writings, from the earliest years of the Christian Church through the medieval period, to conclude that

> [T]he prohibitions against translations were not so much intended to forbid a particularly heinous act, but an attempt to bring order to a chaotic Church. ... The bishops of the Early Church, especially in the East, were trying to allow as much freedom as possible in how the local churches should order their administrative affairs, ruling out what was totally unacceptable. In the case of bishops moving to new dioceses, it was generally agreed that rogue translations were not acceptable. ... Translations effected in an orderly manner were permitted if they were seen to be for a good reason, and if they received the approval of the broader Church ...
>
> *(Sommar 1998: 87–88)*

In short, it was expected that a translation should benefit the bishop being translated, his new congregation, and the church as a whole—though at various times, each of these constituencies could play a dominant role. The perspective of an ambitious individual was not always aligned with a long-term strategy of the church whose position on episcopal translations seems to be defined chiefly in relation to the idea of stewardship, the optimal management of both spiritual and material resources.

Meanwhile, translations of church officials were becoming ever more strongly entangled and explicitly identified with issues of power dynamics, governance and influence, especially at the multiple interfaces of secular and ecclesiastical authority. As Sommar points out, "the fact that bishops were willing and able to translate is evidence of their changed role in the post-Constantinian church. The bishops were now professionals in service to the Empire" (1998: 3). The Pope, the Emperor and other monarchs stood to be powerfully affected by episcopal translations—for better or for worse—and were therefore keenly interested in sanctioning them. It is difficult to establish how exactly these translational strings were attached and who tugged at them; what we know for certain is that they carried significant tensions. Louis Thomassin in his monumental work on church discipline (1678–1679) admits that "in France, Spain, and England, translations were made until the ninth century without consulting the pope at all, by bishops and kings" (Percival 1886: 34). Yet, papal and imperial authority could occasionally be involved in "un-translating" some bishops. For example, when ... from grounds of simple ambition, Anthimus was translated from Trebizonde to Constantinople, the religious of the city wrote to the pope, as also did the patriarchs of Antioch and Jerusalem, and as a result the Emperor Justinian allowed Anthimus to be deposed.

(Percival 1886: 34)

Inevitably, tensions would arise between various centres of power: every now and again, church authorities would protest "against the constant translations made by the secular power" as "the Emperors of Constantinople were often absolute masters of the choice and translations of bishops" (ibid.). Thomassin concludes that "no translations could be made without the consent of the Emperor, especially when it was the See of Constantinople that was to be filled", while pointing to parallels on the British Isles in relation to the patriarchal thrones of imperial cities: "The Kings of England often used this same power to appoint to the Primatial See of Canterbury a bishop already approved in the government of another diocese" (Percival 1886: 34–35).

Translations in Britain

Indeed, the British Isles offer us a valuable showcase because of their distance to the Imperial Capital (and the papal centre of power), and a considerable sense of independence. Especially the last two centuries preceding the eventual breaking away from the Roman Catholic Church in the 1530s are important to understand the complexity of translations. Kathleen Edwards (1959) argues that before the early fourteenth century the practice of ecclesiastical translation had not been common. "The bishops, once appointed, still normally expected to remain in their sees for the rest of their lives"; in fact, "during the twenty years from 1307 to 1327 only one bishop was translated to a second see" (Edwards 1959: 77–78). This scarcity of translations was a politically stabilizing element. Edwards points out that "when a bishop had been born in the diocese he was later to rule, it often happened that he was more ready to adopt and sometimes to lead political opinion in his part of the country"—this, in her view, is one of the factors which "help to account for the absence of any united political action by the episcopate" in that period (1959: 77).

Soon enough, however, tensions between the two main centres of authority began to intensify, often manifested in translations of carefully selected individuals. In his analysis of the power play between the pope and the kings of England (especially Edward II and Edward III) in the management of the church hierarchy, John Highfield describes "a working compromise" which had been established and continued to be effective for several decades. Considering the question: whose candidates were in fact chosen?, Highfield speculates that

From the date when Edward III established secret contact with John XXII early in 1330 a great many choices were undoubtedly those of the king in

> which the pope concurred. But ... there were other important lay and ecclesiastical influences which were respected at the Curia. In any case the pope and cardinals might choose in anticipation a royal clerk or the favourite of a nobleman. They thereby indicated that, although they thought it important that a bishop should be acceptable to those who mattered politically, they did not think it essential to consult the lay powers. Beyond that the pope is found staking out a small corner of the field of episcopal patronage for his own men. This he could do in less important sees or when a series of translations gave him a special opportunity. But it cannot be proved that the increased numbers of translations were a direct attempt by the papacy to increase its control of episcopal patronage. Indeed, they may have been prompted by a desire to promote the successful.
>
> *(Highfield 1956: 134)*

As these comments demonstrate, episcopal translations cannot be reduced to a means of exerting political influence, though it is clear that they were used for this purpose by both the church and the state against each other. Whatever their outward-facing strategic role, translations must also be recognized as part of an internal administrative system rewarding success and loyalty. Especially in late medieval period, "the Welsh sees were being looked upon as the first step on the ladder for promising English civil servants who expected later to be translated to richer English sees" (Edwards 1959: 76). Meanwhile, in England, the prospect of translation was having a discernible effect on the quality of the bishops' ministry:

> [T]he bishops' ties with their dioceses were becoming less close, and they were normally spending less time in diocesan work than their predecessors in the thirteenth century. This has sometimes been attributed to the increasing number of royal clerks and other outsiders provided to bishoprics by the pope in accordance with the king's wishes, and to the much more frequent custom of translating bishops from one see to another. An ambitious man, appointed from outside, having no local family connexions, and hoping soon to be translated to a richer see, might well not have the same interest in his diocese as his predecessors who had normally spent the rest of their lives in it.
>
> *(Edwards 1959: 52)*

This suggests that in the English context (and likely elsewhere), episcopal translation had become a favourite vehicle of professional and socioeconomic mobility for ambitious men of the church, provided that they enjoyed a high enough pedigree and strong connections in the first place. These pre-conditions should not be ignored since "the medieval church did not normally offer a career open to talent through which the low born could rise to positions of power and responsibility" (Edwards 1959: 53). In this sense, translations affirmed and further advanced existing privilege rather than created it.

The promotion of success could extend beyond the perspective of a single individual—a translation often benefited entire cities and communities. William Camden, the author of *Britannia*—a monumental topographical and historical survey of Great Britain and Ireland—in some cases sees translation as a key factor of urban development. The following entry devoted to Chichester illustrates that the relocation of a bishop's residence—another subtle inflection of translation—was nothing short of a watershed moment:

> Chichester, in British *Caercei*, in Saxon Cissan | ceaster, in Latin *Cicestria*, ... a pretty large city, and wall'd about; built by *Cissa* the Saxon, the second King of this Province; taking also it's name from him. ... Yet before the Norman conquest it was of little reputation, noted only for St. Peter's Monastery, and a little Nunnery. But in the reign of William 1. (as appears by Domesday book) *there were in it* 100 Hagae, *and it was in the hands of Earl Roger†; and there are in the said place 60 houses more than there were before: It paid 15 pound to the King, and 10 to the Earl.* Afterwards, when in the reign of the said William 1. it was ordain'd, that the Bishops Sees should be translated out of little towns to places of greater note and resort, this city being honour'd with the Bishop's residence (which was before at *Selsey*) began to flourish. Not many years after, Bishop *Ralph* built there a Cathedral Church, which (before it was fully finish'd) was by a casual fire suddenly burnt down. Notwithstanding ... it was raised up again; and now, besides the Bishop, has a Dean, a Chaunter, a Chancellor, a Treasurer, 2 Archdeacons, and 30 Prebendaries. At the same time the city began to flourish; and had certainly been much frequented and very rich, had not the haven been a little too far off, and less commodious; which nevertheless the citizens are about making more convenient by digging a new canal.
> (Camden 1695: 167–168, original emphases)

Given the contrast in status, prosperity and population levels before and after the transfer of the bishopric seat, it is not an overstatement to say that the history of Chichester is divided into two distinct eras: Before and After Translation. The arrival of the bishop triggered a chain reaction that hardly left a stone unturned: from the city's material and symbolic landscape (the construction of a cathedral), to its social and economic development (the wide range of new ecclesiastical offices and roles), to its regional significance, down to the level of ambition of its citizens who felt emboldened to venture into a major infrastructure project. In this relatively short passage, Camden makes the comment that the city "began to flourish" not once but twice, as the consequences of an episcopal translation snowball into all spheres of life.

Translations during the Reformation and Counter-Reformation

At about the same time that King Henry VIII of England was translating himself and his country out of the increasingly uncomfortable embrace of the Roman

Catholic Church, a young student of law in Paris, named John Calvin, had a similar change of heart. What was initially personal inner turmoil, within several years developed into a full-scale theological programme, presented in his *Institutes of the Christian Religion* whose ever-expanding versions he kept publishing, in Latin and his own translation into French, throughout his life. Having taken refuge in Geneva which had shortly before rebelled against the Catholic Church, Calvin was able to persuade the city council to pass a number of laws regulating various aspects of private and community life, which "effectively transformed his adopted city into the so-called Protestant Rome" (Watt 2020: 1). Given the strong emphasis Calvin put on church governance and on discipline more generally, it is not at all surprising to find that his *Institutes* contain detailed provisions in this regard. Their Chapter 3, specifically concerned with "the teachers and ministers of the church, their election and office" (Calvin 1989: 315), starts by establishing the ground rules and defining ideal conditions. The fundamental assumption, filtering down the set of detailed regulations, is that God "alone should rule and reign in the Church, … preside and be conspicuous in it"—though it is immediately added that, in the absence of his visible presence and directly audible voice, he

> uses the ministry of men, by making them, as it were, his substitutes, not by transferring his right and honour to them, but only doing his own work by their lips, just as an artificer uses a tool for any purpose.
>
> *(Calvin 1989: 316)*

This view of a strictly instrumental role of human authority gives it maximum power and minimum accountability. Tools merely execute the master's will and intention—they do not interpret it and have no agency of their own. Calvin's chief concerns are order, unity and protection: he stresses "the strongest bond of unity … by which believers are kept together in one body" and admits "that the Church cannot be kept safe, unless supported by those guards to which the Lord has been pleased to commit its safety" (1989: 316–317). Even though, in the course of his argument, he makes references to the New Testament image of church as the body of Christ (Ephesians 4:4–16), this is a remarkably inert body. It is not meant to move or even, at the very least, keep growing; rather, it is preoccupied with simply preserving its integrity and entrenching itself:

> Whoever, therefore, studies to abolish this order and kind of government of which we speak, or disparages it as of minor importance, plots the devastation, or rather the ruin and destruction, of the Church. For neither are the light and heat of the sun, nor meat and drink, so necessary to sustain and cherish the present life, as is the apostolical and pastoral office to preserve a Church in the earth.
>
> *(Calvin 1989: 317)*

Despite the brief mention of sustaining and cherishing its life, the perils facing the church—devastation, ruin and destruction—evoke a static structure (such as a building) rather than a living organism. This impression is confirmed and indeed reinforced when we get to the principles that apply to the positions of authority. Calvin is concerned with "those who preside over the government of the Church" (1989: 317), not those who lead it. Again, it is potentially deceiving that his favourite title is "pastor"—that is, etymologically, "shepherd"—as he declares that "what the apostles did to the whole world, every pastor should do to the flock over which he is appointed" (1989: 320). In this paradigm, pastors are not to worry about leading their flock to greener pastures; rather, they are "set as watchmen in the Church" (ibid.) (see Figure 2.2). "Our present purpose ... is not to enumerate the separate qualities of a good pastor", writes Calvin with beguiling sincerity, "but only to indicate ... that in presiding over the Church they ... must train the people to true piety by the doctrine of Christ, administer the sacred mysteries, preserve and exercise right discipline" (ibid.).

This brings us straight to the question of official mobility in Calvin's churches. The *Institutes* declare:

> While we assign a church to each pastor, we deny not that he who is fixed to one church may assist other churches, whether any disturbance has occurred which requires his presence, or his advice is asked on some doubtful matter.
>
> *(Calvin 1989: 320)*

FIGURE 2.2 The Reformation Wall in Genewa, Switzerland, with statues of the four main proponents of Calvinism: William Farel, John Calvin, Theodore Beza, and John Knox.

© Olrat | Dreamstime.com

What is immediately striking in this passage is the dynamics—though one would rather be tempted to say "statics"—of the default relationship between the pastor and his church. Not only is there no sign of mutual agreement (as in the early Christian communities discussed earlier) but the church is denied any agency and becomes fully objectivized. In this model of top-down governance *par excellence*, churches are assigned to pastors, not pastors to churches. Ironically, pastors do not have much say either: they are "fixed to one church" and have "duties assigned" to them. Sometimes they "may assist other churches" but only when there is a risk of serious disturbance—arguably, of a magnitude greater than disturbance brought about by a guard (another of Calvin's favourite ecclesiastical terms) who temporarily abandons his post. There is no doubt that this is a concession, an emergency measure, not a description of a regular or desirable practice. In principle, translation of church officials is banned

> to maintain the peace of the Church, ... lest all should become disorderly, run up and down without any certain vocation, flock together promiscuously to one spot, and capriciously leave the churches vacant, being more solicitous for their own convenience than for the edification of the Church.
>
> *(Calvin 1989: 320–321)*

The choice of vocabulary here is very telling. Even though the word *translation* is not used, the practice is implied to be subversive, chaotic and frenzied—typical of a maniac running up and down with no reason, sense or purpose. Alternatively, the interest in being translated to another church is attributed to a lack of moral compass, to wanting discernment and no independent judgement, to whimsical weakness of character, or simply to a pursuit of one's own benefits—all equally dishonourable options. Calvin's opposition to ecclesiastical translation is not much different from that articulated in the Nicene Canons some twelve hundred years earlier—in both cases "great disturbance and discords that occur" being the main objection—but he wraps it in new layers of contempt, ridicule and condescension.

The phrasing of the *Institutes* concerning the translation of church officials, "This arrangement ought, as far as possible, to be commonly observed, that every one, content with his own limits, may not encroach on another's province" (Calvin 1989: 321), sounds disturbingly close to what could be a joint closing statement at a meeting of the Five Families summoned to discuss their zones of operation across New York City. To prevent any such associations with illicit or ungodly conduct, Calvin musters the heaviest rhetorical artillery: "Nor is this a human invention. It is an ordinance of God" (ibid.), and goes on to invoke a broad range of biblical instances in which the apostles appointed and ordained presbyters in the early church, with a strong intention for these appointments to be permanent and unbroken by translation. The following admonition, "Let every one, then, who undertakes the government and care of one church, know that he is bound by this law of divine vocation" (ibid.), sounds fairly plain and one would expect the argument to be thereby concluded.

Except it is not. Like so many others before him, Calvin is keen to leave a small crack in this otherwise impenetrable ban, and softens his dogmatic position:

> not that he is astricted to the soil (as lawyers speak), that is, enslaved, and, as it were, fixed, as to be unable to move a foot if public utility so require, and the thing is done duly and in order; but he who has been called to one place ought not to think of removing, nor seek to be set free when he deems it for his own advantage. Again, if it is expedient for any one to be transferred to another place, he ought not to attempt it of his own private motive, but to wait for public authority.
>
> *(Calvin 1989: 321)*

In the end, despite the invocations of "an ordinance of God" and "law of divine vocation", translations appear to be a threat not so much to heavenly arrangements as to terrestrial ones. As long as they are "done duly and in order", and especially "if public utility so require"—in other words, as long as they do not openly challenge the structures of authority—translations can and should be allowed, even in the most dogmatic socio-religious systems. The Law of Expediency trumps all other laws.

If there ever was a point on which both the doctrine and practice of the Protestant churches were virtually indistinguishable from those of the Roman Catholic Church, translation surely occupied that rare shared ground. One of the leading figures of the Counter-Reformation, Cardinal Robert Bellarmine,

> disapproved the prevailing custom of translations and protested against it to his master, Pope Clement VIII, reminding him that they were contrary to the canons and contrary to the usage of the Ancient Church, except in cases of necessity and of great gain to the Church.
>
> *(Percival 1886: 35)*

Save for the appeal to the higher authority (which would have been impossible for Protestants who rejected any such idea), Bellarmine's argumentation closely mirrors Calvin's as it draws on both the dogma and the apostolic tradition. In fact, the notion of "great gain to the Church" which could justify suspending the application of ordinary rules echoes the Jesuit motto *ad maiorem Dei gloriam*, "for the greater glory of God". If one has a glorious enough end in sight, the means of attaining it become open to negotiation. Having heard Bellarmine's case, "[t]he pope entirely agreed with these wise observations, and promised that he would himself make, and would urge princes to make, translations only 'with difficulty'" (ibid.). The strong link between translation and gatekeeping was highlighted again, this time by papal authority.

Translations remembered

Percival concludes his "Excursus on the Translation of Bishops" on a somewhat resigned or even resentful note: "But translations are made universally, all the world over, today, and no attention whatever is paid to the ancient canons and discipline of the Church" (1886: 35). In the footnote, he adds "I believe this is true of all churches, Catholic and Protestant, having an episcopal form of government"—and this is the real crux of the matter. Episcopal translations are an inseparable element of a governance structure which combines vertical and horizontal strings of dependency and influence. They are effectively attempts to square a circle. In the larger economy of preventing administrative chaos and discouraging opportunist attitudes, translations are a means of rewarding the loyal and ensuring the best use of exceptional talent beyond a local site that had become too small for it. Even though, strictly speaking, they concern individuals, their effects are felt by communities.

Like the translations of relics, which often became pivotal points in the history of local communities and were commemorated by annual feasts (see Chapter 3), so the translations of bishops would be long remembered in their dioceses. Sometimes they were described as truly providential. Here is one notable example. In his collection of records and documents relating to the Isle of Man and the Diocese of Sodor and Man, William Perceval Ward (1837) laments the deplorable condition of the Manx Church in the early decades of the nineteenth century: "Somewhere during this period a great blot fell upon the Diocese, and complaints were made, not without good reason, by Bishops in England, that unworthy men, unconnected with the Island, were admitted into Holy Orders, to the great disgrace and injury of the Church at large". Fortunately, bishop George Murray who upon his nomination "found great irregularities practised in some of the Churches, and a general carelessness pervading by far too large a proportion of the Clergy" undertook major work of disciplinary purification by "suspending some and degrading others: a necessary discipline, which cannot be enforced in England with the same promptitude". Apparently, by the time Murray was translated on to Rochester in 1827, "these irregularities, and this carelessness ... had vanished from the [Manx] Churches"; not only that, but in the nine years in office he "succeeded in raising funds sufficient for the building and rebuilding of eleven new Churches and Chapels" (ibid.). In fact, in his own address, Murray goes so far as to suggest that "if the ancient discipline of the Church were lost, it might be found in all its purity in the Isle of Mann" (ibid.), with a subtle hint at himself as a near-messianic figure. The impartiality and robustness of this story of moral, administrative and economic restoration is called into question when we consider that its author, bishop Ward, was bishop Murray's immediate successor, undoubtedly keen to partake in his success—but even so, episcopal translations remain its major milestones.

Similarly detailed records are not always available or easily accessible. However difficult it is to reconstruct the various pastoral, political and pragmatic reasons underlying translations of bishops, their fact (and often, direction) is a trace of the complex dynamics between individuals, communities, offices, and localities. In some cases, browsing through the lists of bishops made available online by notable sees of various hierarchical churches, all we find is a mere indication that a translation occurred at a certain point. Can anything about the significance of episcopal translation be gleaned from such scarce evidence? Let us take a closer look at several such lists.

The See of Oxford, funded by Henry VIII, enumerates 43 bishops between 1542 and the present.[1] Typical entries look like this:

1628–1632: Richard Corbet
(formerly Dean of Christ Church; translated to Bishopric of Norwich in 1632)
...
1665–1671: Nathaniel, Lord Crewe
(formerly Rector of Lincoln and Dean of Chichester; translated to Bishopric of Durham in 1671)
1674–1676: Henry Compton
(formerly Canon of Christ Church, translated to Bishopric of London in 1676)
1686–1688: Samuel Parker
(formerly Archdeacon of Canterbury; died 1688)
...
1766–1777: Robert Louth or Lowth
(formerly Bishop of St David's; translated to Bishopric of London in 1777)

In this inventory, translation is never used to describe the installation of a new bishop of Oxford, only his departure to another destination. In cases such as Richard Corbet's and Henry Compton's that would be understandable (since they had already held pastoral positions at an Oxford church before they were appointed bishops) but the list also includes others who had held episcopal offices elsewhere, such as Robert Louth, "formerly Bishop of St David's". Could this signal another semantic nuance of the term, highlighting the status of the "donor"? It would be consistent with the overall axiological trajectory of the translational movement, either of saints and their relics (see Chapter 3) or church officials. If translation always proceeds towards a place of higher significance and prestige, it would make former episcopal posts logically appear as inferior—perhaps, then, refraining from using this designation by the "receiving" bishopric is an act of terminological courtesy? Several other documents support this working hypothesis. The list of bishops of Norwich covers a period of nearly a thousand years, stretching back to the late eleventh century when the see was first moved to the city following the construction of the Norwich Cathedral.[2]

Among 71 bishops, 15 are described as "translated to" various places (most often to Ely, with eight translations between late thirteenth and eighteenth century), but there are no corresponding "translated from" descriptions for the 14 bishops who came to Norwich from elsewhere. These "inbound translations" are simply hinted at by specifying the previous title while "outbound translations" are spelled out explicitly. For example, the entry on Edmund Freak (bishop of Norwich 1575–1584) reads "Bishop of Rochester, translated to Worcester 1584" and on Sir Thomas Gooch (Norwich 1738–1748), "Bishop of Bristol, translated to Ely 1748". A bishop who features on both lists, Richard Corbet, is described as "translated to Norwich" according to the Oxford record but the Norwich inventory does not even mention his previous office.

Regardless of the dominant focus on where the translation is headed, we also find examples of "inbound translations" mentioned in official records. The Bishopric of Bangor in Wales, dating back to the founding of the monastery in the early sixth century, is among the oldest on the British Isles. Out of its 86 bishops, 20 are described as "translated to" another see (the earliest one in 1109, the most recent in 1809) but seven are also "translated from" elsewhere (between 1737 and 1830).[3] Interestingly, two successive bishops experienced double translation: William Cleaver (in office 1800–1806), was "translated from Chester; translated to St Asaph" and John Randolph (1806–1809) "translated from Oxford; translated to London". In the local Welsh context in that particular decade, translation must have appeared as a default mechanism whereby bishops were both installed and sent off. With an exception becoming a rule, one can understand the reasons for Percival's dismay that "no attention whatever is paid to the ancient canons and discipline of the Church" (1886: 35).

To complicate matters further, in the much younger Roman Catholic Diocese of Shrewsbury dating back to mid-nineteenth century, translations are viewed from the perspective of the individual rather than the place.[4] Among the ten bishops, three experienced translation. Edmund Knight, the second incumbent, is described as "translated to Shrewsbury on 25th April 1882" and subsequently "translated to Flavias 28th May 1895"; the seventh incumbent, John Aloysius Murphy, was "translated to Cardiff on 26th August 1961"; finally, the ninth incumbent, Joseph Gray, was "transferred to Shrewsbury 30th September 1980". Setting aside the slight terminological variation in the last record, all four translations mentioned in the Shrewsbury list were "outbound". Similarly, of the four translations involving three of the former bishops of Motherwell, two were to Motherwell, and two others to Botrys and Glasgow—but all were "outbound".[5]

Even though one can find mentions of both "translations to" as well as "from", the overall weight of evidence suggests that the concept of episcopal translation is predominantly "target-salient". Looking at the complete trajectory of the transfer, the destination is usually more important than the origin. In its ecclesiastical sense, translation—even when it is remembered—is generally forward-looking.

A translation in the times of COVID-19

To complete this survey of episcopal translations, let us take a closer look at one of the most recent ones. On 18 January 2020, the United Diocese of Glasgow and Galloway of the Scottish Episcopal Church published a press release announcing the election of its new bishop. The exact wording of the announcement is worth noting:

> The Right Reverend Kevin Pearson was today elected as the new Bishop of Glasgow and Galloway. Bishop Kevin is currently the Bishop of Argyll and The Isles and his election to Glasgow and Galloway represents a historic "*translation*" of a Bishop from one See to another. The See of Glasgow and Galloway became vacant in 2018 following the retirement of the Rt Rev Dr Gregor Duncan … Bishop Kevin will take up his new post at a service of installation later in the year, on a date to be announced in due course. …
>
> Bishop Kevin was elected to Glasgow and Galloway by the Episcopal Synod, a body comprising the Diocesan Bishops of the Scottish Episcopal Church. In accordance with the Church's canonical process, the right of election had passed to the Episcopal Synod, following previous processes of vocational discernment within the Diocese of Glasgow and Galloway.[6]

Several elements in this text deserve a mention. First, the electoral character of the appointment carries considerable emphasis. In this relatively short press release of ten brief paragraphs (each containing only one or two sentences), election is mentioned no fewer than twelve (!) times, starting with the title. Based on this account, there can be no doubt that translation is neither a mere transfer from one place to another nor a result of an individual decision (let alone whim) but an outcome of a long, robust, extensive, collective deliberation process by various bodies, running through several stages and following a strictly prescribed procedure. The Chair of the Episcopal Synod and Primus of the Scottish Episcopal Church, Bishop Mark Strange, quoted in the later part of the text, said:

> I warmly welcome the unanimous election by the Episcopal Synod of Bishop Kevin as Bishop-elect of the Diocese of Glasgow and Galloway. The election follows a period of vacancy and since the right of election passed to the Episcopal Synod during the summer of 2019, the Bishops have continued to listen carefully to the views of the Diocese and to engage in a process of ongoing prayer and discernment throughout the autumn.

This is the second time in this short text that "the right of election" is mentioned as having passed to the Episcopal Synod, implying that the "previous processes of vocational discernment" at a local level had been inconclusive. Reading this statement, one can hardly shake off a sense of over-elaborated defensiveness. The insistence on the legality of the process and its democratic character (four references to election in just two sentences) is prefaced by a remark that the decision was unanimous, and sealed with the assurance of due devotional care being taken throughout. The translation is pictured as occurring at an intersection of worldly and spiritual realities, and being attuned to the demands of both.

Though invoked only once, translation carries a lot of weight in this text. Not only is the word italicized but also put in defamiliarizing inverted commas and immediately defined: "his election … represents a historic *'translation'* of a Bishop from one See to another". Surely this announcement could have been made without it—there is more than enough emphasis on rightful election—but the use of what is presented as a specialist term, amplified by a sense of momentousness ("historic"), additionally mystifies and legitimizes the episcopal appointment. This link with the past is picked up by several other press outlets. "UK News in Brief" published online in *Church Times* on 24 January 2020 starts with the news of "Bishop Pearson translated to Glasgow & Galloway" and, having announced the appointment, goes on to state that "It is the first translation of a bishop in the Scottish Episcopal Church since the 1930s". The rarity of the event not witnessed for several generations, combined with a sense of tradition and embeddedness in complex ecclesiastical processes, has an authenticating effect. That this validation is indeed necessary soon becomes clear. Before quoting the same statement on the "right of election" by the Primus that we know from the earlier press release, it is mentioned that bishop Kevin Pearson "was elected by the Episcopal Synod unanimously, after previous processes of vocational discernment within the diocese failed to reach an agreement". This is the first and only explicit reference to the difficulties, disagreements and tensions that must have preceded the process of translation. The pre-emptive insistence on legitimacy, consideration, and unanimity finally makes sense.

Another press release published on the official website of the Scottish Episcopal Church on 7 April 2020 brings a different distribution of emphases.[7] By then, the pressures of the COVID-19 pandemic and the implications of the national lockdown largely dominate the update on Bishop Kevin Pearson's upcoming translation. Repeating his message to the receiving diocese, Bishop Mark Strange makes reference to the coronavirus restrictions:

> Clearly the present situation has caused me to consider how the process [of translation] could be best conducted without creating a further delay. Therefore following a meeting of The College of Bishops, at which we agreed that Bishop Kevin could be instituted by deed, signed by all members of the College, I can now tell you that Bishop Kevin will become Bishop of Glasgow and Galloway on the 1st July 2020.

An unprecedented global health crisis is calling for extraordinary measures. A collective, ceremonial and corporeal installation of a new bishop, in re-enactment of the earliest apostolic tradition, is not possible in the times of COVID-19. However, some residual elements of a haptically authenticated succession remain in the act of formal institution: an official deed is to be circulated among all electors for their signatures. A special video "The Welcome" published on the website of the diocese in early July 2020 starts with the footage of several bishops signing and dating the deed that carries a large red wax seal as they "confirm, support and allow the installation of bishop Kevin". This is followed by a succession of all-too-familiar Zoom screens featuring hundreds of parishioners from the many congregations in the diocese, keen to introduce themselves and extend their welcome.[8] The sense of celebration, pride, and anticipation is undeniably kairotic; we will see a similar atmosphere of communal excitement surrounding the ceremonial translations of relics (discussed in Chapter 3).

At the same time, this entirely virtual translation seems to have brought about a curious grammatical effect. The press release announcing the decision to proceed by deed is entitled "Bishop Kevin translates to Diocese of Glasgow and Galloway on 1 July".[9] The same syntactic structure is repeated in the opening paragraph: "He will translate to the Diocese of Glasgow and Galloway on 1 July 2020". In its only two occurrences in this text, the verb *translate* is used intransitively in the active voice. To the best of my knowledge, this usage is not attested previously (except in specialist academic studies such as Sommar 1998). Episcopal translations are normally described in the passive voice and one would expect that Bishop Kevin, like so many others before him, would also "be translated". However, in the absence of a public ceremony and a college of bishops visibly performing the translation, Bishop Kevin has no choice but simply "to translate". He is definitely not "translating himself"—that would imply a sense of agency which beyond any doubt lies with the electors. At the height of the pandemic, propelled by a force that has no perceptually obvious source yet is fully binding in official terms, Bishop Kevin Pearson translates to his new diocese.

This translation, performed in Western Europe in the 2020s, highlights many of the main themes explored in this and the following chapter. An undeniable sense of momentousness and celebration is tinted with implicit but clearly perceptible tension, signalling undercurrents of potential controversy, discord and power struggle. Though focused on an individual, translation is not within any single person's gift. Instead, it both depends on and powerfully affects groups and communities. Not only is it authorized and performed by a collective body of the episcopal college (in itself a bundle of interlocking links, both horizontal and vertical) but it also establishes and highlights complex translational bonds between the sending and receiving congregations (likely involving a wide spectrum of reactions: from a sense of pride and camaraderie, to hurt, disappointment, and resentment). A translation changes the dynamics of the entire structure within which it occurs. The original announcement of 18 January 2020 closes with the following admission: "The Bishops are aware that, in electing Bishop Kevin, this will in due course create a new episcopal vacancy in Argyll and The Isles and we will look forward to supporting that Diocese as it seeks a new Bishop". By creating a real gap in its wake, one translation immediately calls for another.

Episcopal translationality

Throughout this chapter, we have seen that a translation of a bishop is not merely a matter of a decision (one of the dominant tropes in the discussions of textual translations) but rather of action that occurs across a multifarious network of influences and relationships. That complexity and distributed agency are arguably the reasons why the term *translation* continues to be used in this context: it has an advantage over simpler, non-specialized notions, such as for example *(re)appointment, move* or *transfer*. A technical term implies a specialized action involving elaborate processes and official institutions. Ecclesiastical translation is seen as hugely consequential and capable of bringing both significant benefits and causing serious problems. That is why, over the centuries, it has been so strictly regulated, prohibited from becoming the default mode of appointing leaders in the church and only allowed in special circumstances in which the potential gains would outweigh the losses. Initially, this gave the term *translation* negative connotations—as something undesirable, disruptive, and therefore discouraged—that only recently seem to have been cast off. This axiological shift arguably follows the growth of the hierarchical structure of the church and the transfers of power within it. A bishop is no longer responsible for one congregation with which he is intimately bonded; he now oversees multiple churches within the diocese, which makes his local connections more dispersed. Consequently, the previous spousal relationship founded on exclusivity gives way to a managerial model which foregrounds corporate benefit.

However, all this does not conclusively establish the experiential character of ecclesiastical translation, which is the main argument of this book. To make that point, we need to reach deeper into the material substrate. Similar to the translation of relics (to be considered in Chapter 3), episcopal translations created a felt connection between the two communities at both ends of the process—and if a bishop continued to be translated on, between all his previous, present, and future sees. Just like in the Middle Ages, especially in the Carolingian period, relics were translated as "gifts of friendship"—even if oftentimes offered and received under coercion—so the translations of bishops between sees could be viewed as acts of goodwill as well as elements of larger power games. Whatever the sentiments surrounding them, translations had profound implications in all spheres of life, from symbolic to material. The incoming bishops brought with them not only certain views and convictions, specific behavioural and verbal habits as well as ways in which, from now on, things were to be done but also important artefacts and an entourage of people to be reckoned with—all of which must have transformed the complex material and social dynamics of the diocese.

In this way, translations were experienced by the communities involved—especially the receiving one—but what about the bishops themselves? Their experience of translation must have been even more obvious. In his essay "Imaginary Homelands", Salman Rushdie notes in a tangential, parenthesized remark that since "the word 'translation' comes, etymologically, from the Latin for 'bearing across'. Having been borne across the world, we are translated men" (1982). If this was ever true of anyone, it was definitely true of countless bishops over the last two millennia—and not in an imaginary way or a figurative sense but in the most literal, direct, even etymological use of the term. Rushdie goes on: "It is normally supposed that something always gets lost in translation: I cling, obstinately, to the notion that something can also be gained"—and that could not have been any closer to the experience of translated bishops, either. Why would you allow yourself to be translated or aspire to it if you were not going to benefit from it in some way? The only concern was to ensure that the gain was publicly perceived as not exclusively or predominantly your own. Of course, the bishops have nearly always been the privileged few—regardless of whether or not they were translated—and their experience of translation was one of elevation towards an even higher status, greater significance and more wealth. But, with all sense of proportion, that translational gain is not radically different in axiological terms from the experience of translation, however painful, that Salman Rushdie or Eva Hoffman write about. They too would probably agree that, despite all its harrowing effects, the translation they underwent—even if they did not quite choose it at the time—was somehow worth the anguish, bringing Rushdie "one of the more pleasant freedoms of the literary migrant to be able to choose his parents" and "open[ing] the universe a little more" (1982), and Hoffmann (1998 [1989]) "a mending of fractured linguistic identities" (Pas 2013: 65). At the very least, in retrospect, one's own experience of translation is cherished rather than resented. I grant that episcopal translation does not have to be transformational in psychological terms—that is surely not its main import. What it highlights are the complexities of forging and severing connections between people, communities and locations in the larger framework of authority, influence and service.

All these various threads—material, geographical and symbolic—converge in the practices involving the pallium, a special ecclesiastical vestment in the Roman Catholic Church, which will provide the concluding focus for this chapter. Its rich symbolism and elaborate ceremonial protocol is briefly explained in the *New Catholic Encyclopedia*:

> The pallium is a circular band about 2 inches wide, made of white wool, and worn over the chasuble about the neck, breast, and shoulders. It has two pendants, one hanging down in front, the other in back. ... The pallium is made (at least partially) from the wool of two lambs—suggesting Christ, the Lamb of God and the Good Shepherd—blessed each year in Rome (on Jan. 21, the feast of St. Agnes, in her basilica on Via Nomentana), presented to

the pope, and sent to the Benedictine Sisters of St. Cecilia in Trastevere. There they are cared for and shorn and the wool is used for weaving the pallia, which are blessed by the pope in the Vatican basilica on June 28, the eve of the feast of SS. Peter and Paul. Then the prefect of pontifical ceremonies places them in a silver urn, enclosed in the Altar of the Confession and over the tomb of St. Peter in the Vatican basilica. The same prefect, to whom the keys of the cabinet are entrusted, takes the pallia, as needed ..., and places them at the disposal of the cardinal protodeacon or whoever is entitled or delegated to proceed to their imposition.

(New Catholic Encyclopedia *1967, vol. X: 929*)

Before its official service begins, the material substance of the pallium is itself translated several times as it undergoes a process of authentication accompanying its production. In the course of ceremonies temporally aligned with important feasts, it comes into direct contact with the pope himself not once but twice—first as the two lambs and then the completed vestments are presented to him for blessing. The pallium is handled only by designated officials and treated with the utmost respect, second only to that enjoyed by the elements of the Eucharist. It is carefully guarded and locked away until it is ready for conferment upon an individual with whom it will form an unbreakable bond.

The pallium carries with it a long legacy, stretching back to the early church period. It began to be worn "in the 4th century by bishops of the Eastern Churches and the Bishop of Rome to emphasize the episcopal dignity and pastoral office"; "in the 6th century, the pallium was conferred by the pope on bishops of the Latin Church, especially metropolitans, until it gradually became a symbol of the metropolitan office" (*New Catholic Encyclopedia* 1967, vol. X: 929). It has since been a "manifest indication of that sovereign power which flows, as it were, from the head of the apostolical church, to the several ecclesiastical members thereof" (Bernard 1731: 135). The pallium is conferred in a public ceremony that involves taking an oath of allegiance to the pope—it is only at this point that a metropolitan bishop acquires the full authority of his role:

> An archbishop, therefore, who has not received the pallium may not exercise any of his functions as metropolitan, nor any metropolitan prerogatives whatever; he is even forbidden to perform any episcopal act until invested with the pallium. Similarly, after his resignation, he may not use the pallium; should he be transferred to another archdiocese.
>
> *(Braun 1911: 427)*

The pallium has been described as "an episcopal badge of office" (Braun 1911: 429) or "a badge of ... ministerial function" (Bernard 1731: 135). This is a very fitting description. In fact, the closest modern secular analogy would be to a police badge: insignia of officially delegated authority, non-transferrable and only valid in the jurisdiction for which it was conferred. The pallium is likewise restricted in personal and geographical terms. The Code of Canon Law is very clear on this point:

> §2 The Metropolitan can wear the pallium, in accordance with the liturgical laws, in any church of the ecclesiastical province over which he presides, but not outside the province, not even with the assent of the diocesan Bishop.
> §3 If the Metropolitan is transferred to another metropolitan see, he requires a new pallium.
> (Code of Canon Law, n.d., book II, part II, section II, title II, chapter II: Metropolitans)

In short, even when a bishop is translated, his pallium remains untranslatable. However, unexpected insights for episcopal translation are revealed in archbishops' solemn burial ceremonies:

> When an arch-bishop dies his pall is buried with him, and if he is buried in his own diocese it is laid on his shoulders; but if out of it, on his head. If an arch-bishop has been translated to several sees, all his palls must be buried with him; that of his last archi-episcopal see is laid on his shoulders, and the rest are laid under his head.
> (Bernard 1731: 135)

Given the role of the pallium as the badge of office, it is not at all surprising that it should be buried with its holder. In analogous secular contexts, rulers and other public officials are often laid to rest in full ceremonial garb which includes their insignia: crowns, spectres, rings, medals, uniforms, and so on. What is noteworthy here is that the previous pallia are also included in this interment. After all, they are functionally sterile: once a translation to a new see has been completed, they have no official or practical role any more. They become non-objects. They cannot be left for the successors. Nor can they be worn as testimony of their wearer's illustrious career progression. Unlike a newly awarded medal that does not threaten or cancel any previous distinctions but rather complements them, a new pallium supersedes the previous one, annulling it for all intents and purposes. This would suggest that an episcopal translation is irreversible and final, and any links between the bishop and his previous diocese are forever severed to make room for the full authority of the incoming metropolitan.

But paradoxically, they are not. Any previous pallia, though entirely bereft of any official authority or even symbolic value, continue to mediate—privately, to the archbishop, for the rest of his lifetime; publicly, to others, at the point of his death—that complex meshwork of connections between a person, community, time and place, which by now are no more than a faint memory. Faint, yet important enough to make one final, material and symbolic appearance. I find no better word to describe this simultaneously powerful and elusive effect than *translationality*: an experience of connecting, through material, sensory mediation, with another reality across time and space.

Notes

1 http://www.oxfordhistory.org.uk/bishops/list.html Accessed 31 October 2022.
2 http://peterowen.org.uk/bishops/norwich.html Accessed 31 October 2022.
3 http://www.bangorcivicsociety.org.uk/pages/hisso/bishops.htm Accessed 31 October 2022.
4 https://www.dioceseofshrewsbury.org/about-us/bishop/previous-incubents Accessed 31 October 2022.
5 https://www.rcdom.org.uk/previous-bishops Accessed 31 October 2022.
6 https://www.glasgow.anglican.org/new-bishop-elected-for-glasgow-and-galloway/ Accessed 31 October 2022.
7 https://www.scotland.anglican.org/bishop-kevin-translates-to-diocese-of-glasgow-and-galloway-on-1-july/ Accessed 31 October 2022.
8 https://www.glasgow.anglican.org/the-welcome/ Accessed 31 October 2022.
9 https://www.scotland.anglican.org/bishop-kevin-translates-to-diocese-of-glasgow-and-galloway-on-1-july/ Accessed 31 October 2022.

3
HOLY BONES
Translations of relics

The Mediolanum translation

In 386 CE, Ambrose, the bishop of Mediolanum, the then capital of the Western Empire, had just finished building one of the several new churches around the city. This was part of his strategy to consolidate the influence of the followers of the Nicene creed (recently pronounced as the only orthodox and legitimate expression of the Christian faith) and further suppress other factions, especially Arians, who still enjoyed imperial support and whose power therefore could not be ignored. Ambrose's situation was quite precarious: building and even dedicating the basilica was not enough to guarantee control over it, even though this was "the first Christian church to have been named after its founder" (Freeman 2011: 16). More spectacular, truly unprecedented measures were necessary. In a letter to his sister, the bishop recounts:

> [A]fter I had dedicated the basilica, many, as it were, with one mouth began to address me, and said: Consecrate this as you did the Roman basilica. And I answered: "Certainly I will if I find any relics of martyrs."
>
> *(Ambrose 1896: 436–437)*

It is telling that the first translation of holy relics of this breadth and scale in the Western church was born out of thinly veiled imperial aspirations and in the spirit of open competition with Rome. "Rather than resorting to another *translatio* from a city better endowed with a Christian pedigree than his own 'sterile' Milan, Ambrose vowed to equip his new church as requested" (McLynn 1994: 211). Even more thinly veiled was Ambrose's intention to be seen as responding to a bottom-up trend, something we could describe in economic terms as popular

DOI: 10.4324/9781003382201-4

demand—though in addressing it, he decided to exceed popular expectations. For this plan to work, one essential ingredient had to be secured: a divine intervention, a sign from above. The Mediolanum translation, to fulfil its role in consolidating the status of the city, its church and its bishop, was to be nothing short of a miracle. In addition, time was clearly of the essence. Given the urgency of his predicament, it is little wonder that no sooner had Ambrose made his promise than he felt in his heart "a kind of prophetic ardour" (1896: 437). Upon this declaration, "the whole city must have experienced something of a shock wave, as friends and foes alike braced themselves to see how the bishop would fulfil his self-imposed task" (McLynn 1994: 211).

From there, events unfolded exactly as one could have predicted. Ambrose soon experienced a miraculous vision in which the location of the remains of two previously unknown martyrs was revealed to him, and proceeded to recover them in the most extraordinary circumstances:

> God favoured us, for even the clergy were afraid who were bidden to clear away the earth from the spot .... I found the fitting signs (Lat.: *signa convenienta*), and on bringing in some on whom hands were to be laid, the power of the holy martyrs became so manifest, that even while I was still silent, one was seized and thrown prostrate at the holy burial-place.
>
> *(Ambrose 1896: 437)*

From the beginning of this quest, both divine favour and conveniently "fitting signs" were evident. Those "on whom hands were to be laid" is Early Christian code for people who suffered from otherwise incurable conditions, notably demonic possession, and could only hope for supernatural healing. Ambrose, once again, is careful to distance himself from any sense of agency: the violent seizure of the possessed person who was thrown to the ground as if to visibly demonstrate the martyrs' magnetic attraction happened without one word being spoken by the bishop. Indeed, the only words spoken on this occasion apparently came from the demon who implored the martyrs to show mercy and addressed them as Gervasius and Protasius, thus revealing their identity (McLynn 1994: 211). No one could doubt that a holy place had been found—but that was just the beginning of a series of astonishing incidents. In the excavated grave, Ambrose declares, "We found two men of marvellous stature, such as those of ancient days. All the bones were perfect, and there was much blood" (Ambrose 1896: 437). Needless to say, these miraculous events attracted huge attention: "During the whole of those two days there was an enormous concourse of people" (ibid.). The presence of this great cloud of witnesses must have provided further validation to the extraordinary nature of the find, and at the same time safeguarded a proper level of public recognition and widespread endorsement against suspicions of fabrication. A sense of momentousness and excitement was building up:

Briefly we arranged the whole in order, and as evening was now coming on *transferred* [Lat: *transtulimus*] them to the basilica of Fausta, where watch was kept during the night, and some received the laying on of hands. On the following day we *translated* [Lat: *transtulimus*] the relics to the basilica called Ambrosian. During the *translation* [Lat: *transferimus*] a blind man was healed.

(Ambrose 1896: 437; Latin text according to Ambrosius n.d.; emphasis added)

In his description, Ambrose is using the common compound verb *transferre*—here, inflected for tense (past and present), voice (active), mood (indicative), person (first) and number (plural). Even though he is drawing on it with remarkable consistency in this passage, there is no reason to suggest that he is attributing to it the specialized sense which will only emerge in the following centuries. What is clear, however, is that even though described using rather ordinary vocabulary, this early instance of relic translation is presented as inspiring extraordinary events. As we saw, miracles started to occur even before the relics were unearthed and continued overnight after the first hasty translation to Basilica Fausta. But it was only the following day, when the relics were set upon litters and carried along in a public, joyful procession to the newly built basilica named after the bishop (see Figure 3.1), that witnessed a truly miraculous translation. In a sermon preached right after this ceremony, Ambrose recalled some of its elements and fleshed out their significance thus:

> For not without reason do many call this the resurrection of the martyrs. ... You know—nay, you have yourselves seen—that many are cleansed from evil spirits, that very many also, having touched with their hands the robe of the saints, are freed from those ailments which oppressed them; you see that the miracles of old time are renewed ..., and that many bodies are healed as it were by the shadow of the holy bodies. How many napkins are passed about! How many garments, laid upon the holy relics and endowed with healing power, are claimed! All are glad to touch even the outside thread, and whosoever touches will be made whole. ...
>
> The glorious relics are taken out of an ignoble burying-place, the trophies are displayed under heaven. The tomb is wet with blood. The marks of the bloody triumph are present, the relics are found undisturbed in their order, the head separated from the body. ...
>
> Let these triumphant victims be brought to the place where Christ is the victim. But He upon the altar, Who suffered for all; they beneath the altar, who were redeemed by His Passion. [...] Let us, then, deposit the sacred relics, and lay them up in a worthy resting-place, and let us celebrate the whole day with faithful devotion.

(Ambrose 1896: 437–438)

FIGURE 3.1 The Basilica of St Ambrose, Milan, Italy.
© Roberto Binetti | Dreamstime.com

If, until now, Ambrose was downplaying his agency to foreground the supernatural discovery of the relics, once they have been publicly translated to the basilica, his restraint in this regard had evaporated. Halfway through his sermon, he declared: "Though this be the gift of God, … I have obtained these martyrs for you" (Ambrose 1896: 438). By the following day, when he preached another sermon to rebuke those who doubted the merits of the martyrs, his reputation and that of the newly translated relics had coalesced into one. Invoking a range of theological arguments as well as witnesses' testimonies, Ambrose announced the miraculous power of the relics that "the devils themselves cannot deny, but the Arians do" (1896: 439). This biting remark brings us back to the religious and political context which inspired the quest for the relics in the first place. The Mediolanum translation—which started an avalanche of similar events in the following centuries—offers a glimpse into the broader philosophical, religious, and social economy of the cult of relics.

Relics and translation

Veneration of holy people, or saints—a term back then reserved predominantly for martyrs—appears to have been limited and localized at first, but with the legalization of the Christian religion by Emperor Constantine in the early fourth century, started to expand (Eastman 2018: 676). One of the earliest records of the localized cult of relics concerns the martyrdom of Polycarp. After this elderly bishop of Smyrna was burned in the arena for his faith around 155 CE,

> Polycarp's congregation later searched the pyre for his relics, gathering up 'his bones—more precious to us than jewels, and finer than pure gold'.

These they 'buried in a spot suitable for the purpose' where they could gather annually to celebrate "the birthday of his martyrdom".

(Duffy 2018: 154)

At such "suitable spots" outside city walls, the saints were venerated in an increasingly ritualized fashion, as stories of their extraordinary lives and martyred deaths were regularly read and recited, their spiritual intercession sought, and their miraculous power anticipated. Around the time of Ambrose, by the end of the fourth century, the ritual of pilgrimage—visiting designated holy sites to honour holy people and gain their favours—had been well established among Christians who "flocked to the graves of the martyrs, and treasured oil or water or cloth which had come into contact with their blood or bones", seeing in them "a channel of divine healing and consolation" (Duffy 2018: 155). In 403 CE, Jerome complained about Rome: "The city is stirred to its depths and the people pour past their half-ruined shrines to visit the tombs of the martyrs" (Jerome 1892: 190). His comment reflects the frustration and anxiety felt by many bishops. Their seats, the basilicas, contained within city walls, did not incorporate the tombs of the martyrs as did those suburban shrines that were now becoming rival centres of worship (Bartlett 2013: 10).

An answer to this threat of losing both religious and social significance was found in translation: "the problem was solved by moving the bodies of the martyrs under the cathedral altars. The charisma of the saint was thereby united to the power of the institution" (Duffy 2018: 155). "The lives and deeds of these early martyrs may have been varied but they were united in sainthood by their violent deaths, subsequent exhumations, and the 'translation' of their bodies into relics" (Nafte 2015: 210).

But what exactly are relics? The English term derives from the Latin *reliquiae*, meaning "remains", and a form of the Latin verb *relinquere*, to "leave behind, or abandon"; traces of which we can hear in the English verb *relinquish*: to release, put aside, give up, let go, renounce. Thus, a relic is something left behind that continues to bear witness to the extraordinary, supernatural and miraculous character of the person it was once a part of. With time, three classes of relics were established, the Latin names indicating their respective origins. First class relics, *ex ossibus*, are bones, so in the strict sense, what remains of the saint's body. Second class relics, *ex indumentis*, are parts of clothing that the saint used or owned, and sometimes also certain objects of personal use (for example, combs); this implies that they had been in physical, intimate contact with his or her body over an extended period during their lifetime. A special subcategory of this class were the *brandea*, cloths dipped in the blood of the martyrs (Wilson 1983b: 340). Finally, third class relics, *ex linteo*, are objects, usually fabrics, which had touched the body of the saint or relics of the first class; for example, a piece of a shroud used to cover the body or on which the bones rested. The key conceptual element here is thoroughly material, substantial, and haptic: it is the physical touch that creates the mystical link. Parallels to the central rite of the Roman Church come to mind: "[t]he saint was believed to be present in his or her relics, as Christ was present in the Eucharist" (Duffy 2018: 156). Just as ordinary bread and wine during the Eucharist are in their essence transubstantiated into the real body and blood of Christ (though their physical properties remain unaffected), so an otherwise ordinary piece of matter becomes a sacred object by coming into physical contact with a saint or their relics of a higher class.

The tradition of translating the relics of martyrs and other saints and depositing them under the altar originated in the Eastern Church, possibly under the inspiration of this vision from the Book of Revelation (6: 9): "And when he had opened the fifth seal, I saw under the altar the souls of them that were slain for the word of God, and for the testimony which they held" (*King James Version* 1978). Constantinople, as the new capital city of the Roman Empire, was in particular need of holy bodies and saw a number of notable translations—including the saints, Andrew, and Luke—as early as the mid-fourth century, followed by many others (Wilson 1983a: 4; Kracik 1994: 99). Ambrose's translation of the relics of Gervasius and Protasius seems to have been one of the first acts of this kind in the West, and one that gave rise to a widespread tradition. To realize the scale of the ever-increasing demand for the relics of saints, especially from the eighth century onwards, let us note that in the seven years of his pontificate (817–824), Pope Paschal I ordered around 2,300 translations of saints from the catacombs to the numerous basilicas in Rome—on average, that is roughly one per day! From the Early Middle Ages, a ritual translation of a martyr's relics from their original place of burial (or from a less worthy site) to the most sacred place in a church was a form of canonization confirming the saintly status and, as such, was subject to the control of bishops, synods, and popes (Wilson 1983a: 6). In fact, until this day the act of canonization is alternatively described as elevation to the altar. Recognized saints were not "buried in the ground like ordinary mortals but … raised above it in shrines, cases and caskets. … [T]heir solemn 'translation' to such elevated places was often the means of proclaiming their sanctity" (Wilson 1983a: 10). A translation did not inaugurate the process of acquiring sainthood but rather crowned it (see Figure 3.2).

Thus one of the first observations relevant to the work of relic translation is that it was an act of complex elevation—spatial as well as social, to use the division suggested by Roman Michałowski (1983). In the first instance, a saint's remains were found somewhere low, both in physical and symbolic terms: usually buried deep in the ground, covered from view. It was only thanks to "fitting signs" declared by someone in authority that they were recognized for what they really were, leading to their physical and symbolic elevation. Secondly, during the ceremony of translation, the relics were carried on litters or in specially crafted reliquaries or fereters, lifted for everyone to see, and some to touch. As we will see from various testimonies, translation by definition proceeded from a less to a more worthy place: it was always upwards, never downwards. The initial act of

FIGURE 3.2 The silver reliquary of St Adalbert (Wojciech) of Prague in the Gniezno Cathedral, Poland.
© Mariamuz | Dreamstime.com

burial of a martyr, committing the body to the ground in the original interment, was never described as a translation. Instead,

> translation was the solemn process of transferring, or in some cases restoring, the relic to what was considered its rightful place, or to a place of greater authority or higher status befitting the holiness of the once whole individual or item.
>
> *(McAlhany 2014: 443)*

How did relics become available for translation? Two basic situations were possible: either hitherto unknown relics were discovered—a case usually described in Latin as *inventio*—or those held in one place and in possession of one group were transferred to another and handed over to new custodians, more or less willingly. The various modes of circulation will be discussed in some detail later; at this point, it is important to note that regardless of the method of acquisition of the relics, their translations—despite being an undeniable result of human efforts—were usually claimed to have had originated with a divine intervention. Somewhat paradoxically, relics as cultural constructs were "considered at one and the same time to be both subject and object, a person and a thing" (Nafte 2015: 217), and did not fall squarely under human volition or control. Ambrose's vision is a perfect case in point. Sometimes an angel would reveal the place of burial of a martyr who had been forgotten, as with St Evermarus of Leodium (Liège), who seeing the stubborn unbelief of the priest who had received the vision, eventually had to whip him into obedience so that a translation could be performed (Michałowski 1983: 7–8). At other times, the saint himself would intervene, as did St Januarius who appeared to a certain woman in a dream, expressing his desire for his body to leave Napoli and its sinful citizens and be reunited with his people in Beneventum (Michałowski 1983: 3). Similarly, after two centuries of resting in a tomb in a forecourt of the basilica named after him, Saint-Germain-des-Prés, the saint revealed his wish for his remains to be translated to a more prominent position in the church, which he specified with remarkable precision. All these instances point to something we saw earlier in Mediolanum: though performed at critical historical junctures, often in the wake of important (though not necessarily strictly religious) events or in anticipation of them, translations were presented as part of a providential plan, as something with supernatural rather than natural origins.

This is not to say that the divine plan could not have been aided by human intention, action or inaction, or only understood retrospectively—in fact, most translation accounts were written precisely to explain the circumstances surrounding the original act of translation (which may have predated the writing by several centuries) or justify the selection of the place. Given their miraculous power and, even more importantly, their role in instituting sacred places, relics soon became precious commodities. "Although *translatio* was often a key component in the creation of a saint, there was no standard practice common throughout the early Church, and perhaps many of these ceremonies were responses to specific political needs" (Wycherley 2015: 73). Like in Ambrose's case, they could be used to consolidate religious and political authority by invigorating popular piety and enthusiasm, and mobilizing support.

One aim of translation practices "was to dramatize relics so that they became a public demonstration of sacred power. And this power could be channelled to achieve the ends of the celebrant who controlled it" (Freeman 2011: 17). The themes of influence and power will be fleshed out later. The relevant observation here is that it was not only the relics whose status was elevated through translation; the receiving place was also being endowed with a new, higher rank. Every city, town or village where a church was being built had to secure relics of martyrs or other saints. With time, this became a condition on which a new church's dedication depended. Under the canon *Item placuit* of the Fifth Council of Cartage from 401 CE, no new altar could be built unless relics were secured for it (Geary 1978: 20); this requirement was reiterated by the Seventh General Council of Nicaea in 787 CE (Wilson 1983a: 4). Needless to say, this had far-reaching implications for the entire economy of relics, their discovery, "production" and recognition.

Writing about the origins of the translation of relics in the late fourth century and the beliefs that first inspired it, Peter Brown observes: "If relics could travel, then the distance between the believer and the place where the holy could be found ceased to be a fixed, physical distance" (1981: 89). In this sense, the translation of relics may be viewed as an opposite of pilgrimage. This central trope, the movement of one party towards the other, is at the heart of one of the classical formulations of the translational problem by Friedrich Schleiermacher (1813/2012: 49). Who should be left in peace, and who should bear the inconvenience of travel? A pilgrimage required nothing of the saint who was indeed being left in peace; the entire effort, expense, danger and inconvenience were on the person visiting a holy place. In translation, this distribution of agency was fully reversed: it was the relics that were being removed from their previous place of rest to be transferred to a new community that awaited them. One can say, in Schleiermacher's terms, that the author was not only brought closer to the reader but ceremoniously installed in the reader's own site. But unlike textual translations, in which the transfer is metaphorical (ideas and meanings do not travel but rather emerge in a new context), the translation of relics is corpuscular: an actual movement through space is involved, and there is a resulting absence in the original location. No wonder that, in some cases, communities in possession of relics were ill predisposed to the prospect of their loss, and force had to be invoked. Some translations had to overcome resistance and hostility; others were simply performed by force, deceit or outright theft.

In any event, the translation of relics was governed by the same right that applied to textual translations, which proves that calling both practices by the same word was not accidental but conceptually motivated. In his famous *Letter to Pammachius*, Jerome invokes the authority of the translations by Hilary of Poitiers (c. 310–367) who "by right of victory carried the meaning as if captive into his own language" (Jerome 2012: 25; cf. Garceau 2018). "Like slaves, relics belong to that category, unusual in Western society, of objects that are both persons and things" (Geary 1986: 169)—in relation to relics, the notes of possession, captivity or subordination may have been somewhat toned down, but the right of victory still stood. If the custodians of relics managed to defend them against thieves or raiders, it was due to the protection of the saint who granted victory. However, if some relics were captured and translated by force or deception, without any supernatural resistance, this was a clear sign that the previous guardians did not show enough devotion or simply did not deserve them (Kracik 1994: 104). It is worth bearing in mind that

> Thefts of relics introduced a further difficulty since most were said to have taken place during some period of invasion, destruction, or other sort of cultural discontinuity. Hence the cultural symbolism of the relic, its identity, was usually lost or at least placed in doubt. This difficulty was recognized by contemporaries, and the very literature from which we learn of these thefts is largely an effort to overcome this loss of continuity … In any case, the *translatio* and the other hagiographic texts written about the saint are the means by which his identity is standardized and stabilized during this perilous move from an old to a new symbolic context.
>
> *(Geary 1978: 8–9)*

The need to develop a justifying and stabilizing narrative around stolen or forcefully removed relics was often fulfilled by *translationes sanctorum* ("translations of the saints"), a specialized literary genre which evolved out of the basic hagiographical writings, *vitae* ("lives of the saints"). A good example is the translation of St Cyprian from Carthage occupied by barbarians to the just and glorious kingdom of Charles the Great (Michałowski 1983: 20–21). We will reflect on the function of *translationes* more fully when discussing issues of authenticity in later part of this chapter. For now, suffice it to say that history is written by the victors—and the history of glorious and festive translations is no exception.

The translation of St Nicholas

These intricate power struggles and several other relevant aspects are foregrounded in another notable translation that occurred later than those mentioned so far, towards the end of the eleventh century, and was described in *The Translation of Saint Nicholas, Confessor*. We know it from two primary records: that of Nicephorus, thought to have been written in Latin shortly after the saint's relics' arrival in Bari (which occurred on 9 May 1087), translated into English by Charles W. Jones (1978), and an anonymous report in Greek from the thirteenth century, translated into English by J. McGinley and H. Mursurillo (Anonymous 1980).

Both accounts begin with a familiar invocation of divine inspiration amidst religious and political turmoil. During the reign of Emperor Alexius, when "the foreign and infidel hordes that had migrated through the Roman Empire were being pacified and the bold Normans who had voyaged thither had been beaten and dispersed" (Anonymous 1980), Almighty God in his providence determined that it was time for the city of Bari and indeed the entire province of Apulia "to be visited and ennobled by a most propitious and lasting splendor" (Jones 1978: 177). This general and pious aspiration was soon translated into rather concrete actions as some certain "wise and illustrious men"—who turn out to be merchants—decided to set sail to Antioch in Syria on what appeared to be a regular trading mission, with their ships "laden with grain and other merchandise" (ibid.). This time, however, the cruise was to include an important halfway stop, made either on the way over or back, as the merchants made plans to drop anchor in the Byzantine city of Myra (present-day Demre in southern Turkey), come on land, take the body of St Nicholas and bring it to Bari.

Both versions of the story are remarkably direct on this point and unapologetically embrace the viewpoint of the Barians, who do not deem it necessary or relevant to explain their right to the holy body but simply assert their intention "to possess and take pride in him as in a great fortune and inseparable treasure" (Anonymous 1980). Unlike in some other translations, there was no direct supernatural intervention. Apparently, the fact that the region around Myra had fallen to the Turks in the previous decade must have felt like a sufficient reason to translate the relics to a safer and more worthy place. Despite repeated denials of "pursuing mercantile and selfish interests" (ibid.), a sense of commercial enterprise is never far removed, especially as the Barians find out that their Venetian competitors—in the later account described as "brothers", likely in the spirit of Christian comradery against the Islamist occupants of Myra—had conceived of the very same plan. They were likely hoping to replicate the success from nearly three centuries before, when two merchants aided by a pair of Greek monks managed to steal the relics of St Mark from Alexandria and bring them to Venice, concealed under haunches of pork to avoid the scrutiny of the Egyptian guards in an act of "blatant piracy" (Nicol 2008: 24). This time, not only were the Venetians headed for Antioch "for similar commercial reasons" as the Barians but they also had equipped themselves with formidable "iron instruments" to break open the church floor and get to the holy corpse (Jones 1978: 177).

Here comes the first sign of divine providence: despite their logistical advantage and a record track of divine favour, the Venetian merchants were denied success by God, who instead decided to give their plan and its fulfilment to the men of Bari (Anonymous 1980). But God clearly helps those who help themselves: Nicephorus is at pains to demonstrate that the Barians spared no effort, hard work or wit to outdo not only their Italian competitors but also the Greek custodians of the relics and the Turks who were occupying the area (but luckily had not plundered the basilica). The record of the events that transpired in Myra emphasises, in equal measure, God's favour but also the undeniable merits of the Barians who, depending on the situation, sometimes acted politely and respectfully, and at other times assertively or coercively, with remarkable determination. The storyline at this point is full of twists and turns and is so artfully narrated that it is worth quoting the account (in McGinley and Mursurillo's translation) at length:

> Disembarking, then, at Myra, these privileged mariners, after approaching the sacred and holy grave of the Blessed, and after bowing down with great humility, ... made an act of reverence. Then, after they found monks watching beside the holy grave of the Blessed, they requested them to make known to them where the saint's body lay. The monks, thinking that they had made the request in order to reverence the body, with sincerity and kindheartedness complied with their desire and showed them the place where the body of the holy prelate was. The monks afterwards questioned them somewhat sharply, "Why you men, do you make such a request? You haven't planned to carry off the remains of the holy saint from here? You don't intend to remove it to your own region? If that is your purpose, let it be clear that you parley with unyielding men, even if it means our death. For we have rid ourselves of all fear. We won't allow this to be done, we are not going to take after the Iscariot who became a traitor to his own Saviour and Master. Away with any such thoughts!
> ...
> They then who made their request humbly enough as reasonable men, made reply to the monks in humility: "Why surely indeed we admit to you

that for no other purpose did we disembark here than to take the holy remains of our inspired Father. We beg you, then, for your acquiescence, to be our helpers in this, and let not our efforts be in vain." And the monks replied: "The saint truly will not allow this to come to pass, and he will not consent to have his body touched. But if you would listen to our advice, make off from these parts with all speed, before the townspeople hear of what is going on and put you to death."

The men that made this request, then, seeing that they had answered in bitterness of heart, changed their tactics accordingly as it is written elsewhere: "The best course to be pursued is the one that is the least obnoxious," and they said: "Look you, that we have not disembarked here of our own will, but we have been sent by the Pope of Rome and by the Archbishops and Bishops and authorities at Rome associated with him and the whole Council. For all of these arrived in our city of Bari with a large host and the diverse armies of the west, enjoining on us to accomplish this work, and bring back to the Pope the remains of the saint without fail. Why even the saint himself, appearing in a vision to the Pope bade him do this with all haste. And you if you want, accept suitable recompense from us, that we may depart in peace and benevolence."

(Anonymous 1980)

By then, the Barians had tried all possible means of persuasion: respectful observance of local customs, flattery, appeals to the conscience and religious authority, bullying, and bribery—all evidently permitted in pursuit of a higher end. It is worth noting that at least some confusion in these negotiations was likely due to difficulties in interlingual translation: at some point, the guardians were confused "thinking because of an inadequate mastery of languages that they [i.e. the Barians] were asking for the place of oblation" (Jones 1978: 178). However, as the conversation progressed, arms were drawn, and tools produced, doubts about the visitors' true intentions must have been quickly dispelled. When none of the more peaceful tactics worked, and the local monks remained unpersuaded and uncooperative, the merchants of Bari abandoned hope for a non-violent outcome and simply forced their way into the tomb (see Figure 3.3), to the horror of the custodians. In distress, one of the monks who was holding a glass vial filled with the fragrant oils miraculously secreted by the saint's body dropped it and heard it crash on the stones. Yet, when collectively examined a moment later, the vial turned out to be intact. This was immediately interpreted as the supernatural sign that

the will of God and the saint acquiesced in removing his remains from there. For the visitors now had full assurance that the saint was escorting them, and saying: "Here is the tomb in which I lie; take me then, and depart; for the people of Bari are to be forever protected by my intercession."

(Anonymous 1980)

FIGURE 3.3 Damaged sarcophagus in the church of St Nicholas in Demre (ancient Myra), Turkey.
© Romica | Dreamstime.com

Now that the human resistance was largely overcome, there came the time to face the resistance of the earthly matter. At that point, Matthew, apparently the most hot-blooded of the Barians,

> put down his sword, and, taking up a huge mallet, hammered with great force at the cover of the floor, which was over the oil-exuding tomb, and straightway shattered it. And digging into the hole, led on by the welling favor of the sacred oil, they discovered a second cover which was the lid on top of the splendid chest. When they had opened this but half way …, the aforementioned Matthew, unable to restrain the ardor of his heart, having no care for himself lest he suffer any harm, beat upon the cover with great strength and shattered it to dust. And when they had opened it, they saw the glory of God, for they found it filled with sacred oil … After this, Matthew, putting aside all fear from his heart, fully clothed as he was, descended into the sacred and holy tomb. And while he was descending within, and dipping his hands into the sacred oil, he beheld the venerable remains glowing like coals of fire, fragrant above all fragrance. And taking them in his hand he kissed them and caressed them endlessly. And he handed them over to the two aforementioned priests. From these portents it was clear to see that Bishop of Christ was bestowing himself on the Italians. …
>
> At this juncture, Matthew, taking up the sacred remains, held them carefully. One of the two priests …, taking them as they were and placing them in his cloak, took possession of them with clear conscience. … And when

the men had been assembled and had taken up their arms, they, together with the priest bearing the sacred remains on his shoulders, repaired to their ships, praising the ineffable providence and benevolence and power of God. When those who were in the boats heard the great force of their hymn which they were singing to Christ the Saviour concerning this bishop, with inexpressible joy they accosted and received their fellow sailors, and adding their own praise to theirs, they lauded their Lord ...

(Anonymous 1980)

The removal of the relics wreaked havoc in the community of Myra. The citizens of the city, having found out what had happened, flocked to the wharves, dismayed and heavy-hearted, many of them throwing themselves into the sea and grabbing hold of the oars and rudders of the Italian ships, pleaded with the Barians not to depart without leaving a share or some small portion of the saint's body. The Italians firmly declined and appealed to a sense of justice, pointing out that after more than seven centuries of enjoying the saint's protection, healings and blessings, it was now time to share him with other Christians and let him "give light to the western world" (Anonymous 1980). In this way, the translation was to serve the purpose of an equitable distribution of divine favour.

Thus began a long journey back to Bari. The remains of St Nicholas were reverentially placed in a small wooden chest, and the ships set sail westwards. Tossed back and forth by both adverse and favourable winds, interpreted as the expression of the saint's will to visit or avoid certain places, and accompanied by countless other supernatural signs that appeared along the way, at last the ships arrived at the Italian shores, and the final stage of this long translation commenced:

[W]hen they had come into the city harbor and had placed the sacred remains in the casket and were welcomed joyously by the townsmen and their fellow citizens, they narrated to them how they had acquired the sacred remains of our holy father Saint Nicholas. ... And carrying the casket from the ships, they placed it within the altar of St Benedict, while the sailors carefully guarded the monastery gates lest they be deprived of the holy relics by some stratagem.

(Anonymous 1980)

Having invested so much of their skill, determination and wit, the merchants of Bari were not taking any chances (see Figure 3.4). Their fears appeared to have been justified, for there ensued an armed clash with the men of Archbishop Ursus who had attempted to seize the remains by force and carry them away. But the Barians, once again, were able to defend their treasured possession and, at that point,

FIGURE 3.4 Seventeenth-century icon of the translation of the relics of St Nicholas of Myra.
Muzeum Historyczne in Sanok, Poland. Public domain.

> [T]he large crowd of citizens immediately bore off the venerable remains from the monastery of St Benedict, singing "Kyrie eleison" and other suitable and sacred hymns. And taking the remains from the gate of the harbor, they brought them to the royal praetorium and placed them in the altar of St Eustratius the great martyr. … And this altar, together with other sacred altars that were in the praetorium, was razed to the ground, in order to erect there the holy and sacred altar of our inspired Father Nicholas …
>
> Be it known therefore that St Nicholas was translated from Myra in Lycia eleven days before the Kalends of May and entered Bari on May 9 at the first evening of watch.
>
> *(Anonymous 1980)*

Even though the account of the translation itself ends here, its effects on the people of Bari carry on: that very night and the following morning, forty-seven men, women, and children suffering from various sicknesses were cured—for each of the forty-seven sailors who stepped on land in Myra to claim St Nicholas's relics (while some stayed on the ships). Miraculous healings of both bodies and souls, experienced by dozens, continued over the following days. On a more mundane level, all participants in the translation received remarkable recognition and remuneration. Several lists compiled in the twelfth century give us their names and detail the rewards they received from archbishop Elias. Each of the sixty-two sailors secured for himself and his heirs the following privileges: "burial place next to the wall of the Basilica, pew for man and wife, clerical appointment in the college without fee if desired at regular stipend, full support as pensioner on quitting secular habit" (Jones 1978: 200). Clearly, the rewards of translation cascaded down a spectrum of interlocking spheres: spiritual, social, and economic.

Totus corpus

The extensive accounts of the translation of St Nicholas give us insight into several essential aspects of the translation of relics but also raise some fundamental ontological questions. How are the remains of saints to be viewed in terms of their completeness and integrity? Martyrs, almost without exception, met violent deaths, were often tortured and mutilated, and their bodies were subjected to the most horrific treatment, both before and after death. As we remember from Ambrose's account of the discovery of the Mediolanum martyrs in 386 CE, the bodies, though decapitated, were "found undisturbed in their order" (Lat. *inviolatae reliquiae loco suo et ordine repertae*) and "all the bones were perfect" (Lat. *omnia ossa integra*). The translation of the body of St Pusinna from Châlons-sur-Marne to Herford in 860 CE, made within several years of the event, also stresses the value of receiving the *totum corpus*, all [that remains] of a human body, rather than just some of its parts (Michałowski 1983: 2–3; cf. Shuler 2010). Likewise, the account of the translation of two notable martyrs from roughly the same period makes clear that "the whole Florentius" and "the whole Hilarius" were sought and eventually obtained by the new custodians in Bonneval Abbey, even though earlier attempts had been made to only hand over some parts of their remains (Michałowski 1983: 3). Coming back to the translation of St Nicholas—even though he was a "confessor", not a martyr, and had died of natural causes at a relatively advanced age—Nicephorus's account still emphasizes that, upon discovery, the saint's relics were carefully examined and found intact, and only then tenderly arranged in a silk cloak for the journey to Bari. However, when the adverse winds made it evident the mariners had lost divine favour,

> [T]hey began to accuse each other that some one among them had pilfered something from the relics of the saint. ... Because, if any had dared to do so, they would have to consider what could be done with whatever came from the holy body so that they could return it to its proper place. Then five of the sailors made known that they had something from the holy relics. When they had returned it and put it down with the lot, these five and the rest of the company swore that no one of them had any more of the holy relics. By this incident, no one was left in doubt that it was in accordance with the will of God. It was God's will that they should be delayed until the relics of the holy body were rendered intact. They were thereby given to understand that the confessor of God himself willed that his relics should never in any way be divided.
>
> *(Jones 1978: 176)*

In the cases described above, the value of the relics depended on their integrity and completeness. The translation of St Nicholas especially demonstrates that the success of the entire translational mission hinged on first retrieving and then delivering the whole body of the saint: hence the initial examinations at the grave, the investigation followed by oaths on the ship, and the public interment at the final destination. The task of translation—at least in theory—consisted of a complete removal of the holy body from the original site, followed by its full deliverance, intact, into the receiving site. Here is a perfect incarnation of the idea of loss-free translation: not a hair must be missed.

And yet, the insistence on completeness that we find in this translation account—and many others—comes across as suspiciously overemphatic and strategically pre-emptive, as if the idealistic aspiration was to make up for an imperfect execution. Such an impression is hardly surprising if we bear in mind that this distinct hagiographical genre emerged precisely to explain, justify or defend the translations of relics—which implies that, more often than not, these events tended to stir controversies, fuel disagreements, and raise suspicion.

Once again, translation's complex socio-political entanglement is impossible to ignore, and St Nicholas's example is a perfect case in point. Despite what the two translation accounts mentioned above would want their readers to believe, the rivalry between the Barian and the Venetian crews was not over when the former beat the latter in reaching Myra, recovered the saint's body and quickly made away with it. Only a decade or so later, as part of what we now call the First Crusade, sailors from Venice also arrived in Myra to find the Church of St Nicholas nearly deserted, with the mass celebrated only once a month.[1] Given the much lower levels of protection and resistance than those faced by their rivals from Bari several years earlier, the Venetians had little trouble taking possession of a few boxes which turned out to contain the remains of two bishops, St Theodore and another St Nicholas (the uncle of Nicholas of Myra), and placing them promptly on board their ships. Apparently not entirely satisfied with these finds, some sailors decided to return to the church one last time and, following a sweet scent, broke through several floor layers under which they found a copper urn with the inscription "Here lies the Great Bishop Nicholas, Glorious on Land and Sea". This was the real treasure they were after, so the Venetian mariners seized it right away, though before departure—unlike the unscrupulous Barians—did not forget to leave some relics (presumably, of other saints) to the archbishop of Myra, along with a sum of money as compensation for the damage caused to the church. The expedition returned to Venice in 1101 and, after some disagreement about the most fitting place where to deposit them (reminiscent of the controversies in Bari), the relics—consisting of some five hundred, mostly small, bone fragments—were finally secured under the high altar in the church of San Nicolò al Lido.

In relation to the overarching questions explored in this book—what is translation and what does it do?—we must reflect on why the removal of the remaining relics of St Nicholas's from Myra and their installation in Venice is not commonly described as a translation, and seems never to have inspired elaborate hagiographic accounts corresponding to those originating in southern Italy. Why were some relics of St Nicholas *translated* to Bari in 1087, but merely *brought* to Venice in 1101? What did the two crews do differently?

Posed this way, this question exposes a key feature of relic translation. The difference is clearly not a matter of technology or procedure. In both cases, similar acts were performed: floors smashed, crypts broken into and precious bones excavated. The moral conduct of the translators was not any different, either: they all tried various strategies and, finding polite requests ineffective, had no reservations against resorting to deceit and violence.

What signals some critical difference is the broad—historical, ideological, religious, social and psychological—context of reception. The citizens of Bari had no reason to doubt that they were witnessing the first-ever arrival of the authentic and, to their knowledge, complete relics of St Nicholas. By contrast, when the Venetian ships returned from the First Crusade carrying the "residual" remains of the saint, the Bari relics had not only been publicly translated but also ceremonially interred in the basilica by Pope Urban II more than a decade earlier. In these circumstances, the merchants of Venice could not describe their mission as a translation, at least not openly. Nor could they credibly insist—as did the Barians—that they had the "whole" and intact saint, but only some, and rather fragmented, parts of his skeleton. Importantly, they did not have the skull, apparently the most valuable part among all relics (a view reflected in early medieval terminology: a saint's skull was not called *cranium* but rather *caput* in Latin [in Old Franconian, *chef*], "head" [Michałowski 1983: 3]), which had been taken to Bari. But paradoxically, this fact may have helped support their claims of authenticity. Had the Venetians declared to have recovered the entire body (or at least the parts doubling those held at Bari), this would inevitably challenge the authenticity of the Barian relics; instead, what was brought to Venice was presented as the parts that the first plunderers overlooked and left behind in their carelessness and haste. Thus the Venetians, despite their chronological handicap, were able to outdo their rivals in terms of diligence, piety and reverence shown by making sure that the crypt in Myra was swept clean. All of the saint's relics were removed (though the task may have been made easier for them by the unfortunate Myrans, who, after losing the majority of the large relics in 1087, appear to have collected the remaining small bones into the copper urn, only to lose them too in 1100!). Not surprisingly, a codex written some three hundred years later by the Venetian nobleman Antonio Morosini presents a somewhat different version of events—though we should note that he was a secular chronicler, so his account is not a translation in the hagiographical sense. Still, according to him, it was apparently the sailors from Venice who first obtained the relics of St Nicholas but, on the journey home, were forced to make a stop at Bari to replenish their food supplies. When the Barians found out that the body of St Nicholas was on board, they refused help, but since the Venetians "were in great need they were forced to give them one of the arms of St Nicholas, and it was put in place honourably during the year of Our Lord 1095" (*Morosini Codex*, §033.00).

The controversies about which city had the true and real body of the saint carried on for nearly nine centuries during which the crypt in Bari mostly remained sealed, although with time the idea of *totus corpus* became somewhat relativized (for reasons discussed above). It was only in 1953, due to some extensive structural work required around St Nicholas's tomb, that it was opened in the presence of a special pontifical commission, chaired by the archbishop of Bari, and the task of examining the bones was entrusted to Luigi Martino, professor of human anatomy at the University of Bari, assisted by his colleagues Alfredo Ruggieri and Luigi Venezia.[2] Before being reinterred in the renovated crypt four years later, the bones were inventoried, measured and X-rayed, allowing a skeleton reconstruction. They were found to be highly fragile and brittle—after all, they had rested in Myra for some 740 years, and then another 870 in Bari—and mixed with some stones and gravel which may have been collected in haste from the original tomb by the merchants-sailors. However, the central fact established beyond doubt in the mid-1950s was that the saint's *corpus* held in Bari was by no means *totus*. In 1992, a similar examination was commissioned in Venice, and Luigi Martino was again put in charge to ensure the continuity and credibility of the enquiry. Even though the Venetian collection of relics, as mentioned earlier, was in a much worse condition and included some five hundred small bone pieces and chips, Martino was able to conclude that they were complementary to the bones in Bari, and had come from the skeleton of the same man. Again, it should be stressed that we are not talking about a neat division of easily distinguishable parts. Rather, the two collections of bones appear to have been gathered in a somewhat random fashion: for example, elements of both femoral heads are in Venice but other femur parts rest in Bari. Since femurs are the longest and one of the most characteristic parts of the human skeleton, it seems unlikely that their incompleteness would have been missed when they were first found and brought to Italy. This means that the eleventh-century translation of St Nicholas's relics involved an imagined and perceived, rather than actual, totality of the *corpus*. Thus medieval practices of *translatio reliquiarum* demonstrate a more general translational principle: though it may, for ideological reasons, be presented (and perceived by the public) as a complete and exhaustive transfer, the real business of translation deals with partiality.

Pars pro toto

This observation leads us directly to another key aspect of the economy of relics, especially in the later periods, when their cult was spreading aggressively. Luigi Martino's examinations in the 1950s and 1990s revealed some other striking similarities between the two collections of St Nicholas's relics. In Bari, one vertebra was found to show a thin slice of bone removed with a sharp knife; in Venice, a similar sharp cut was found at the top of the left long arm bone. That small pieces of holy bones were cut off, presumably as "independent" relics, signals a key perceptual and ideological shift. The demand for totality, likely tied to a sense of local pride and tangible benefits enjoyed by the hosts of holy sites, must have been counterbalanced by the conviction that a part may legitimately and sufficiently stand for the whole. This principle of *pars pro toto* meant that the tiniest relic was viewed as carrying in itself the fullness of the saint's power. Already in the fourth century, Gregory of Nazianzus declared that even drops of the martyr's blood and "small tokens of their passion"—that is, their relics—"are as powerful as their bodies" (Eastman 2018: 679). A century later, Theodoret of Cyr in *The Cure of Pagan Maladies* insisted that "though the body has been divided, its grace has continued undivided. And that little particle and smallest relic has the same power as the absolutely and utterly undivided martyr" (Jurgens 1979: 241). Consequently, it was not unusual for a small body part to be described as *corpus* (Gagov 1948; Michałowski 1983: 2; Kracik 1994: 102). "These body parts, even in fragments, were not symbolic of sainthood, or indicators of a divine presence, but the absolute physical embodiment of the departed. A sliver of bone or a wisp of hair represented the entire person" (Nafte 2015: 212). In theoretical terms, this can be described as "distributed personhood": the saints, "as agents, they were not just where their bodies were, but in many different places (and times) simultaneously" (Gell 1998: 21)—except that the relics offered grounds for claiming bodily, not just imagined presence.

Of course, apart from philosophical deliberations and theological arguments, considerations of a more mundane nature were quickly coming to the fore. As demand soared and the number of primary relics remained stable (unless the remains of new saints were discovered), removing parts of the saints' remains became increasingly common in order to give—or, more likely, sell—them to others. Analysing the qualitative changes in the cult of relics between antiquity and the early medieval period, Jan Kracik (1994) notes that especially the seventh and eighth centuries saw a rapid increase in the number of relics in the West, as the churches in Gaul performed numerous translations and inventions, involving also lesser known saints. In their role as the funders of cathedrals and monasteries across their empire, the kings of the Franks demanded real bones from the popes in Rome, and were not prepared to accept relics of lesser classes, such as the *brandea*. Consequently,

> [t]o the communities fortunate enough to have a saint's remains in its church, the benefits in terms of revenue and status were enormous, and competition to acquire relics and to promote the local saint's virtues over those of neighboring communities was keen.
>
> *(Geary 1986: 176)*

But the inventory of holy bones could only stretch so far and partitions become inevitable. Here we see the qualitative change announced by Kracik: as a holy body was being divided, and its parts offered as gifts (or sold) to other communities of believers, not only did its power not diminish but it was multiplied. While a saint during his or her lifetime had been bound by ubication (location in a particular place), relics enabled ubiquity, as each sacred part was treated as manifestation of the saint's presence (Kracik 1994: 103). "In 1291 the Dominican theologian Oliver de Tréguier went so far as to argue that a division of relics allowed a greater accumulation of prayers when one added the totals at the shrines where they were honoured" (Freeman 2011: 143). By the same logic, partitioning a body helped alleviate a sense of loss inevitably produced by removing all relics (as was the case in Myra), and created a unique bond between the two or more communities on the opposite ends of the translation process. Complex patronage dynamics were at play: as bishops distributed the relics in their possession among their dioceses or even beyond, "rather than diffusing the importance of the central sanctuary, these gifts increased both its prestige as the central location of the cult now known more widely and the prestige of the ecclesiastic" (Geary 1986: 183).

As a result, it is more of a rule than an exception to find the relics of a saint dispersed over a large area. To illustrate this phenomenon, let us supplement the diachronic view with a synchronic perspective and turn once more to one of the most widely translated saints of all times. According to St Nicholas Center,[3] while the primary relics of the saint are located in the crypt of the basilica of his name in Bari, and in the second major repository in Venice, some relics are also kept in various Roman Catholic and Orthodox churches in: Austria (Wilfersdorf); Belgium (Sint-Niklaas); Bulgaria (Sofia and Bourgas); Canada (Napierville [a finger], Ottawa and Toronto); Denmark (Slangerup); England (Brighton); France (Corbie [a finger], Lille [a tooth], Saint-Nicholas-de-Port, Lorraine [a finger brought from Bari in 1090], and Toulouse [a finger bone]); Greece (Amarynthos, Apikia and Portaria); Germany (Brauweiler; Halberstadt [a finger originally in St Sophia in Constantinople], Nikolausberg, Panschwitz-Kuckau [a tooth], and Worms); Italy (Rimini [upper arm] and Tortorici); the Netherlands (Utrecht, Maastricht and Meijel); Palestine (Beit Jala); Romania (Targu-Mures and Bucharest); Russia (Buzhaninovo, Kazan, Kemerovo, Petrozavodsk, and St Petersburg); Scotland (Aberdeen); Spain (Murcia); Switzerland (Fribourg); Ukraine (Irpin, Kiev, and Lviv); and at least twelve different locations in the United States—including in the St Nicholas Greek Orthodox Church in Manhattan, New York, adjacent to the Twin Towers of the World Trade Center and buried in their collapse on 11 September 2001. Visualizing this extensive network of churches and shrines spanning three continents gives us an idea of the multiple intersecting currents of influences, at least in theory all traceable to the body of a single saint.

Surely, it would be naïve to assume the authenticity of all or even most of these relics. Especially when a legend emphasized the importance of a part of a saint's body, it was not surprising to find that particular part multiplied and claimed by various locations (Jones 1978: 201). Therefore, any systematic attempt to tally these relics is bound to lead to rather embarrassing conclusions. For example, "[a] nineteenth-century census of relics revealed more than thirty heads of John the Baptist" (ibid.). In his own informal count, Jones identified as many as seventeen teeth of St Nicholas held separately from bodies (1978: 202). Still, in several cases scientific examinations have given credence to the traditionally held convictions. In 2017, Tom Higham and Georges Kazan of the Oxford Relics Cluster at Keble College, Oxford University, tested some micro-samples of a pelvis fragment from St Martha of Bethany Church, Shrine of All Saints, in Morton Grove, Illinois, USA (previously held in Lyon, France). Using radio-carbon dating, they were able to confirm the relic's age to the fourth century, which would correspond to St Nicholas's time of death (Coughlan 2017; see also Kazan 2018). Although a comparative DNA analysis with other bones attributed to the saint has not yet been conducted—the risks associated with such a study would likely be too high for the religious institutions involved—Higham and Kazan' findings stand out from the dominant scientific experience in which "many such relics … turn of to be much later inventions" (Coughlan 2017).

To give just one high-profile example: radiocarbon testing, analysis of blood stains, and an examination of some plant and mineral fragments have confirmed that one of the best known relics in the Roman Catholic Church, the Turin Shroud (see Figure 3.5), in which the body of Christ was allegedly wrapped during the few days between his crucifixion and resurrection, comes from the right area, Palestine, but definitely not the right time, having been created

FIGURE 3.5 The Holy Shroud of Turin, Italy.
© Perseomedusa | Dreamstime.com

sometime between 1260 and 1390 CE, rather than twelve or thirteen centuries earlier. "The Catholic Church … refuses to comment on the authenticity of the Shroud, saying that it is purely a scientific question" (Freeman 2011: xii). But the scientific answers do not seem to convince those who believe the relic is genuine and continue their veneration.

Authenticity and authentication

So far, the notion of authenticity has been implicit in our discussion of the economy of relics, and especially their translation, but now it starts to demand fuller treatment. It would seem logical to assume that the power of the relics of the highest class, *ex ossibus*, comes from their ontological identity with the body of the saint: once a person of flesh and blood, now reduced to bones. But this assumption soon becomes problematized as a complex network of conflicting tensions is revealed. The obvious difficulty is that "[t]he most eagerly sought after relics in the medieval period—bodies and portions of bodies—were superficially similar to other corpses and skeletons universally available" (Geary 1986: 174). Barring some structural injuries or severe disfigurements, skulls, let alone other bones, have no special features and do not enable reliable identification—at least not without specialist examination that only became possible relatively recently. Worse still, a human skeleton in its entirety is distinctive enough but in separation small bones or their fragments may be difficult to tell from those coming from animals. Geoffrey Chaucer's depiction of the Pardoner in *The Canterbury Tales*— whose collection of relics included "a pilwe-beer" (pillowcase) claimed to be "Oure Lady veyl", "a gobet of the seyl Peter hadde" (a piece of sail) as well as "pigges bones"—though thoroughly comical, does not seem entirely implausible or terribly exaggerated. The problem must have been very real, since the church law was introduced in the late Middle Ages to the effect that "the relic should be of a size sufficient for them to be recognizable as parts of human bodies; very small relics may not be used" (Beal, Coriden, and Green 2000: 1439; cf. Nafte 2015: 212).

The value attached to relics "required the communal acceptance of three interrelated beliefs": first, that the individual in question was a saint; second, that his or her remains deserve to be prized; and third, "that the particular corpse or portion thereof was indeed the remains of that particular saint" (Geary 1986: 175), and it is this last criterion that we are concerned with here. A specific set of remains could be identified with a particular saint by considering extrinsic or intrinsic criteria. The former category included examinations of the tomb or reliquary, as well as "documents called *authenticae* found either in the tomb of the reliquary itself, or in the descriptions of the burial of saints in hagiographical texts" (Geary 1986: 177). It is worth stressing that relics as objects of veneration required fuller translational engagement than did textual materials, such as manuscripts. Whereas "a manuscript will always have some potential significance to anyone capable of reading it" (Geary 1978: 5), regardless of any variations due to cultural horizons and symbolic functions, as will representational works of visual art which normally "carry an intrinsic code comprehensible within a relatively wide cultural tradition" (6), bare relics have no such intrinsic code. Instead, they need to be embedded in a signifying context extraneous to the relic itself: "a reliquary with an inscription of iconographic representation of the saint, a document attesting to its authenticity, or a tradition, oral or written" (ibid.). This was particularly important when problematic, "unauthorized and illegitimate" translations were performed: "a relic that had been stolen could not maintain the authority of its previous context and had to be invested with an entirely new authority, invented or forged, though still recognizable as part of the same set of values (McAlhany 2014: 443).

Inasmuch as these authenticating processes were carried out officially and in public by local bishops, and witnessed by both lay and clerical audience, they ultimately relied on a number of assumptions regarding the genuine character of the documents, the veracity and precision of the hagiographical accounts, and the trustworthiness of the long chain of human agents involved in the transmission and authentication of the relics. In short, it was up to church officials to declare the authenticity of relics based on guarantees issued and examined by that same church, so these "external examinations" (McAlhany 2014: 443), despite their name, were entirely internal to the ecclesiastical structures. Described in these terms, this self-certification amounts to evidential circularity and would not of course meet the standards of an independent legal process in our times—but we must continue to bear in mind that in the period we are considering the authority of the church was practically unquestionable as well as inseparable from secular power; even if it was not fully trusted it could not be openly challenged.

However, setting their evidentiary value aside, these official processes were not the only means of authenticating holy relics, and likely not the most important one. As Geary explains,

> The most telling evidence usually came from the supernatural intervention of the saint himself, who indicated where his remains were to be found. Then, during the process of determining the relics' authenticity, the saint would often show by miraculous intervention that they were indeed genuine. Thus the initial impetus for the consideration of a possible relic often came in the form of a vision in which the saint appeared to a holy person and revealed where his remains were to be found.
>
> *(1986: 177)*

Of course, in this case authentication was also directly tied to authority, since the person who received the visions would have been "a revered member of the local religious community, a person who commanded respect and authority, by virtue of his office or of his own saintliness"; and "[w]hen a vision came to a person of more humble status, its interpretation was often the responsibility of someone of superior status" (Geary 1986: 177–178). Up to this point, the value of the testimony relied on the status of the witness.

But then came an important development as a wider group of participants became involved in the identification and authentication processes since these revelatory visions usually led to a popular search by the community, be it a monastery or an entire village. When found, the relics would confirm their authenticity by performing wonders. How these miraculous events were observed, experienced and validated is another matter but a certain degree of public scrutiny seems to have been essential. Geary notes that this expectation "for the relics to prove themselves efficacious was reinforced by the custom, in existence by the ninth century, of submitting relics to an ordeal by fire to determine if they were genuine" (1986: 178).

Translation had a key role to play in this process of authentication. Corpses were being translated from the status of ordinary human remains to that of sacred relics "through a public ritual emphasizing both the identity of the remains with those of a saint and the actual miraculous power exercised by that saint through these particular remains" (Geary 1986: 178). The range of the miracles could be very wide, and they appealed to different senses. One of the most popular signs which not only accompanied the relics but also in many cases enabled their discovery in the first place was their strong, wonderful smell. This olfactory testimony must have been particularly powerful as it instantly established the supernatural character of the holy bodies against the repugnant odour of putrescence released by ordinary corpses. It had an immediately authenticating effect: "to encounter a scent was to encounter proof of a material presence, a trail of existence which could be traced to its source" (Classen, Howes and Synnott 1994: 205). In ancient Christianity, "heavenly perfume" and "sweet fragrance" often marked sites and moments of special divine presence: a rededication of a previously desecrated church, a death of a saint, or an encounter with holy relics (Harvey 2006: 65). Importantly, responses to olfactory stimuli are to a certain extent instinctive and cannot be easily controlled, suggesting an external intervention. In the same way as the foul stench of sin produced repulsion, the sweet scent of relics created attraction. But not only that: smells "participated in effecting the processes they represented. Odors could cleanse, purify, ward off, or heal; they could contaminate, polute, endanger" (Harvey 2006: 2). By inhaling the sweet scent of the relics, a Christian could not only recognize sainthood but also have a share in it: literally fill his or her lungs with an air of holiness.

Public translations created highly prized opportunities to experience this sensory encounter with the saint through his or her fragrant relics. By the fifth century, incense practices were commonly incorporated into Christian ceremonies, including burial processions and the translations of relics from one place to another, with perfumed air serving as "a marker that the person or occasion was of exceptional importance or worth" (Harvey 2006: 75). Since the main purpose of many translation accounts was to dispel any doubts around the authenticity of the relics (Michałowski 1983: 10), mentions of exceptional olfactory sensations are very frequent. For example, when the Barian sailors shattered the cover of St Nicholas's crypt in Myra, they found it filled with sacred oil,

> And immediately such an odor was wafted up to them that they seemed to be standing in Paradise. And not to them alone was the odor vouchsafed, but it pervaded even to the harbor to those in the ships. Immediately then, illuminated by the perfumes, they recognized that it was unquestionably within their power to carry off the remains of the saint.
>
> *(Anonymous 1980)*

In their article "The Smell of Relics: Authenticating Saintly Bones and the Role of Scent in the Sensory Experience of Medieval Christian Veneration", Paul Brazinski and Allegra Fryxell describe a range of practices that may have contributed to the relics' "distinctive scent" (2013: 8). They quote ceramic evidence, such as the use of *ampullae* or pilgrim flasks to serve as containers for sanctified liquids, as well as *unguentaria*, narrow-necked flasks containing perfumed oils or unguents (in some cases also suspended incense). These were often placed in the vicinity of relics which thus became exposed to aromatic fluids; in other cases, the construction of reliquaries enabled the relics to be directly infused by fragrant substances poured by pilgrims as offerings (2013: 9). Brazinski and Fryxell conclude that "[a]rchaeological evidence of contraptions for dispensing or carrying liquids, in addition to recent chemical analysis, … suggests that relics did have a uniquely marked smell in the medieval world" (2013: 9). This could mean that "across Medieval Europe, a relic's particular scent was known and used as a means of both evaluating authenticity and shaping the experience of relic worship in general" (2013: 13). A translation, then, could be authenticated by smell.

Other sensory perceptions were also taken as confirmation of the genuineness of the relics. Especially in Frankish churches, "elevations and translations of relics were commonly the occasion for a sudden burst of postmortem miracles" (Smith 1990: 320). Sometimes the holy bodies were so light that those carrying them did not feel their weight at all, as in the case of St Januarius (Michałowski 1983: 3, 20); at other times, conversely, the relics became so heavy that no one could lift them until the saint's will or wish was fulfilled, as with St Germain (Michałowski 1983: 8). "*Brandea*—pieces of cloth that had touched the saint's bones—were believed to become heavier from the contact" (Duffy 2018: 156). Relics could defy the laws of physics. A boat carrying the remains of St Vivian crossed the river without any propulsion, simply in response to the ardent prayers of the monks fleeing with their patron from their enemies (Michałowski 1983: 18). Similarly, when St Bartholomew's sarcophagus was thrown into the sea by godless people, instead of sinking down, it miraculously floated to the island of Lipari, where the local bishop received the remains with due reverence

(Michałowski 1983: 22). Often, the haptic and the olfactory sensations co-existed, and relics would give off pleasant odours when touched (Geary 1978: 4).

Whereas touching a relic and, in some cases, smelling its scent, required physical proximity, sight allowed much broader access for many worshippers at once—and without the risk of damage, theft, or undesirably close inspection. Since relics did not visually differ from ordinary bones and were not decorative in themselves, they were routinely placed in elaborate containers for purposes of veneration. With the increasing fragmentation of the relics in circulation, the distinction between relics and reliquaries became quite blurred, especially when reliquaries started to be shaped like the body part they held. "It is apparent that the function of a reliquary was more than just to protect the bones: it organized the holy remains" (Arponen, Maijanen, and Immonen 2018: 170) and presented them in a recognizable form: as a human bust, skull, foot, or arm (cf. Bagnoli et al. 2011).

> From the twelfth century onwards, "speaking reliquaries" proliferated, shaped to represent the relics they contained: head and bust relics to contain skulls, feet reliquaries for foot bones or sandals, and perhaps most strikingly of all, arm relics, dramatic life-sized objects of silver and gold which brandished, beckoned or seemed to bless the pilgrim. In fact, not all such 'speaking reliquaries' contained arm bones: they might simply hold assorted collections of relics, but their dramatic form powerfully represented the dynamism believed to reside in the relics, and could be used to powerful effect in the liturgy and processions manipulated to touch or bless.
>
> *(Duffy 2018: 160)*

Indeed, if relics of the first class could impart some of their character onto the objects that had been in close contact with them, then this surely applied to reliquaries. Bernard d'Angers, in his chronicle from 1010, describes a procession in which a richly ornamented reliquary containing the head of St Foy received passionate veneration:

> [T]he crowd of people prostrating themselves on the ground was so dense it was impossible to kneel down …When they saw it [the reliquary] for the first time, all in gold and sparkling with precious stones and looking like a human face, the majority of the peasants thought that the statue was really looking at them and answering their prayers with her eyes.
>
> *(Freeman 2011: 81)*

Commenting on the relics encased in gold statues Charles Freeman suggests that "it was as if the reality of the fractured bones and decayed flesh had to be glorified in gold and precious stones if its true value as the body of a saint could be recognized" (2011: 82). The Fourth Lateran Council in 1215 converted this practice into law when it made it mandatory for all relics to be placed in containers (Freeman

2011: 143). There is little doubt that the sense of awe inspired by the beauty and opulence of the reliquary extended to its otherwise unimpressive contents, but just as importantly, the reliquary offered an excellent opportunity for a powerful statement of status and wealth of the relic owners, and must have been a source of local pride (see Figure 3.6). In addition to their religious role, consisting of "injecting vitality into everyday spiritual life" (Freeman 2011: xiii), relics "fulfilled many other functions, as prestige items, money-spinners, talismans against disaster, and as the focus of community identity" (xiv).

This local perspective is another key to understanding the logic of authenticity. Given that "different communities often disagreed, even violently, over which one possessed the genuine relics of a particular saint" (Geary 1986: 178), it was clearly in the interest of its custodians to affirm the authenticity of their relics rather than undermine it. No great honour was to be gained from discovering that one's own community had misdirected their worship, misplaced their trust, or been fooled by obtaining counterfeit relics. Consequently,

> [t]he identification of false relics and the determination of genuine claims ultimately rested on very pragmatic, functional evidence: if the relics worked—that is, if they were channels for supernatural interventions—then they were genuine. If they did not, they we not authentic, regardless of the strength of external evidence.
>
> *(Geary 1986: 178)*

FIGURE 3.6 A golden reliquary containing the relics of merchant and martyr Saint Cugat in the Basilica de Santa Maria Del Mar in Barcelona, Spain.
© David Pillow | Dreamstime.com

The hopes and expectations that the relics would "work" must have run high and originated within the host community, since "relics, especially famous ones, enhanced the spiritual capital of churches and brought them visitors, donations, and financial benefits" (Arponen, Maijanen, and Immonen 2018: 152). This pragmatic aspect also helps us understand authentication as an ongoing process rather than a one-off event. After all, what good is there in relics that appear to have lost their miraculous powers? They are no better than counterfeits or no relics at all. "Once relics had received recognition—had come to be perceived as genuine and efficacious—their continuing significance and value depended on their continued performance of miracles and on their relative value compared with other relics and other sources of power" (Geary 1986: 178).

Therefore, translations whereby relics were being (re)discovered, examined, and carried around in triumphant processions had an undeniably authenticating function: they "publicized their existence and created or strengthened their cult" (Geary 1986: 178). In fact, these ceremonies were so important that "relics long recognized and venerated were periodically 'lost' and 'rediscovered'" (ibid.). This brings to mind George Steiner's observation that "every generation retranslates its classics, out of a vital compulsion for immediacy and precise echo" (1998: 30). Echoes, however precise, fade with time, so in order to continue to reverberate they must be regularly reinitiated; by the same token, as long as echoes are audible, there is no need to doubt or question their source. Geary quotes the example of St Mark who had been the patron of Venice since his initial translation from Alexandria in the ninth century, and yet his relics "were rediscovered in the eleventh century in the course of restoration of the Basilica of St Mark—an orchestrated revitalization ritual that enhanced the value and importance of the saint in the community" (1986: 178). The formal examination of relics in an attempt to authenticate them was practically and pragmatically inseparable from the solemn celebration of the miracles they effected, and the benefits—both spiritual and economic—that they brought. This is another reason why translation celebrations were incorporated into the liturgical calendar and performed regularly on the feasts associated with the particular saint. One of the most famous examples which has survived through the centuries until our times is the triannual feast of liquefaction of St Januarius's blood stored in two small ampules in Naples. The following description of the ritual, drawn from Wikipedia, is worth quoting in full as it captures the thoroughly commercialized character of the contemporary celebrations:

> For most of the time, the ampoules are kept in a bank vault, whose keys are held by a commission of local notables, including the Mayor of Naples; while the bones are kept in a crypt under the main altar of Naples Cathedral. On feast days, all these relics are taken in procession from the cathedral to the Monastery of Santa Chiara, where the archbishop holds the reliquary up and tilts it to show that the contents are solid, and places it on the high altar

next to the saint's other relics. After intense prayers by the faithful, including the so-called "relatives of Saint Januarius" (*parenti di San Gennaro*), the content of the larger vial typically appears to liquefy. The archbishop then holds up the vial and tilts it again to demonstrate that liquefaction has taken place. The announcement of the liquefaction is greeted with a 21-gun salute at the 13th-century Castel Nuovo. The ampoules remain exposed on the altar for eight days, while the priests move or turn them periodically to show that the contents remain liquid.[4]

Based on this description, today the miracle appears to be little more than a trick aimed at dazzling the audience (the archbishop's actions bear a striking resemblance to the theatrical gestures of a typical magician!) and devoid of any discernible spiritual component. Unsurprisingly, various scientific studies, though unable to obtain direct access to the relics guarded by the Catholic Church and thus limited to analysing similar material, are unanimously sceptical of any miraculous action being involved, since liquefaction may also be achieved by shaking, heating, or through a chemical reaction. If the investment of various authorities, both ecclesiastical and secular, in perpetuating the popular belief in the miraculous behaviour of the relics is still evident in certain pockets of twenty-first century Europe, it would doubtless have been much stronger many centuries ago. To most, authenticity is secondary as long as there is a miracle—or magic—to behold. What matters is the gaze of the beholder.

Finally, we must recognize another powerful means that served to authenticate the relics and their translations: *translationes sanctorum*, already mentioned several times. In a largely oral world, these "translations of the saints" provided narratives explaining and justifying the movement of relics, and in many cases carried considerably more weight when written down. A performative reality was being translated into a textual one: ready to be read aloud, quoted, studied and carried beyond the here and now of the events it sought to immortalize. Citing the opinion of Guibert, a twelfth-century abbot of Nogent, saints worthy of veneration should enjoy the support of *scriptorum veracium traditio certa*, "unimpeachable written evidence" which could "clarify the relationship of physical relic to spiritual truth" (Smith 1990: 309), and the same could have likely been said about their translations. To be properly recognized and receive the attention they deserved, translation events needed to be documented. The many translations we have from Carolingian churches share a number of common elements: "the testing of the relics, liminal miracles as the procession reaches the threshold of the saint's 'home,' the ceremony of arrival and enshrining accompanied by healings and gifts to the saint" (Smith 1990: 334). As Michałowski (1983: 4ff) demonstrates, *translationes* may be distinguished from their sister genre, *miracula*, devoted to recording holy signs and supernatural events, in that they only focus on these miraculous elements insofar as they helped explain how (or why) the translation of relics occurred.

Michałowski (1983: 10–11) suggests that translations were written for a number of reasons: (1) strictly religious, to praise the saint and glorify the blessing imparted by him or her on the community in possession of the relics, and thereby give expression to the chronicler's own piety; (2) educational, to provide clues regarding religious life and theological debate, as well as historical, in relation to both the history of the relics themselves and of the institution in possession of them; (3) utilitarian, to raise the prestige of the institution and defend its estates, or encourage the donations of new ones (Michael Spring sums this up in his light style: "[t]he authors of these translations ... hoped to spread the word that Saint So-and-So was moving into a new neighborhood after a long, gruelling escape, and was reopen for business at a better address" [2015: 174]); and, to a large extent encapsulating all the previous functions, (4) evidentiary, to affirm the authenticity of the relics and dispel doubts in this respect. Still, given that the translations were invariably produced by and within the communities that were the destination of the translation process—the target readers, to use the disciplinary jargon—"the propagandistic function of these texts and their public liturgical nature demanded that they reflect values and attitudes espoused by their audiences, if they were to be effective" (Geary 1978: 9). In short, their documentary role must be accepted with caution; rather, they should be viewed as acts of preaching to the converted—or at least to positively predisposed potential converts.

Summing up, it is hard to resist the conclusion that in the broader economy of relics, scientific verification or independent examination cannot outweigh the power of belief—whether understood in strictly religious terms or as complex psychological, emotional, social, and economic investment. As Geary puts it, in relation to relics, "'authenticity' means less identity with a particular saint's body than efficacy in terms of communal needs" (1986: 181). At the same time, admitting that the recognition, veneration, and translation of relics follow faith-based or otherwise imagined trajectories does not make their influence any less real.

Relic translations as "trace element" of social interactions

Just as textual translations may be studied as evidence of linguistic, cultural and material exchanges between various communities as part of the broader power dynamics, so translations of relics provide us with rich material documenting all kinds of influences in medieval Europe. The historian Peter Brown claims that "the transfer of relics ... can serve the historian as a faithful 'trace element' that enables him [or her] to take an X-ray photograph of the intricate systems of patronage, alliance and gift-giving" (1981: 89) that linked the various parts of the late Roman Empire across geographical distances as well as over cultural, political and class divides. He goes as far as to hypothesize that

> if the translation of relics had not gained a major place in Christian piety, the spiritual landscape of the Christian Mediterranean might have been very

different. It might have resembled that of the later Islamic world: the holy might have been permanently localized in a few privileged areas, such as the Holy Land, and in "cities of the saints", such as Rome. There might have been a Christian Mecca or a Christian Kerbela, but not the decisive spread of the cult of major saints, such as Peter and Paul, far beyond the ancient frontiers of the Roman world, as happened in Europe of the dark ages. Elsewhere, the holy might have been tied to the particularity of local graves that enjoyed little or no prestige outside their own region.

(Brown 1981: 90)

Instead, the widespread translation of relics established a whole new web of cult sites, superimposed on the existing, "strictly 'geographical' map of the availability of the holy, which had tied the *praesentia* of the saints to the accidents of place and local history" (Brown 1981: 91), significantly transforming the religious, cultural and political landscape of medieval Europe. It (re-)established and (re-)emphasized hierarchies of dependence and subordination, both on individual and collective levels—so much so that tracing its patterns offers us unique insights into patronage and politics among the Christian elites of the late Roman Empire, and indeed the very emergence of these social classes:

> In the first place, the translation of relics symbolized the newly achieved solidarity of an empire-wide class. The late fourth century saw the formation of a new Christian elite of bishops and noble pilgrims ... [who] found themselves increasingly committed to the wide and dangerous world of the new Christian empire. ... The new members of this Christian elite were in an exceptionally strong position to encourage the discovery and translation of relics. Their wide journeys and their unanswerable social prestige made it easy for them to appropriate and to give their stamp of authority to fragments of the holy. ... Relics offered a way of expressing both protection and solidarity.
>
> *(Brown 1981: 93–95)*

Many of these translations were predominantly unidirectional and therefore indicative of power hierarchies, when

> [t]hose who possessed the holy, in the form of portable relics, could show *gratia* by sharing these good things with others, and by bringing them from the places where they had been exclusively available to communities scattered throughout the Roman world.
>
> *(Brown 1981: 89)*

In his studies of relic translations in the Carolingian era, Michałowski (1981; 1983) demonstrated the role played by them as "gifts of friendship" in instituting and consolidating bonds of "fraternal love" between both individuals and groups.[5] From the mid-eighth century, the popes in Rome, having no shortage of relics in the city's catacombs, were strategically offering them as gifts to increasingly powerful Frankish churches in the north, in the hope of strengthening the mutual ties (Geary 1986: 182–183). Of course, these gifts did not come without some strings attached. The direction of the translation highlighted the dynamics of patronage, subordination and dependence, though as the power balance was gradually shifting north, it would be more adequate to speak of interdependence: the papal "gifts" were not simply being offered but increasingly expected, if not demanded. As noted before, the practice of parcelling the holy remains to give them to carefully selected beneficiaries did not diminish the value of the relics "but rather enhanced it, since their value lay not in the bones themselves as alienable objects, but rather in the relationships they could create as subjects" (Geary 1986: 183). In other cases, friendships were authenticated not so much between the donor and recipient communities as between the "translators" themselves—as when Hildebert received a vision to recover and translate the relics of St Vincent, but it was only his monastic brother Audald who was able to complete it following Hildebert's unexpected death, despite the scheming of many powerful ecclesiastical figures (Michałowski 1983: 28).

At the same time, Brown's claim that "behind every relic that was newly installed in its shrine throughout the Mediterranean, there had to lie some precise gesture of good will and solidarity" (1981: 89) seems to paint an idealized and incomplete picture of the various social dimensions of translations. Geary takes a much more down-to-earth view that

> although relics were almost universally understood to be important sources of personal supernatural power and formed the primary focus of religious devotion throughout Europe from the eighth through the twelfth centuries, they were bought and sold, stolen and divided, much as any other commodity was.
>
> *(1986: 169)*

His study of furtive translations of relics (Geary 1978) reveals remarkable complexity of this peculiar commodity flow within the "transactional culture" (Geary 1986: 170), in which good will and solidarity were not perhaps as frequent as greed, forgery, deceit, and violence.

Consequently, translations of holy relics provide evidence for all sorts of social interactions—friendly and hostile, open and surreptitious, collaborative and competitive—which relied on "various modes of transfer: sale, exchange, gift, and theft" (Geary 1986: 169). A certain hierarchy of power relations may be discerned here. In the absence of bonds of friendship, a party seeking to obtain relics but unwilling to accept strings of dependency or subordination could do so through a commercial transaction. The trade between Frankish churchmen and Italian merchants in the ninth century is particularly well documented, and the most famous brand name was Deusdona (a very telling name in itself, meaning "God's gift"; in various sources described alternatively as a deacon, swindler and thief) who developed a highly efficient, elaborate system of acquiring bones from Roman cemeteries in the winter months and delivering them to his customers awaiting on the northern side of the Alps in the spring (Geary 1986: 185; Spring 2015), but there were also countless others, including occasional and minor relic peddlers, non-fictional counterparts of Chaucer's Pardoner. Finally, the other end of the power spectrum would have seen "coerced transferrals": either through a non-violent theft of individual relics or during organized raids of the enemy's churches (Geary 1986: 183–184). In these latter situations the term *translation* appears be used with greater restraint but it would probably be premature to conclude that they definitely fall outside of its prototypical meaning.

Kairos!

Despite the broad spectrum of situations in which relics were acquired, which problematizes their translation as an invariable gesture of genuine and simple friendship, it seems plausible to assume that once the translation entered the territory of the receiving community, the process usually gravitated towards a similar cultural pattern. "[R]elics might have been 'invented', bought or stolen" but as they proceeded to be "solemnly and publicly 'translated'" (Wilson 1983a: 27), any doubts about their genuineness, the dubious circumstances of their acquisition, and a possibly questionable conduct of the translators, must have drowned in a widespread sense of excitement. The elements of communal celebration and popular recognition must have been integral parts of any solemn translation of martyrs' relics, which, as noted before, benefitted the receiving community in various ways: by endowing it with extra religious and cultural significance, adding a level of felt security and protection, and providing a tangible economic boost. It must have carried with it a sense of *kairos:* a turning point, a critical juncture, a unique moment coming at the right time.

To give these speculations a more concrete shape, let us return, once again, to the translation of St Nicholas. In the first days of May 1087 in Bari, like in Ambrose's Mediolanum seven centuries earlier and hundreds of miles north, a sense of popular anticipation was being skilfully engineered. Being merchants by trade, the Barian sailors knew full well the laws of supply and demand and were no strangers to marketing techniques. After they left the Greek port of Sukea (Sykia), "they did not deviate from their course at any point" (Jones 1978: 187), though as soon as they sighted the familiar shores, rather than head straight to Bari, they decided to land "at the harbor of St George the great martyr, about four miles from the city" (Anonymous 1980). Having made this symbolic connection between the locally established saint and the newly arriving one—and giving the news of their return a chance to spread across the area—"they set about to fashion a most beautiful casket in order to place therein the venerable remains" (ibid.). Evidently, what was a suitable carrier for the relics in the rough seas would have diminished the splendour of the translation ceremony that was about to take place. Just as importantly, the time needed to build a fitting reliquary could be used to complete the necessary preparations in Bari, further enhance people's enthusiasm, and ensure mass attendance. When all was ready, rather than head to Bari by land (the distance would have been no more than eight miles or thirteen kilometres), the merchants set sail for what must have been the shortest cruise in their maritime career but likely the most glorious one:

> Now after these Barians had set their course for the port of their city, their relatives came to meet them in little boats. They were told how the mariners had brought with them the body of the most blessed confessor. When some of the greeters came to understand that fact, they quickly returned to shore, shouting it at the top of their voices to all those standing around. As the news spread everywhere through the city, everyone ran together in a crowd to witness the marvelous and heartwarming spectacle. The Barian clergy, dressed in their sacred vestments, extending the blessings of heaven, walked down with hurried steps to the port, looking to receive the holy body.
>
> *(Jones 1978: 189)*

Bearing in mind that this was a second landing in a short time, and practically within walking distance of the first "unofficial" one, it is hard to resist the impression that this welcome was carefully staged and eagerly performed. There was something theatrical about the reaction of the greeters in the small boats; likewise, the Barian clergy turned out to be perfectly prepared for their task as they waited, in full ritual gear, for a signal to rush to the harbour. Overall, it is a sense of a "marvelous and heartwarming spectacle" that appears to have constituted the core of a prototypical solemn translation of relics: "[t]he great processions of bejewelled bones and flesh, with music and ceremony to match, provide[d] the theatre of the age" (Freeman 2011: 267).

Yet it would be a mistake to reduce this rich spectacle to following certain ceremonial and social scripts, and to allow the twenty-first-century scepticism to colour our understanding of the religious and spiritual dimensions of relic translations that in their day must have been experienced in extremely powerful ways. Focusing in particular on the late-Roman period, Brown makes a fair point that

> studies of the social and political contexts of translations of relics have revealed with such delightful, and even damaging, circumstantiality the relations and the motives of the principal human participants, that we should not forget the prime giver of good things, who was thought by late-antique men to stand behind the busy story of the discovery, the transfer, the accumulation—even, at times, the bare-faced robbery—of the holy. God gave the

relic; in the first instance, by allowing it to be discovered, and then by allowing it to be transferred.

(Brown 1981: 91)

From such a spiritual perspective, a solemn translation must have seemed nothing short of God's will being realized in front of the very eyes of the faithful in a re-enactment of the *Pater Noster* supplication: "Thy Kingdom come. Thy will be done in earth, as it is in heaven" (*King James Version* 1987). In translations, the *sacrum* and the *profanum* intersected as relics embodied a unique space between heaven and earth (Freeman 2011: xiv). The remains of the saints were being translated to a more worthy place as part of a divine plan. Like Abraham heeding God's call to leave his home in Ur behind and set out to Canaan, a land flowing with milk and honey, so the saint, present in his or her relics, was being brought to a more fitting place of recognition and veneration, inaugurating a new era in the life of the receiving community, which itself took the role of a new Promised Land. As Brown further argues,

> The discovery of a relic, therefore, was far more than an act of pious archaeology, and its transfer far more than a strange new form of Christian connoisseurship: both actions made plain, at a particular time and place, the immensity of God's mercy. They announced moments of amnesty. They brought a sense of deliverance and pardon into the present.
>
> *(1981: 92)*

In the background, further echoes of the Lord's prayer may be heard—"And lead us not into temptation, but deliver us from evil" (*King James Version* 1987)—as Brown goes on: "Nowhere did the silver lining of God's amnesty shine more clearly from behind the black cloud of the late-antique sense of sin than in account of the discovery and translation of relics" (1981: 91). If, as he insists, "a sense of the mercy of God lies at the root of the discovery, translation, and installation of relics" (1981: 92), then translation was a powerful means of administering and experiencing salvation. Consequently,

> In such a mood, the relic itself may not have been as important as the invisible gesture of God's forgiveness that had made it available in the first place; and so its power in the community was very much the condensation of the determination of this community to believe that it had been judged by God to have deserved the *praesentia* of the saint. ... The precise events of the discovery of the relic and the ceremonies surrounding its arrival and installation counted for more than the mere fact of its presence in the city. Many relics lapsed into obscurity after their arrival. What mattered was the arrival itself.
>
> *(Brown 1981: 92–93)*

These observations highlight a translation's kairotic quality as an event "larger than life". Experienced originally in a particular historical moment that witnessed the public transfer of a saint's remains to a place of higher worth, a translation belonged to a linear, chronological order. Even in this sense, of course, it covered much more than just the carrying of some bones from one place to another; rather, it encompassed the entire chain of events surrounding the central act of transfer, with all its semiotic and social context, all the festivities and celebrations. Meanwhile, these acts of solemn translation, like other momentous events, had such a profound impact on the local community that they often became parts of the cyclical order through regular re-enactments anchored in a particular locality, and their annual commemoration in the ecclesiastical calendar also came to be known as a translation. For example, in the liturgical calendar, St Benedict's feasts were initially kept both on the date of his death (21st March) and his translation (11th July); however, since the earlier date always falls in Lent, and therefore could not feature joyful celebrations, with time the anniversary of his translation became the principal feast. Within the same week, the translations of St Thomas of Canterbury (7th July) and St Martin of Tours (4th July) were also celebrated.

It is an important clue that a martyr's translation would sometimes eclipse his or her death in terms of commemorative significance. Solemn translations may be seen as enactments of "the resurrection of the martyrs", as openly declared by Ambrose in his sermon quoted at the beginning of this chapter. The death of a martyr may have taken place long ago, away from the public eye, and only with time would it acquire due recognition, usually by some miraculous events attributed to the saint and often experienced at his or her burial site. In the case of the lesser known, forgotten or simply "invented" saints, little may have been known about the time and circumstances of their death, or indeed their life. Annual translations became the main points of contact with the saint and his or her powers by creating a nexus of memories, hopes and expectations at which the temporal, spatial, and contextual lines intersected.

The benefits and risks of relic translation

So far, we have mostly been analysing translations that could be described as target-oriented: they were usually instigated and conducted by members of the receiving community in hopes of bringing about some benefits. But we should not lose sight of the fact that translations could also be beneficial to the original custodians of the relics, especially if they did not intend to part with them for good. Following this line of enquiry—in his study focussed on Flanders and its neighbouring territories, a region in which relic translations appear to have been particularly common between the tenth and twelfth centuries—Steven Vanderputten demonstrates how the monastic communities "were an effective means of enacting their privileged relationship with the divine" (2011: 143). Especially in the latter part of this period, "while translations continued to be an integral part of the rituals associated with the veneration of saints and the fostering of a sense of community centred on a saint's cult" (145), their significance shifted from the management of the broader social order—by physically emphasizing the primacy of divine law cascading down the feudal power structure—towards the defence of the monks' own domanial interests.

This new monastic and feudal context reveals several ways in which relics functioned explicitly as "tools of power" (Ugé 1999). First, "Flemish monks performed translations as means of manifesting both a saint's presence among the living and the physical reality of his or her lordship over the monastic community" (Vanderputten 2011: 146). Coinciding with important moments in the life of the community, translations were performed not only when dedicating new places of worship but also when property was acquired, and especially when the authority of the patron saint, and his or her order, was to be re-established over disputed estates (ibid.). Translations enacted and visualized the nature of a saint's lordship: reports exist of "*quêtes itinérantes*, during which the saint was allowed (or, in some cases, forced) to visit each of his estates in succession and claim ownership of them" (ibid.). Secondly, often at the behest of secular powers, and typically in the wake of their failure to bring peace and justice, relics were made to appear at public peace-making gatherings to proclaim the divine law reconciliation amidst local feuds, as carefully prepared denunciations of violence were being staged (147–148).

Sometimes translations became opportunities for social interventions—or at least were presented that way. Examples are numerous and go well beyond the historical and geographical context studied by Vanderputten (2011). Freeman (2011: 54–55) recalls a well-documented conflict in sixth-century Gaul, between Queen Radegund and a local bishop Maroveus, in which relics become weapons. When, after many twists and turns in the tussle between these two, a finger of St Mammes was successfully translated from Constantinople and installed in Radegund's nunnery in Poitiers, "sick and possessed people were soon being admitted to be healed as if, it was said, they were supplicants to the royal court" (2011: 55). Another noteworthy case is the translation of St Germain in 756 to a more prominent place in the basilica, briefly mentioned before, designed as an important state affair, performed in the presence of King Pepin (the Short), his young son Charles (who was one day to be known as the Great), and countless bishops and lords. However, when all was ready for the elevation to begin, it appeared that the relics could not be lifted (most likely, by an abbot or another major ecclesiastical figure). Amidst the confusion and embarrassment, someone explained to the king that in one of the royal estates, the servants were being abused and mistreated by the king's officials, and that the saint, by refusing to be lifted, is clearly making a plea on their behalf. The king, keen to appease St Germain, decided to give the estate to him or, rather, to the monks who were in possession of his relics. Only then, miraculously, did the relics become light again and the translation could successfully proceed (see Michałowski 1983: 8).

Translations in the service of peace-making and social improvement offered great rewards to the monastic groups which performed them: not only did they obtain "a recognized status as intermediaries with the divine, but also created a great deal of goodwill towards their own claims and queries" (Vanderputten 2011: 148), and their success in doing so may be attributed, without contradiction, to a mixture of "political cunning and self-interest, psychological tension, [and] a sincere desire for peace" (Koziol 1992: 252). Projecting contemporary labels many centuries back (and somewhat tongue-in-cheek), the functions of these translations could be described as both activist and lobbyist, with a strong emphasis on fundraising or even crowdfunding.

However, the higher the stakes and potential benefits, the higher also the risk. Profitable (at times, perhaps better described as profiteering) translations were not exempt from this rule. Commenting on the twelfth-century work *Miracula Sanctae Rictrudis* by Andreas of Marchiennes, Vanderputten detects signs of "increasingly problematic discourse of relic translations" in the description of St Rictrudis relics being quickly brought back to the abbey promptly after ceremonies had been completed, as the monks knew that "the patroness did not like being transported for lucrative purposes" (2011: 150). In the same work, Andreas gives an account of a spectacularly failed translation mission:

> Some time during the next few years, the hard-pressed monks of Marchiennes decided to bring the relics of Eusebia, the daughter of their patron saint, to England, "where the people were very rich and deprived of saints, which [they thought] would inspire them to make large donations" ... A delegation made the journey to translate the relics, but was met with the general apathy of the English population, who were not at all familiar with Eusebia ... The monks soon ran out of financial reserves for transportation and food, and were forced to sell off the silver shrine that held the relics. A hasty and shameful return followed.
>
> *(Vanderputten 2011: 150)*

Vanderputten notes that the inclusion of the story of a failed translation in a collection

> otherwise devoted to the glorious interventions of Eusebia and her mother Rictrudis indicates that the author considered it useful to warn his fellow monks against the potentially disastrous effects of exposing relics to an audience unconcerned with a particular saint.
>
> *(ibid.)*

This once again demonstrates that far from being a mere transfer, translation depends for its success on a delicate balance of various factors that cannot always be anticipated, let alone engineered. In a contemporary context, this sounds reminiscent of the largely unpredictable fortunes of textual, especially literary translations. Taking into account the details of specific markets, cultural affinities, literary trends, and so on, translators, authors, publishers and translation studies scholars can rarely explain, let alone predict, a commercial success or a failure of a specific translation on a concrete market. It seems that translation has a power to channel undercurrents that otherwise remain invisible and its potential benefits (in this case, viewed in strictly financial terms) tend to be seen as outweighing its risks.

At other times, it was precisely because of some external risks and dangers that translations were carried out, as if by-products of broader historical developments. A series of pagan raids and invasions, especially by Normans, meant that some monks had to flee their monasteries and abbeys, taking with them the most treasured possessions which of course would have included relics of their patrons (Wilson 1983a: 4; Michałowski 1983: 9–10). Some of these relics, saved from profanation, would then have been parcelled out and donated to—or extorted by—the monastic communities in which the fugitives found refuge or experienced hospitality (Kracik 1994: 106). In some cases, these involuntary or forced translations evolved into lengthy peregrinations in which the relics travelled from one convent to another. A good example is the multi-stage translation of St Philibert of Jumièges, whose body, removed from the coastal island of Noirmoutier by the monks fleeing from the Vikings in 836, continued to be carried West, taking refuge at various locations, to settle finally, some forty years later, at a Benedictine abbey at Tournus in present-day central-eastern France, over 600 kilometres away from the original tomb. In this and similar situations, a translation may be viewed without much exaggeration as a strict means of salvation: otherwise, the relics would have fallen into the hands of the enemy and likely been lost.

Modern translations of religious and secular relics

So far, our discussion has sought to establish relic translation as a rich and important part of medieval religious, cultural and social practices. In this quest for a fuller account of the meaning of translation, we highlighted some conceptual elements shared with the traditional understanding of textual, interlingual translation but also signalled other aspects that must have seemed odd and unfamiliar to many readers today. As Geary argues, faced with some of these "seemingly absurd and embarrassing vestiges of early Christian and medieval piety", contemporary scholars tend to downplay their importance as an element of folk religion unworthy of serious academic attention, "and to relegate the entire subject to the level of antiquarian curiosities" (1978: 3). In the remaining part of this chapter, I would like to challenge this widespread perception and its underlying assumptions, and demonstrate how traces of a logic reminiscent of medieval relic translations may still be found in various spheres of life today. The benefits are two-fold: by reflecting on the medieval practices of relic translation we may realize the richness of this broader notion, which in turn may help us better understand some aspects of certain contemporary phenomena which otherwise remain opaque or seemingly unrelated.

Closer to home

Before suggesting parallels and offering extrapolations, it makes sense to ask about more direct links. To what extent are religious relics still venerated and translated today? The example of the annual celebrations of the liquefaction of St Januarius's blood in Naples, mentioned earlier, is not as isolated as it might seem, though it has been largely reduced to a peculiar tourist attraction. Across Europe, there are countless local sites where relics are preserved and displayed, often surrounded by legends of their miraculous power. To focus just on the two countries best known to me, Ireland and Poland, both with a historically strong Roman Catholic heritage, you only need to walk into a major church to find relics—sometimes deposited under the main altar, at other times in one of the lateral chapels or parish museums.

Starting closest to home, St Patrick's Parish Church in Belfast boasts in its treasury a relic of the saint's arm, enshrined in a richly ornamented, medieval silver reliquary (though when it was opened in 1856 after centuries of veneration, it turned out to contain no relic but just a piece of yew wood about a foot long; it is assumed that the relic had been worn out through constant pouring of water through the reliquary to obtain a cure for various diseases). The reliquary is normally on loan in the Ulster Museum (see Figure 3.7)—literally across the street from my office at Queen's University—while another genuine relic of St Patrick is kept at the parish treasury; the two are sometimes reunited "on occasions of high solemnity",[6] which highlights the unique, mutually validating relationship between the relic and its material encasement.

Moving on, about an hour's drive south, St Peter's Church in Drogheda has the severed head of St Oliver Plunkett, a religious leader and a national hero; after his execution in 1681 the Irish Catholics hailed him a martyr, and brought his head to Rome. In the early 1720s, it was translated to Ireland and placed in the custody of an order of nuns, and St Oliver became the patron saint for peace and reconciliation (a hardly enviable remit in the Irish religious and political context!).

A similar distance further south, in Christ Church Cathedral in Dublin, the heart of St Laurence O'Toole (Lorcán Ua Tuathail), a twelfth-century bishop of the city, is on display (see Figure 3.8). His service coincided with the Anglo-Norman invasion of Ireland, and in 1175 he helped broker the Treaty of Windsor with a king of England. After he died on a peace mission in France and was canonized in 1225 because of miracles said to have occurred at his tomb, his heart was translated to Ireland and became a major pilgrimage destination for the next

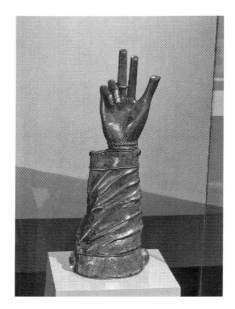

FIGURE 3.7 "Shrine of St Patrick's hand". A silver gilt arm-reliquary on display in the Ulster Museum, Belfast, Northern Ireland.
Photograph by the author

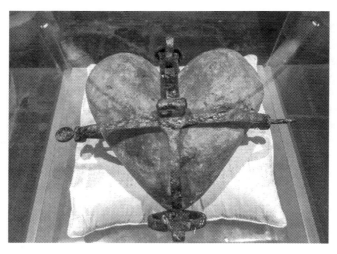

FIGURE 3.8 The heart of St Laurence O'Toole. Christ Church Cathedral, Dublin, Ireland.
© Debra Reschoff Ahearn | Dreamstime.com

eight centuries. A major incident occurred in March 2012, when the saint's heart, housed in a wooden box and displayed in an iron cage, was stolen from the Cathedral. The robbery appears to have been clearly targeted and carefully carried out: the thieves used metal cutters to prise open the iron bars but completely ignored gold chalices and candlesticks, leaving no traces. As the distressed dean of the Cathedral noted at the time, the relic "has no economic value but it is a priceless treasure that links our present foundation with its founding father" (BBC 2012). It is therefore very curious what kind of value it had for the thieves: religious? magical? historical? symbolic? These are only speculations. The fact is that after six years, in April 2018, the Gardaí (Irish police) received a tip-off and proceeded to recover the relic from the Phoenix Park, about half an hour's walk from where it had been stolen. According to one Dublin newspaper, the thieves decided to return the relic because after several of their loved ones died from apparent heart attacks, they thought it was cursed (*Irish Examiner* 2018). On 26 April 2018, the heart of St Laurence O'Toole was presented to the Archbishop of Dublin by a Garda Assistant Commissioner in a solemn ceremony: "a choir sang to mark the heart's return, with churchgoers queuing up to catch a glimpse of the relic and give prayers of thanks" (ibid.). The archbishop thanked those who helped recover the relic, and said: "the return of the heart of Laurence O'Toole to Christ Church Cathedral brings great joy to the people of Dublin as Dubliners" (ibid.). (The fact that the Anglican Church of Ireland considers the saint's heart to be a historical artefact, and not a relic [Flanagan 2019] is a mere technicality.) For his part, the Garda Assistant Commissioner commended officers who he said had "kept their radars on and their minds open" (*Irish Examiner* 2018). The thieves themselves appear to have received only divine punishment, as the police confirmed that no arrests had been made. Later that year, on 14 November 2018, the heart, housed in a specially designed art piece, was ceremoniously reinstalled in its previous resting place that in the meantime had been rejuvenated thanks to generous public funding. On that occasion, the dean of the Cathedral issued the following statement (note the sequence in which the reasons are given):

> I am delighted that we have two such tremendous reasons for celebration at this time. We are deeply grateful for the grant funding from Dublin City Council and Fáilte Ireland that has enabled the redesign and landscaping of our grounds. Further it is my great privilege and joy at this time to be able to return the heart of St Laurence to the people of Dublin.
>
> *(Church of Ireland 2018)*

What is remarkable is that this story—that happened in the twenty-first century Republic of Ireland and was reported in electronic media—might have just as well been recorded, verbatim, in a *translatio* from over a thousand years ago, in one of the Irish kingdoms! The narrative could not have followed the classic pattern any closer, interlacing explicit statements with more or less subtle hints. After the miracle-working relics are stolen (for unknown but apparently non-commercial reasons), the saint intervenes by inflicting a series of mysterious deaths on the families of the thieves—no one could fail to link cardiac arrests to an affront against a sacred heart!—and commands the repentant villains to return his relics, with the help of the valiant Guardians of the Peace (a literal translation of *An Garda Síochánai*), to its newly re-elevated, rightful place of rest in a joyful public ceremony involving high ecclesiastical and secular officials. The roughish thieves receive both punishment and forgiveness (likely, also some spiritual enlightenment), the miraculous power of the saint is re-established and enhanced, and the community of the faithful experiences a religious, symbolic, and economic uplift.

Similar stories abound elsewhere, involving both old and new saints. In the wake of Pope John Paul II's death and funeral and in response to the widespread popular call *Santo Subito!*, a beatification procedure was initiated in the Vatican in preparation for his official canonization. This created an immediate and truly unprecedented demand for relics. The pope's body was buried in its entirety (the calls from his native Poland to be given his heart fell on deaf ears of the College of Cardinals) but it soon turned out that those in his immediate circles who were blessed with foresight had managed to secure, over the years of medical treatment, some ampules with his blood, as well as some hair and several teeth. As bodily tissues, these are the relics of the highest class, of which only a finite collection could exist. Though the precise amount is unclear (early reports mentioned "four small containers"), in the several years that followed, the personal secretary to the pope and custodian of his belongings, Cardinal Stanisław Dziwisz, made numerous gifts of the pontiff's precious blood drops. In Poland alone, by 2014, the year in which John Paul II was formally canonized as saint, well over a hundred parishes were in possession of his blood relics which in all cases had been received and installed in official, public ceremonies (Hołub 2014), fully deserving to be called translations (though usually they were not). The papal sanctuary in Kraków-Łagiewniki, visited by several million pilgrims every year, has on display not only the pope's blood in a vial but also the white cassock he was wearing during the assassination attempt in St Peter's Square in 1981, still with blood stains and a hole from the bullet. In addition to the staggering number of the first class relics, there are innumerable holy items of the lower classes which are quickly becoming objects of interest and veneration. Among them is the wooden canoe "Tłusy Bąk" ("fat bumblebee"), used by John Paul II when he was still a bishop. Officially a third class relic, it is displayed in the Museum of Sport and Tourism in Warsaw as "one of the most precious artefacts, much admired by the patrons", its significance is attributed to the fact that "sports activities allowed the pope to be more involved in serving both people and God" (Dziennik 2016, my translation). The ceremony of unveiling the canoe-relic in 2016 was performed by the papal nuncio in Poland and attended by a large group of clergy, including several chaplains, as well as members of sports clubs from all over the country (ibid.). Poland's cult of its beloved pope is by no means limited to main metropolitan centres; a range of smaller towns have their own sacred sites, often symbolically connected to one of the several papal visits. One of many examples is the Museum of John Paul II in Stalowa Wola which has some ornamented vestments as well as a cushion from the papal throne in the Vatican.

To what extent holy relics continue to be subject to the laws of supply and demand is revealed by a series of thefts in the last decade, including from Cologne Cathedral (January 2016) and various Italian sanctuaries: in San Pietro della Ienca (January 2014), Brescii (October 2017) and Spoleto (September 2020)—in all cases, relics of John Paul II's blood were taken. Commenting on the most recent incident, Archbishop Renato Boccardo indicated that the reliquary might have been stolen "for ransom, which has happened in the past with other relics in Italy" (Reuters 2020). By November 2020, the thief had been detained and his house searched but the vial of blood was never recovered; it is speculated that it had been sold to a collector (Smykla 2020). Other thefts seem to be motivated by purely monetary gains: in 2017, a vial containing a piece of St John Bosco was stolen from the Basilica of Castelnuovo d'Asti in the Italian Piedmont, but quickly recovered from the thief who "believed the reliquary contained gold and had planned to sell it" (Montagna 2017). Seeing the quickly multiplying reports such as these, one begins to wonder whether Patrick Geary's work *Furta Sacra: Thefts of Relics in the Central Middle Ages* (1978) may soon see a sequel focused on the twenty-first century.

Relics on the move today

Mobility continues to be an important aspect of relic cult, which highlights their translational character. Some churches do not display their relics permanently but only for special periods of public veneration; behind this practice are possibly security concerns but also, more likely, a typically kairotic logic. Rare, time-bound events by definition have unique appeal in the complex interplay of spiritual, social, cultural and economic factors. A relic on permanent display might risk becoming commonplace and losing some of its attraction. Reaching to a different geographical context, the Manila Cathedral has recently initiated a tradition of promoting the worship of saints by exposing their relics for public veneration but only for short periods—effectively translating them into and out of view. A drop of John Paul II's blood, which arrived in the Cathedral in December 2017 and drew more than 20,000 pilgrims during the first exposition, was then displayed again for just two days, beginning on 18 May 2018 (the saint's birthday), but only from 6am to 8pm. In this particular case, some practical considerations may have been at play, as the Manila Cathedral is in possession of a complete reliquary-calendar containing 365 relics of various saints. Still, the Cathedral's rector promised frequent periods of exposition of John Paul II's blood—but not a permanent installation—and mentioned some plans for the relic to visit the parishes around Manila in 2019 to mark the Year of the Youth (Lagarde 2018). It is evident that the relics' frequent movement, their constant translational stirring both within the Cathedral's walls and across the diocese, is viewed as an integral part of their function. Relics need to be put to work by moving from one place to another.

Some of these peregrinations have a truly global scope. When Monsignor Sławomir Oder was tasked with gathering evidence for the miraculous events associated with John Paul II's relics as part of the canonization process, he started receiving endless requests for his relics (of second or third class). After one million cards with a picture of the pope and a few threads from his cassock, produced by the Roman diocese, were snatched away in a flash, he realized that the demand was insatiable. This prompted him to organize a series of trips, officially termed "pilgrimages of relics". In late 2011, Oder took a vial containing the pope's blood from Italy to Spain, and then to Mexico where it visited all of the country's dioceses; from there to Colombia and several other countries in South America; in 2012 to Nigeria, then to the USA, and to Canada—everywhere drawing huge crowds and inspiring waves of extraordinary events (Hołub 2014; see also Oder and Gaeta 2014). It is worth stressing here that the process of achieving sainthood in the Roman Catholic Church is strictly tied to the requirement for miracles. Beatification may commence only when it is proven that the candidate for a saint played a key part in some miraculous event, usually some supernatural act of healing. Canonization requires proof of another miracle. But if miraculous healings can occur simply through the intercession of a prospective saint, how can this be proven? The proof is translational in nature: that is why in the context of invoking a successful saintly intercession, one often sees mentions of pilgrimages to holy sites and close encounters with relics. A tangible, preferably physical connection in which the spatiotemporal continuum is preserved offers the weightiest and most credible proof. In an ironic twist, the relics need the miracles no less than the worshipers do. That is one of the main reasons why the pope's relics travelled so extensively while the canonization procedures were underway.

By contrast, other movements involving relics are extremely localized and intimate in their character. At Christmas 2011, the Polish tabloid *Super Express* reported that a priest from Legionowo near Warsaw, Tomasz Chciałowski, was taking requests for home visits by a reliquary containing John Paul II's tooth. In an interview, the priest explained that the believers are encouraged to bring the reliquary home for a 24-hour period to give the pope an opportunity to experience ordinary people's lives and thus be better informed to make specific pleas for miracles on their behalf. It is worth noting that the relic—a mandibular canine tooth, partly decayed—was being treated and spoken about in extremely subjectivized terms:

> I want the Pope to experience our everyday life, to see what we do, to know our problems and dreams ... This will help parishioners to open up before the Pope and perhaps see a long-awaited miracle ... You can stay

with the relics in the church or take them home for the night ... You can hug the reliquary and pour your heart out before it ... Bookings requests are accepted from anyone who wants to invite the Pope home ... Whoever admits the Holy Father into their home should show him their normal, everyday live. You can sleep, eat, cry or laugh; anything you would do with a close friend visiting you.

(Super Express 2011; my translation)

The interview concluded with the address and phone number at which "invitations for the pope" were being received. Even if we accept that, under a sensationalizing journalistic licence typical of tabloids, certain elements of this description were made to sound extravagant and raise some eyebrows, they are surely not exaggerated beyond recognition. Similar reactions and attitudes are attested in a range of other situations, including numerous ceremonies surrounding the reception of relics: they are being welcomed, offered bread and salt (symbols of hospitality), brought flowers, fruit baskets, small token gifts, and cards with prayer requests. Participants in translation processions constantly seek opportunities to reach out and touch the relics or at least catch a close glimpse of them, in the same way as fans would seek personal contact, however brief, with a celebrity. By the power of mystical metonymy, the saint himself is present among the community of believers as their friend and ally. It is undeniable that relics "occupy positions in the network of human social agency that are almost equivalent to the positions of humans themselves" (Thomas 1998: x). Once again, the climate of these religious, social and cultural phenomena, including the language with which they are described, is surprisingly reminiscent of what we encounter in medieval *translationes* and chronicles. As they did back then, translations still activate processes of familiarization, taking ownership, and building friendships (both actual and imagined): the saint takes the community under his or her protection while also becoming "its own".

These dual motifs of ownership and friendship find a powerful illustration in relic translations occurring at the very summits of ecclesiastic hierarchies. In the last several decades, relics have been strategically used as instruments of reconciliation between the two branches of Christianity, the Roman Catholic and the Eastern Orthodox Churches, following a series of schisms that plunged them into bitter rivalry for over a thousand years. A major breakthrough in the relations between the Latin and Greek Church occurred at the beginning of the third millennium, when Rome agreed to hand over the relics of St John Chrysostom and St Gregory the Theologian (of Nazianzus), two of the Church fathers particularly venerated in the Eastern Orthodox tradition. The relics had been seized during the sack of Constantinople and brought to Rome in 1204; it was agreed that they would be returned exactly 800 years later. The ceremonies that took place between 27 and 30 November 2004 are amply documented in both written accounts (e.g. NBC News 2004) and videos, offering rich material for analysis.

The documentary commissioned by the Order of St Andrew the Apostle, available on YouTube,[7] is especially relevant because it presents the receiving party's perspective. The translation is consistently framed—beginning with the film's title—as "The Return of the Holy Relics", and the commentary, especially in the first part, treads a thin line between diplomatic gestures of reconciliatory gratitude within the official "dialogue of love" and a discernible sense of hurt and resentment (after all, reclaiming one's own property from the thief can hardly be expected to inspire effusive thankfulness!). The return is presented as proceeding "from Rome to the Church of Constantinople", that is, from a geographical to a spiritual location, which points to historical and religious justice being restored. As most translations of relics, this one also follows a strongly axiological vector.

Watching this short documentary of under thirty minutes, one can hardly miss a poignant turning point, roughly 1/3 into the footage, between the celebrations in Rome and in Istanbul. The Roman ceremony is profoundly official, with thousands in attendance at St Peter's Basilica, including dozens of cardinals and bishops, as well as other clergy members. The glass boxes containing the relics, placed in laced alabaster reliquaries mounted on wooden litters, are wheeled in and brought to the bottom of the steps by a group of clerics. Then, two teams of four lay ushers in dark concierge-style suits lift the litters, ascend to the podium and present the boxes first to the Pope John Paul II, and then to the Ecumenical Patriarch Bartholomew I, for a ceremonial kiss. With the exception of the most solemn moments, the faithful remain seated. A sense of decorum reigns supreme, interrupted only by polite, brief applause when the litters are carried down the steps again, having been officially handed over to the Greeks. After delivering the official and irresistibly diplomatic statements, the two leaders, following the relics gliding away on elegantly dressed platforms, leave the basilica in a slow, dignified procession, to the sound of organ music and the smell of incense. The screen fades to black.

When the story resumes at the airport apron in Istanbul, the atmosphere is palpably different. As the wooden crates containing the relics are being lowered from the cargo bay of the aircraft, the footage cuts to the courtyard of St George's Cathedral in the Phanar quarter of the city, where according to the narrator, hundreds are expecting the arrival of the relics, though the film shows closer to several dozen of both clergy and lay people, rather chaotically lined up along the passage between the inner gate to the complex and the entrance to the church. Many are holding handles and appear to be chatting; at some point, a cat can be seen running across the scene. The atmosphere suggests an extended family gathering rather than an official religious event of the highest calibre. Then a van pulls up in front of the church gate: the relics, freed from their wooden litters and encased in smaller crystal cases wrapped with yellow (St Gregory) and red (St John) ribbons, are carefully, almost lovingly removed by two pairs of priests in golden vestments, and carried up the steps, through the crowded courtyard, and into the Cathedral. The movement is not nearly as ceremonially dignified as was the glide along the smooth expanses of the Roman marble floors—but there is something deeply intimate in how the cases are being rocked along, at all times safely cradled in the arms of the two priests carrying each of them. By then, there are hundreds in the picture, and the procession has to make frequent stops, especially when passing through doorways and narrower sections, to allow the discrete but efficient security guards to push the crowds to the sides. The sound of continually ringing bells is mixed with deep choral chants as the two sets of bones are ceremoniously carried into the Cathedral, through the iconostasis, and around the altar, before being set down on the throne of the Patriarch himself who had given it up for his two ancient predecessors as a sign of veneration. When the camera scans the main nave of the church and the semi-circular balcony around it, the differences to the Roman celebrations from just three days before become striking. There is the question of scale, no doubt: the relatively small St George's is dwarfed by St Peter's (few churches are not!) and has an undeniable cosy ambience to it. But sheer size cannot explain the difference in the atmosphere. The Roman ceremony was solemn and perfectly performed but emotionally sterile. In Istanbul, at the various stages of the ceremony—even when watching it on a screen—one can viscerally perceive the waves of anticipation, excitement, awe, admiration, joy, pride, and emotion rippling through the crowd. Many are spontaneously making the sign of the cross and wiping away tears; when the official service is over, they will be queuing up, thin votive candles in their hands, to kiss the crystal cases and seek a personal connection with the saints who have returned home after eight centuries in exile.

Watching this footage and reading the various materials published around this event, one can have no doubt that these celebrations constitute a translation *par excellence*. Like so many medieval translations in the Middle Ages, the transfer of the relics of St Gregory the Theologian and St John Chrysostom to Constantinople on 30 November 2004 gave rise to a feast now officially added to the liturgical calendar of the Eastern Orthodox Church. "Hymns for the Translation of the Relics", composed especially for this occasion, have also become a part of this Church's tradition ever since. The intuition about an axiological component being inherent to the conceptualization of relic translation, articulated earlier, is confirmed here: the violent, unlawful seizure of the relics from Constantinople in 1204 is never called a translation (at least not by the Eastern Orthodox Christians); instead, the relics are described as having been "taken away" and "exiled" against their own will. A translation is not a mere change of location, community or ownership; the transfer of material objects is wrapped in thick layers of signification and governed by certain conditions.

Although this translation is dominated by profoundly spiritual and historical symbolism, it is impossible to ignore its less visible but no less influential political aspects unfolding out of the limelight and behind the scenes. As we noted before, relics combine the heavenly and earthly perspectives. The "dialogue of love" between the Eastern and Western Churches may occasionally rise to heavenly heights but it also has earthly undercurrents. The official statements are worded with meticulous precision as they oscillate between gratitude and guilt tripping. The Eastern Orthodox Patriarch, following the translation ceremony of the relics which "for eight hundred years ... have been in exile, although in a Christian country—not of their own will, but as the result of the infamous Fourth Crusade which sacked the city in the year of our Lord 1204", expresses the sentiments of his faith community thus:

> Once again, from here, we would like to express our gratitude to his Holiness the Pope of Rome and his curia for their generous decision to return these holy relics to the Church of Constantinople to which they belong. This gesture differentiates them from the deed of their predecessors eight centuries ago, who accepted the spiritual material treasures that had been taken from our city and our Church. The fact that, albeit eight centuries later, the saints are returning to where they have always belonged and justice has been restored, is a joyous event and worthy of special exultation.

When "a kiss of peace" is subsequently exchanged between the Ecumenical Patriarch Bartholomew I and Cardinal Walter Casper, leader of the Vatican delegation, the tension evident on the faces of the Roman officials during the address finally eases. The minefield has been traversed without major casualties. That significant diplomatic hurdles must have been cleared is evident from the narrative on the website where the documentary is housed.[8] It notes the mutual gestures of good will, first by the Ecumenical Patriarch who, for the first time (despite annual invitations) decided to attend the Patronal Feast of the Roman Catholic Church in June 2004, and second, by Pope John Paul II who on this occasion "officially apologized for the tragic events of the Fourth Crusade" (interestingly, the narrator in the documentary refers to it dismissively as "a blanket apology"!). Then, the response of the Bartholomew I is given, to the effect that

> [N]o material compensation was at that time appropriate, but the rightful return of the sacred relics of the two Archbishops of Constantinople would comprise a spiritual restoration of that Church's legacy. The return of their relics would be a tangible gesture of the acknowledgement of past errors, a moral restoration of the spiritual legacy of the East, and a significant step in the process of reconciliation.

Against this background, it is easier to understand the stark difference in the atmosphere felt at the two ends of the translation process. The Vatican is uneasy with the label of a repentant villain, and Constantinople is precariously juggling its dual role as a supplicant and a rightful owner of the relics, its words of gratitude coming through clenched jaws. There is a difference of opinion regarding the historical details: while the Orthodox leaders claim that the relics of both saints were seized by the crusaders in 1204, the Vatican insists that the bones of St Gregory had been brought to Rome already in the eighth century by Byzantine monks feeling persecution (Fisher 2004: 31). Further clues to this tug-of-war are in what is strategically left unsaid or tactfully omitted. None of the official statements by either of the parties mentions that in its magnanimous gesture, the Vatican did not relinquish the entirety of the holy relics but kept a small portion of both saints to be interred in Rome—a fact only picked up, though without comment, by some international media, including NBC News (2004) drawing on Associated Press, and *The New York Times* (Fisher 2004). Various interpretations are possible here, some more likely than others and by no means mutually exclusive: a trace of new bonds of "fraternal love", fashioned on medieval gift-giving practices? a symbolic face-saving act? a gentle slap on the cheek? a mark of the upper hand? Whatever the case may be, these events present us with a dizzyingly broad spectrum of multi-layered factors involved in the translation of relics in the twenty-first century.

Interestingly, this high-profile contemporary translation of relics offers a model example for George Steiner's four-stroke hermeneutic motion: (1) the initial trust mixed with distrust and anxiety, after which comes (2) aggression as "the translator invades, extracts, and brings home", leaving behind "an empty scar in the landscape" (1998: 314), followed by (3) incorporation (which Steiner metaphorically relates to "sacramental intake or incarnation" as well as infection [1998: 315], but not to the translation of relics which would have seemed like a perfect illustration!), and (4) culmination in compensation, restitution, restoration of balance. Whether involving texts of sacred bodies, translation is a negation of entropy: "all capture calls for subsequent compensation; utterance elicits response … A translation is, more than figuratively, an act of double-entry; both formally and morally the books must balance" (1998: 319). One cannot help but wonder whether, had Steiner focused on translations of relics rather than texts, would his model of hermeneutic motion have been any different?

Non-translational solemnity

The foregoing pages demonstrated the existence of contemporary religious practices closely corresponding to medieval relic translations in both performative and discursive terms. Dominant as they may be, it is worth bearing in mind that the definition from the *Oxford English Dictionary* (2022) affirms that translation may designate the transfer involving the remains of not just a martyr or saint but also a "ruler, or other significant person". This is a notable lexicographic foothold which allows us to extend our purview beyond strictly religious contexts (at the same time, *strictly* does not seem like a fully adequate qualification since many burial ceremonies contain some religious element which often cannot be definitively isolated). Importantly, in this broader framework, it makes sense to continue to apply the conceptualization developed earlier, in which the central element of a translation is a movement of the venerated remains to a place of higher honour or status. For this scenario to be invoked, a clear axiological differential between the start and end points is presupposed.

In this sense, some burial ceremonies, no matter how large or significant, lack this key translational component. I am writing these words in the week following the funeral of Queen Elizabeth II on 19 September 2022. This first state funeral in the United Kingdom to be held in nearly sixty years was watched by some 28 million viewers in the UK alone (BBC 2022) and hundreds of millions worldwide, as it was broadcast live by countless television channels and streamed online. It followed both royal and military protocols and carried a full range of religious and secular symbolic significance. To appreciate the sheer scale of these solemn ceremonies it is worth outlining them here.[9] After four days of lying in state, the Queen's coffin was borne in procession on the State Gun Carriage of the Royal Navy—pulled by ninety-eight Royal Navy sailors, with a further forty marching behind—from the Palace of Westminster to Westminster Abbey for the State Funeral Service (see Figure 3.9). Once it was concluded, the Cavalry Last Post was sounded by the State Trumpeters of the Household Cavalry, and the nation fell silent for two minutes. Then the national anthem was sung for the first of many times that day. As Big Ben tolled, the Queen's coffin made its final journey through London: from Westminster Abbey, along Horse Guards, down the Mall to Wellington Arch. The procession included King Charles III and members of the Royal Family, as well as detachments from various British and Commonwealth armed forces. Once the coffin reached Wellington Arch, it was

FIGURE 3.9 Queen Elizabeth II's funeral procession on 19 September 2022. Public domain

placed in the State Hearse. The parade gave a Royal Salute, and the national anthem played again as the State Hearse began its journey to Windsor. There, it travelled via the Long Walk to St George's Chapel, with members of the Royal Family joining the procession in the Quadrangle at Windsor Castle. Minute Guns were fired in multiple locations and the Curfew Tower Bell tolled throughout. From the bottom of the steps, the Queen's coffin, carried by eight pallbearers from the 1st Battalion Grenadier Guards, was borne in procession into the Chapel for the Committal Service. Before the final hymn, the Imperial State Crown, the Orb and the Sceptre were removed from the Queen's coffin and set down on velvet cushions on the altar. At the end of the final hymn, the King placed the Queen's Company Camp Colour on the coffin; at the same time, the Lord Chamberlain broke his Wand of Office and put it on the coffin to signify the end of his service. The coffin was then slowly lowered into the Royal Vault to a lament played by a single piper, as the Garter King of Arms was pronouncing the Queen's styles and titles. The national anthem was sung once more at the conclusion of the service.

The ceremonies lasted over six hours and included multiple transitions between material and symbolic spaces. I recall these details here as proof that it is not the rank of the deceased or the solemnity of the funeral ceremonies that make it a translation. Nor is it transfer itself, however elaborate and symbolically rich. Queen Elizabeth II's last journey, though it followed a complex horizontal and vertical trajectory, was not experienced as a translation because it occurred *within* a single symbolic sphere perceived as an axiological unity. The destination did not hold more prestige than the starting point (if anything, the reverse would be true); in the end, the Queen's remains were lowered, not elevated, and hidden away, not exposed. For the hundreds of thousands of people who lined the streets of London and Windsor that day, watching the funeral profession was no doubt an extremely powerful experience—but arguably not one of translationality.

The same criterion applies to other state and religious burials, no matter how solemn. During the several days preceding John Paul II's funeral on 8 April 2005, described as "history's largest" (*The Independent* 2005), attended by hundreds of religious and political leaders and well as millions of mourners, the Pope's body lay in state in different locations, and was transferred several times as part of the traditional Rites of the Exposition, Visitation, and Interment. In this case, once again, despite following the most elaborate protocols, the ceremonial movement of the pope's body was void of this perceived translationality because it was contained within the Vatican's walls and lacked an axiological vector. I am repeatedly stressing the importance of what is being felt—rather than intellectually registered—to highlight that translationality is largely a matter of perception rather than of any external, objectified criteria. If translation consists of a flow of energy, as in electrical current, it needs an initial potential difference. In both examples given above, no such difference could be discerned.

Secular translations to the Wawel Cathedral

What may count as a contemporary translation, then? Reaching to the cultural and linguistic context with which I am most intimately familiar, I would point to the extended funeral ceremonies of the President of Poland, Lech Kaczyński and the First Lady Maria Kaczyńska, who died alongside 94 other people in a crash of the presidential aircraft on 10 April 2010 near Smolensk in Russia. The disaster, by far the most tragic in the Polish history, had special symbolic significance because the aircraft was carrying the official state delegation to ceremonies marking the 70th anniversary of the Katyń massacre, a mass murder of some 20,000 Polish officers and intellectuals by the Soviets during World War II. This fresh wound sustained directly over an old scar of historical proportions, in close proximity to the place of the massacre, and paired with the unclear circumstances of the crash, led some to believe that it was not an accident but an act of political assassination. In the weeks of national mourning that followed, the rhetoric of symbolic martyrdom was frequently invoked and the casualties were described as "whose who fell" (*polegli*, a term describing an honourable death in combat). The fact that it was Russian soldiers who recovered the mutilated bodies of the victims, and Russian pathologists who performed autopsies, added insult to injury amidst reports of hasty and disrespectful treatment of the remains. It is little wonder, then, that when the body of President Kaczyński was flown to Poland just one day after the crash, and the body of the First Lady followed two days later, both were received with an outpouring of grief accompanied by a sense of relief: the nation had its First Couple returned to it from what had become a cursed, hostile and sinister land. Though the initial separate transfers of the bodies of the presidential couple were described as "repatriation", "return to the country" or "flight back home", *translation* would have been a more adequate term. On both days, tens of thousands lined the streets of Warsaw between the airport and the grounds of the Presidential Palace where Lech and Maria Kaczyńscy then lay in state between 13–17 April 2010; it is estimated that over 180,000 Poles came to pay their respects. The first translation—from the muddy, scarred and bloody airfield in Russia to the seat of the highest office in Poland—had been completed.

In the meantime, following several days of heated political debates about the most fitting resting place, a joint decision was made by the government and the Catholic Church authorities that the President and his wife should be interred not in Warsaw but in the historical capital of Poland, Kraków, at the Royal Castle on the Wawel Hill. This was dictated by a translational logic: faced with an unprecedented sense of national loss, many Poles were keen to see it counterbalanced with a cathartic act of an unparalleled elevation. After a public commemoration ceremony on 17 April 2010 on one of the capital's largest squares, the following morning the coffins of the presidential couple were flown to Kraków in the second stage of their solemn translation. There, following the official ceremonies at St Mary's basilica on the Town Square, the coffins were brought on cannon carriages along the streets of Kraków to the foot of the Castle Hill, and then carried into the Wawel Cathedral—the coronation church of Polish monarchs, nearly a thousand years old—to be subsequently placed in an alabaster sarcophagus in the crypts underneath it. Given its historical, religious and cultural significance, Wawel Cathedral, at the heart of the Royal Castle complex, by far outranks any other symbolic sites in the country. Translating the bodies of the President and his wife into the most sacred of Poland's national shrines became a method of coping with a monumental sense of loss, the more shocking given its tragic and unclear circumstances. This once again illustrates that translation, in the sense we are exploring here, is governed by hearts and not just minds. Even though Kaczyński was an elected head of state and not a monarch, who prior to the disaster was rather unpopular with little chance for re-election and had no personal links with Kraków, he was still awarded the highest funereal honour. This speaks volumes of the historical atmosphere in Poland in mid-April 2010 but also—in equal measure—of the redemptive power of translation.

This was not the first time that the Wawel Cathedral has seen a translation of this kind. As a national shrine, in addition to the bodies of Poland's many kings, queens, and their royal children, it holds the remains of several of the country's most beloved artists and leaders. Among them is arguably the most celebrated Polish Romantic poet, Adam Mickiewicz, who died in 1855 in Istanbul while on a mission to organize Polish forces to fight under Ottoman command against Russia, which earned him the reputation of a political leader of the fight for independence on top of his literary fame. His body was first laid to rest in Turkey for a brief period, but it soon became clear that the extremely strong national sentiments would make a translation to his homeland inevitable. Given that during this period Poland was partitioned between the three neighbouring states and did not exist as an independent political entity, Mickiewicz's embalmed body was brought to Paris in 1856 where it was interred at the cemetery des Champeaux de Montmorency. This half-way translation from a foreign to a friendly and familiar country was definitely welcome but in the long run, understandably, it could not satisfy the desire for what had become the relics of a national prophet. As a result of various political and organizational efforts over the next several decades, it finally became possible to translate Mickiewicz's remains to Kraków in the summer of 1890. The translation was completed on 4 July, becoming nothing short of a once-in-a-generation celebration for the nation craving to regain its independence after a century of foreign occupation. A commemorative book published later that year (*Złożenie ... 1890*) contains detailed descriptions of the several stages of the translation process (with separate ceremonies held in Paris, Zurich, Vienna and Kraków), a collection of official documents, the full text of twelve speeches (six presented on each end of the translation), a complete list of wreaths sent for the occasion from all over the country and from abroad, a bibliography of press coverage, and some two dozen photographs. It is a remarkable work of secular hagiography testifying to and following through on "the elevated thought of translating Adam Mickiewicz's immortal remains from the hospitable French land to his homeland" (*Złożenie* ... 1890: 4; my translation); it documents "one of the most glorious, uplifting and momentous celebrations which had become great, peaceful manifestation of the nation's unquenched life and its determination for independence" (5; my translation). Some excerpts from the eulogies given at the exhumation of Mickiewicz's remains in Paris, capture the spirit of the moment well:

> Soon ... the crowds longing to see these long-awaited remains will welcome them with their aims lifted to the heavens, with sighs of reverence and love. The land of the fathers will tremble with joy, embracing the mortal remains of the immortal son; the royal canopy will open to receive the king of national inspiration and feelings ... His word is spreading even farther across our plains and forests, penetrating the society's depths: it soothes like balm, comforts like liquor, warms up those who are cold, and elevates the thoughts of all. ... These ashes of this great seer and sage, the nation's master and teacher, its comforter and prophet, must be present in our fathers' land with us and among us, to inspire irresistible endurance, unfaltering sacrifices and never-ending work for the future.
>
> (*Złożenie* ... *1980: 22–24; my translation*)

Despite being a secular ceremony, it was framed in rich spiritual imagery strongly reminiscent of medieval solemn translations of relics, including the affirmation of special bonds of friendship between France—where the poet had found refuge (for many years he was a professor of literature at the Collège de France) as well as a temporary resting place after death—and his homeland to which his body was now being returned. Mickiewicz was explicitly called a prophet and comforter (a title which in the Christian tradition belongs to the Holy Spirit), his remains were for all intents and purposes treated as sacred relics, and his literary legacy was attributed miraculous powers active in the psychological, emotional and social domains, benefitting both individuals and communities. This quasi-mystical rhetoric and extremely lofty style likely jar our modern ears but at the same time provide important evidence of conceptual continuity between medieval religious practices and secular ceremonies of the modern era. Translations of relics did not cease with the post-Enlightenment decline of belief and the diminishing role of institutional religion. The same elements that defined medieval translations continue to be present in events celebrated much closer to our times.

To complete the account of the series of secular translations to the Wawel Cathedral and bridge the gap between Mickiewicz's in 1890 and Kaczyński's in 2010, two other events deserve a mention. Juliusz Słowacki, the other great poet of Polish Romanticism who, like his literary rival Mickiewicz, was also involved in the resistance movement, died in 1849 in Paris and was buried at the Montmartre cemetery. The idea of translating his remains to Poland first emerged at the beginning of the twentieth century but had to wait several decades for the right political climate. Only in 1927 did Józef Piłsudski, the main architect of the Second Polish Republic re-established after World War I, and a great personal admirer of the poet, command that Słowacki's body be recovered and interred at the Wawel Cathedral in the crypt of national poets (which until then had held only one). This translation was notable not so much for its beginning and end points—which it shared with Mickiewicz's—but its path. Following the exhumation in mid-June 1927, the coffin with the poet's remains was placed on board the navy vessel ORP Wilia which brought it to the country's borders in a symbolic gesture by the newly born Polish Navy. From the port city of Gdańsk, Słowacki's remains were carried upstream the Wisła river on board the paddle steamer "Mickiewicz" (note another symbolic layer!). Before reaching the capital city of Warsaw, the steamer stopped at various river towns along the route to enable spontaneous acts of veneration and respect by the local people. From Warsaw, after a mass celebrated at St John's Cathedral, Słowacki's bones were brought to Kraków by train, exactly two weeks after the exhumation in Paris, and after solemn funeral ceremonies in the courtyard of the Wawel Castle, laid to rest side by side with Mickiewicz's. The unique historical context in which this translation was taking place, following the regaining of Poland's independence, explains the peculiar peregrination strikingly reminiscent of medieval practices involving the relics of saints. Here, the poet's relics were at once reclaiming the Second Polish Republic as their homeland and were being themselves reclaimed by it, as they followed the symbolic waterway from its sea border, to the political centre (Warsaw), and on to the spiritual, religious, and religious heart (Kraków), where they were deposited in the place of the highest honour, among Poland's monarchs.

Only eight years later, in 1935, the body of Marshall Józef Piłsudski, one of the greatest Polish statesmen and the *de facto* head of state, repeated the last section of his favourite poet's journey. This time, the translation was unique in that it had been skilfully planned and orchestrated by its own subject while he was still alive. In a short note made a few weeks before his death, Piłsudski wrote: "They may want to bury me at Wawel, who knows. Let them!" (1935; my translation). It is easy to be fooled by this apparently speculative phrasing; however, considering the popular admiration and respect the Marshall enjoyed (and carefully cultivated), it should rather be read as a strong suggestion if not indeed a command, veiled only in the thinnest layer of conventional modesty (several lines down in his last will, any traces of shyness were entirely gone when Piłsudski referred to himself as "Poland's greatest knight" [my translation]). Already two years earlier, during a visit to the Wawel Cathedral to celebrate the 250th anniversary of the Battle of Vienna at the tomb of its victorious commander, King Jan III Sobieski, Piłsudski dropped a hint that "perhaps some room could be found there" for himself, too (Kowalski 2015). When it came to confirming these informal arrangements as a matter of urgency, the staunch resistance of Cardinal Adam Sapieha, the curator of the Cathedral, was overrun by a direct petition to the pope Pius XI who immediately granted his approval (a high testimony of Piłsudski's diplomatic skills even after his death!).[10] The Marshall had his lifelong dream fulfilled, and after five days of funeral ceremonies held in the capital, his silver coffin was translated by rail to Kraków (some railway sections had been built especially for this purpose); despite the late hour, thousands of people lined up along the tracks to pay their respects. On the morning of 18 May 1935 in Kraków, some quarter of a million mourners formed a procession over ten miles long—a funeral march of a scale never seen before or since in Polish history (Kowalski 2015). Escorted by representatives of all military commands, a cannon carriage drawn by six black horses brought the venerable remains from the main railway station to the Town Square for a requiem mass in St Mary's Cathedral, and from there to the Wawel Castle. To the sound of 101 cannon salutes, Piłsudski's body in a glazed silver coffin was interred in the central crypt of St Leonard, side by side with the marble sarcophagi of Jan III Sobieski (d. 1696) and Tadeusz Kościuszko (d. 1817). As President Ignacy Mościcki put it in his farewell eulogy:

> The royal shadows have gained a new companion of eternal sleep. No crown on his temples, no sceptre in his hand. And yet, he was the king of our hearts and master of our fate ... the mighty Sovereign of Polish Hearts and Souls.
>
> *(1935; my translation)*

In this brief speech of under three minutes, hearts were mentioned no fewer than six times! The prevalence of this imagery was hardly accidental. Hours after Piłsudski's death, in fulfilment of his will, his heart was removed to be buried alongside his mother's remains in Vilnius (present day Lithuania, but at the time still a Polish city) exactly a year later. (Coincidently, the hearts of two of his neighbours in the crypt, Sobieski and Kościuszko, had also been removed and both rest in Warsaw). This transfer of hearts directly continues the line of medieval translational practices. Just as a saint may be simultaneously present at various geographically distant churches which are nevertheless allied in the veneration of their patron, so the relics of the great leaders are partitioned and strategically distributed in an effort to (re-)establish symbolic bonds, fostering a sense of shared national pride and common legacy. The emergence of these imagined yet powerful links between various places, communities, and times is among key translational effects.

Due to limitations of space, I cannot discuss any more relic translations here, but need to stress that despite the selection of examples (dictated by my own lived experience from Central and Western Europe and the focus on English in this predominantly semasiological quest), the cult of relics is not limited to a single religion.

FIGURE 3.10 The Chairman Mao Memorial Hall on Tiananmen Square in Beijing, China. © Leonid Andronov | Dreamstime.com

"Indeed, albeit to differing degrees of importance, many major world religions—including Buddhism, Hinduism, and Islam—have traditions of venerating the earthly remains of holy persons or objects that have been in contact with them" (Arponen, Maijanen, and Immonen 2018: 151; see also Wheeler 2006, Strong 2007; Meri 2010; Aymard 2014; Hooper 2014; Collinet, Parsapajouh, and Boivin 2020; McGregor 2020). Not only that: translational effects in the presence of venerated human remains are not confined to religious settings. Even in openly non- or anti-religious political and cultural contexts one finds sites of memory and cult animated by a promise of translationality, however meekly wrapped in the folds of the local ideological rhetoric. Think of Lenin's Mausoleum in Moscow, the Chairman Mao Memorial Hall in Beijing (see Figure 3.10) or the Kumsusan Palace of Sun in Pyongyang—what are they if not secular shrines, destinations of pilgrimages and portals to a mythical past? Traces of translationality may be found wherever the physical extends into the metaphysical.

(How) can these bones live?

In the opening pages of her poignant and compelling study *Can These Bones Live? Translation, Survival and Cultural Memory* (2007), Bella Brodzki makes the following comment:

> We are most accustomed to thinking of translation as an empirical linguistic maneuver, but excavating or unearthing burial sites or ruins to reconstruct

traces of the physical and textual past in a new context is also a mode of translation, just as resurrecting a memory or interpreting a dream are acts of translation.

(2007: 4)

The solemn translation of relics—both religious and secular—which indeed proceeds through searching ruins, unearthing burial grounds and excavating crash sites, is perhaps the best example of this entanglement of the material and the textual, of memories and dreams, of mourning and hope, of the past, present and future. Beyond their obvious physical context, corporeal transfers occur in an imagined, symbolic dimension. This means that translation is irresistibly transformative:

> In the process of being transferred from one realm or condition to another, the source event or idea is necessarily reconfigured; the result of translation is that the original, also inaccessible, is no longer an original per se; it is a pretext whose identity has been redefined.
>
> *(Brodzki 2007: 4)*

Approaching this insight from the conventional realm of translation studies—the domain of languages, texts and "translation proper"—it is easy to trivialize it by lumping it together with the usual objections against invariance, commensurability, equivalence, isomorphism, and so on. Things change in translation, we know that much. But that is not (only) what Brodzki is saying. While admitting that "[t]hrough the act of translation, remnants and fragments are inscribed—reclaimed and reconstituted as a narrative—and then collected collectively; that is, altered and reinscribed into a history", she stresses that this history "also undergoes alteration, transformation, in the process" (2007: 6). One aspect of this transformation has to do with the passage of time:

> Even if, hypothetically, it were possible to excavate a body, a text, an image, or even a memory intact, the necessarily delayed, translated context of such an excavation would be transformed in the interval between the moment of production and the moment of its translation.
>
> *(Brodzki 2007: 4–5)*

Once again, this is not just an affirmation of the obvious reality of *panta rhei*. Rather, translation "defines a space around itself in which vital change occurs" (Blumczynski 2016b: 344). That change is vital in a profoundly etymological, not just a rhetorical sense: it marks a liminal point between life and death. Let us listen to Bella Brodzki again:

> To cross the threshold from life to death and from death to afterlife is to be translated, to be in translation. Translation is the mode through which what

is dead, disappeared, forgotten, buried, or supressed overcomes its determined fate by being borne (and thus born anew) to other contexts across time and space.

(2007: 6)

This is how bones can live: animated by translationality.

In the next chapter we will explore some further aspects of this phenomenon. My contention is not only that a range of contemporary practices and phenomena—both religious and secular—still reverberate with echoes of the ideas that fuelled the imagination and excitement around the translation of relics in late antiquity and the Middle Ages, but also that these elements of modern culture may be meaningfully understood and experienced translationally.

Notes

1 I am following the account compiled by the St Nicholas Centre, https://www.stnicholascenter.org/who-is-st-nicholas/real-face/relics-in-the-lido-of-venice Accessed 31 October 2022.
2 In this section, I am following https://www.stnicholascenter.org/who-is-st-nicholas/real-face/anatomical-examination Accessed 31 October 2022.
3 https://www.stnicholascenter.org/who-is-st-nicholas/relics Accessed 31 October 2022.
4 https://en.wikipedia.org/wiki/Januarius Accessed 31 October 2022.
5 A more subtle example of this tracing function is the translation of Queen Æthelthryth, whose uncorrupted body was elevated to the altar some sixteen years after her death, in 695 in Ely; it is the earliest translation in England of which we have record, "and an indication that the Anglo-Saxon kingdoms were now borrowing rituals from France" (Freeman 2011: 65).
6 https://saintpatricksbelfast.org.uk/our-parish/relic-of-st-patrick/ Accessed 31 October 2022.
7 https://youtu.be/dfXskSyAJc8 Accessed 31 October 2022.
8 https://www.goarch.org/-/the-return-of-the-holy-relics-of-st-gregory-the-theologian-and-st-john-chrysostom Accessed 31 October 2022.
9 I am drawing on the official information from https://www.royal.uk/state-funeral-her-majesty-queen-0 Accessed 31 October 2022.
10 Cardinal Sapieha, despite having to put up with this coercion when the kairotic sentiments were at their highest, was determined to push back—in both a figurative and literal sense. Just two years later, in 1937, under the pretext of preservation concerns (in the initual period, Piłsudski's glass coffin attracted 25,000-strong crowds every day) and some ceremonial irregularities, he unilaterally decided to place the Marshall's body in a metal coffin and move it to a much less prominent crypt under the Tower of Silver Bells, practically by the exit of the royal tombs. This "de-translation" of Piłsudski's remains by a few notches in the symbolic hierarchy is a further proof of the complex interplay of authority, power, pride, and ambition cutting across the official and public dimensions. (For a fuller account of the controversy around Piłsudski's burial at the Wawel Catherdral, see Kowalski 2015.) In another symbolic gesture, the sarcophagus of President Kaczyński and his wife was placed in the vestibule to this farthest crypt in 2010.

4

FROM GIFT SHOPS TO THE CUSTOM SHOP

Translationality for sale

The previous two chapters devoted to corporeal translations have demonstrated that translational relationships are fundamentally constituted by a sense of connection felt even after the material transfer of the symbolic bodies has ceased and is only discernible in its echoes. Although translations as historical acts occur at concrete spatiotemporal junctures, their influence extends far beyond these anchor points. In a translational economy, the historicity of a transfer is not as important as its re-enactment, memory and perception. This is not very surprising. We know from Descriptive Translation Studies that a translational status is awarded based on conviction rather than any external evidence. Notoriously tricky to circumscribe and define, "assumed translations"—as Gideon Toury calls them—are "all utterances in a target culture which are presented or regarded as translations, on any grounds whatever" (2012: 27; see also Pym 2014: 73–74). To these traditionally translational grounds, I would add an experiential dimension advocated throughout this book: translationality may be felt.

A brief methodological note is in order here. The discussion in this chapter will venture beyond the remit of a semasiological account, which means that the descriptive commitment must be temporarily suspended. The phenomena illustrated by the examples given below are not, to my knowledge, labelled, presented or regarded as translations, either explicitly or implicitly. Still, even in the absence of the terminological marker, the key elements observed in the corporeal translational movements offer a powerful conceptual framework against which a range of cultural phenomena may be better understood.

The museum experience

To be able to experience translationality, we first need to internalize a certain kind of psychosomatic sensitivity. In doing so, we may be aided by invoking the

DOI: 10.4324/9781003382201-5

type of emotion sometimes felt when visiting contemporary secular counterparts of sacred shrines: museums and art galleries. It is that peculiar feeling of transcendence and awareness of coming into close contact with "the real thing". Time freezes as you realize that the same bit of matter now separated from you by a single pane of glass once lay on the moon's surface or was touched by Leonardo da Vinci's paintbrush. Apart from the anticipation of some miraculous effects, I see no reason to regard this reaction as qualitatively different from the emotions that must have been evoked by religious relics approached in good faith. The more famous the object, the higher the expectations tend to run: in the imagination, it becomes larger than life. That is why relics, unimpressive in themselves, were placed in sumptuous reliquaries. That is also why in museums, where artefacts are usually displayed behind glass, it is not uncommon to hear reports of feeling underwhelmed or disappointed: is *that* it? As the old chestnut goes, the Mona Lisa is smaller than you think. The ceiling of the Sistine Chapel—when you finally get to see it after a long stroll through the Vatican, following endless, suspense-building signposts—does not seem dramatically different from hundreds of other frescoes found in Rome, across Italy or in other parts of Europe. And yet, despite the crowds and amidst the regular admonitions of the Vatican guards ("Silence! No photographs!"), one may still feel that familiar translational tingle. "I am looking at the walls once painted by Michelangelo". "I am standing in the room where so many popes have been elected, as will the next one".

To be clear, I am not arguing that works of art radiate some kind of irresistible aesthetic power—a view rather famously ridiculed by John Berger in his classic BBC television series *Ways of Seeing* (later made into a book). He invokes a hypothetical visitor to the National Gallery in London who, before seeing Leonardo's cartoon *Virgin on the Rocks*, would likely be primed by his or her previous knowledge to feel something like this:

> I am in front of it. I can see it. This painting by Leonardo is unlike any other in the world. The National Gallery has the real one. If I look at this painting hard enough, I should somehow be able to feel its authenticity. The *Virgin on the Rocks* by Leonardo da Vinci: it is authentic and therefore it is beautiful.
>
> (Berger 1972: 21)

Berger points out that such feelings, naïve as they may seem, "accord perfectly with the sophisticated culture of art experts" (Berger 1972: 22) who have a tendency to discuss works or art "as though they were holy relics: relics which are first and foremost evidence of their own survival" and who study such objects' past "in order to prove their survival genuine". Yet, as Berger observes, the emphasis on

> the spiritual value of an object … can only be explained in terms of magic or religion … And since in modern society neither of these is a living force, the

art object, the 'work of art', is enveloped in an atmosphere of entirely bogus religiosity.

(ibid.)

It is a fair point and Berger is right in calling it out. However, my suggestion of translationality which may sometimes be experienced at historical or cultural shrines has little to do with the aesthetic or artistic value of the objects displayed therein. Gell notes that "[t]he innumerable shades of social/emotional responses to artefacts (of terror, desire, awe, fascination, etc.) in the unfolding patterns of social life cannot be encompassed or reduced to aesthetic feelings" (1998: 6). Translationality profiles an imaginary journey through time and space, activated at and by a special site. It cannot be experienced anywhere else, except by acknowledging the distance which remains constitutive of the experience ("We are only a few blocks away from Ground Zero"). An anthropological theory of art, as formulated by Gell, concerns "social relations that obtain *in the neighbourhood* of works of art" (1998: 28; emphasis added).

The power of sacred sites and objects ("sacred" in any sense that generates translationality, not necessarily religious) is that they act as time machines. The temporal dimension is compressed as one makes a translational connection with a site of a momentous event or a special person's imagined presence. In fact, *presence* is precisely the right word in this context because it highlights the temporal nexus. The same John Berger who exposes the "bogus religiosity" surrounding the works of art, offers the following description of a viewing experience:

> It is as if the painting, absolutely still, soundless, becomes a corridor, connecting the moment it represents with the moment at which you are looking at it, and something travels down that corridor at a speed greater than light, throwing into question a way of measuring time itself.
>
> *(1972)*[1]

When you encounter what you believe to be an authentic relic or a shrine, the past becomes absorbed into the present. That is the experience of translationality.

Lest this should sound overly exalted and sublime, I would argue that a similar translational impulse prompts us to collect shells from that special beach: we want to take a part of it with us to capture the precious moments. Memories need a material substrate, and this is precisely what souvenirs provide: be they pebbles, fridge magnets, cups, or art albums. This must be one of the first lessons taught to aspiring curators in the museum and art gallery industry: make sure that the patrons exit through the gift shop. Monetize that translational impulse. By the way, why are these commercial outlets called gift shops? Who are the gifts sold there intended for? In part, for others, no doubt: family members or friends who are not with us on this occasion, and who we want to give a token of this experience as an expression of love or friendship. But to someone who did not experience this translationality herself and has no memory of it, it will likely matter little whether her Velázquez poster comes from a shop at the Prado museum or at Madrid airport. It seems to me, then, that the shops at the contemporary historical, cultural and artistic shrines give their patrons a chance to purchase a special kind of gift intended for oneself: a souvenir. A souvenir is effectively a spontaneously constructed relic. What distinguishes it from its ordinary lookalike is precisely its translationality: an ability to invoke a meaningfully felt connection across time and space.

As we reflect on this further, it may be helpful to explore the distinction between relics and replicas, which I would like to illustrate with a recollection of a personal experience. The Altamira cave complex near Santillana del Mar in Cantabria, northern Spain, is famous for its prehistoric charcoal and polychrome art featuring animals and human hands, created over thousands of years, with the earliest paintings dating to around 35,000 years ago. When the site was first explored in modern times (around 1879) and the artwork was interpreted as Upper Palaeolithic by Spanish archaeologists, the scholarly community initially doubted its authenticity because of the exceptional artistic quality of the paintings and their excellent state of preservation. The Altamira cave art was deemed too perfect to be true, and the man who first reported its discovery on his land, Marcelino Sanz de Sautuola, was even accused of forgery. It took more than twenty years, and similar finds at other places across Western Europe, for the Altamira caves to become internationally recognized as authentic and start building their iconic status as "the Sistine Chapel of Palaeolithic art" (Jones 2001: 3). The exquisite artwork (see Figure 4.1), paired with the awareness of the swathes of time that separate us from the Stone Age artists, inspires profound reflection about humanity itself.

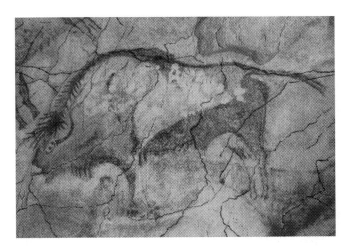

FIGURE 4.1 Palaeolithic rock painting in the Altamira cave, Santillana del Mar, Cantabria, Spain.
© Jesus De Fuensanta | Dreamstime.com

Throughout the twentieth century and well into the twenty-first, Altamira has continued to draw crowds of visitors. In 1985 UNESCO declared it a World Heritage Site. Usually, on a spring or summer day, you may need to wait in a queue for an hour or more before you get to the minimalist museum complex, integrated into the green fields and meadows that surround it. Once inside, visitors work their way through the permanent multimedia exhibition "Life in the times of Altamira", some temporary displays, a workshop room, a café, and the inevitable gift shop before heading to the entrance of the main attraction: the cave. It is only at this point that many realize that what they are about to see is the Neocave, a full-scale reconstruction of Altamira as it was between 22,000 and 13,000 years ago—not *the real thing*. The actual cave is located about a hundred metres east of the museum and "is temporarily closed to visitors to ensure its proper conservation" (as mentioned in the final two lines of the official museum leaflet). This "temporal closure", imposed in 1977, by now seems rather permanent, and there are currently no plans to reopen the cave for the public. The natural reliquary has been sealed.

From the perspective of conservation efforts, this was the only reasonable decision. Over the years, the carbon dioxide and water vapour brought into the cave by a large number of tourists started to damage the prehistoric paintings. The relics were being exhaled out of existence. What the visitors are being offered today is access to an exceptionally well-made replica, described by the *New York Times* travel advisory as a "cloned grotto ... where every bump and fissure of the original stone has been reproduced ... [using] the charcoal and ocher pigments, along with the tools and techniques of the ancients" (Jones 2001, 3). Steps and platforms, along with an electric lighting system, make for a very convenient and streamlined viewing experience. About 2,000 visitors pass through the Neocave daily (compared to some 25 who were admitted to the *real* Altamira cave when limited access was trialled in the 1980s, before a complete closure). There is no doubt that many of them leave duly impressed. But for some—myself included—the dominant emotion is that of thwarted hopes and disappointment at what turned out to be an encounter with a replica, not a relic. Perhaps simply standing outside the real cave and peeking from a distance, even if unable to catch any meaningful glimpse, would have generated some translational ripples (similar to finding oneself in front of a building with a commemorative plaque saying that someone notable had lived, worked, or stayed there for a brief period). The Neocave, however masterfully executed and praiseworthy for its conservational function, was in my perception translationally sterile.

This kind of experiential difference may be partially explained by what Walter Benjamin in his 1936 essay "The Work of Art in the Age of Mechanical Reproduction" calls "aura". In Benjamin's view, an object's aura is tied to its uniqueness and presence, of which there can be no replica; it is that part of an object's existence that cannot be multiplied or transmitted. In fact, reproducing a work of art destroys that aura because "the technique of reproduction detaches the reproduced object from the domain of tradition. By making many reproductions it substitutes a plurality of copies for a unique existence" (Benjamin 2019: 171). Benjamin observes that "[f]rom a photographic negative, for example, one can make any number of prints; to ask for the 'authentic' print makes no sense" (2019: 174). That is certainly true—and yet, I would suggest that the logic of "aura", and the strict ontic distinction between relics and replicas that underlies it, is only partly applicable beyond the context of (re)production of visual art. For there are situations in which these two categories seem to coalesce—or at least problematize each other.

As we leave behind the museum experience (likely picking up a few souvenirs from the gift shop on the way out), one thing is certain. The power of translationality extends beyond the spiritual and the aesthetic. Anything that captures human imagination and inspires excitement—anything that can become an object of desire—immediately throws up the question of value, both symbolic and material. It is often asserted that certain works of art, much like religious relics, are "priceless"—but this is rarely an absolute statement of fact, more often an advertising strategy aimed at maximizing desirability. After all, priceless objects change hands all the time. They are exchanged for other objects, sold and bought, traded for an infinite spectrum of monetary and symbolic benefits—but also stolen, looted, and extorted. Moreover, the history of religion and history of art know countless heists as well as hoaxes; precious objects may not only be taken away but also copied. By applying to the material as well as metaphorical transfers, translationality allows us to account for the twin economies of theft and forgery. But it would be a mistake to reduce translationality to these negative contexts and implicate it in the problematic discourse of authenticity. Instead, in the following pages I am going to demonstrate that—according to a translational logic—relics and replicas need not be mutually exclusive but may function as complementary or even overlapping categories. This convergence is found, perhaps surprisingly, in some musical instruments, particularly electric guitars.

The power of the axe

The iconic status of the electric guitar for a range of genres in contemporary music—especially blues, rock'n'roll, jazz, and various kinds of metal—is obvious and needs little proof. Unlike other instruments that come in generic shapes and sizes (how many distinctive models of a violin or a trombone can you think of?), the electric guitar is remarkably malleable (see Figure 4.2). As a result, some models and their manufacturers are immediately identifiable with certain artists. Few people would know the manufacturer of Miles Davis's trumpet; meanwhile, it is hard to miss the label "Gibson" on B.B. King's black semi-hollow guitar "Lucille"—both names are proudly engraved, using mother of pearl inlays, on the headstock, making "this elegant instrument … instantly recognizable" (according to the description found on the website of a leading guitar vendor). Pat Metheny is usually pictured with a natural maple semi-hollow Ibanez. For Angus Young of

FIGURE 4.2 A variety of electric guitar models.
© Mike Monahan | Dreamstime.com

AC/DC, that would be Gibson SG Standard. For Jimi Hendrix, Eric Clapton, David Gilmour, Jeff Beck, Stevie Ray Vaughan, and hundreds of others—Fender Stratocaster, the most popular electric guitar ever. For Bruce Springsteen, Albert Collins, and Susan Tedeschi—Fender Telecaster. For Carlos Santana—PRS. For Kaki King—Ovation. For Tom Petty—the Rickenbacker 660. For Jimmy Page of Led Zeppelin—Gibson Les Paul, except in "Stairway to Heaven" where Page plays a distinctive doubleneck Gibson EDS-1275. Queen's Brian May usually plays his own model "The Red Special" which he designed and built with his father in the 1960s because he could not afford any of the major brands. The list could go on—the point is that famous guitarists are often identified with not just a generic guitar but with a particular shape, model, and manufacturer.

Of course, the visual properties are just one element of the link between the artists and their signature instruments. Since solid body electric guitars are essentially slabs of wood rather than resonance boxes, their tonal qualities do not depend on their shape or even the kind of wood used for the body and the fingerboard but rather on the kind of pickups, their configuration and adjustable settings. (Beyond the guitar itself, the tone will of course be further modulated by various pedals, effects, amplifiers, speakers, and so on). All these material factors, combined with the artist's playing technique (by far the most important element but understandably not particularly highlighted in advertising materials), offer almost unlimited but at the same time strongly channelled possibilities for developing a characteristic tonal style. Many famous guitarists, and surely most of those mentioned above, are instantly recognizable for their distinctive tone. Keith Richards of the Rolling Stones, who reportedly has a collection of around three thousand guitars, once jokingly said: "Give me five minutes and I'll make 'em all sound the same" (Santoro 1986). To sound like Mark Knopfler or Gary Moore is the ambition of millions of aspiring guitarists.

Given the cult surrounding musical heroes, it comes as no surprise that various artefacts owned or used by them achieve the status of relics (technically, of the second class) and become objects of both commercial and cultural interest. As other kinds of desirable collectables and memorabilia, they are bought and sold at auctions and displayed in museums. If in the domain of visual art, "from the point of view of the da Vinci cultists, the *Mona Lisa* is thematically perceived, not as an image, but as a sacred relic of Leonardo, the semi-divine creative hero" (Gell 1998: 57), then the same principle applies to the instruments owned or played by the semi-divine musical heroes. In April 2019, the Metropolitan Museum of Art in New York organized "Play It Loud"—"the first major exhibition in an art museum dedicated entirely to the iconic instruments of rock and roll"[2]—putting on display over a hundred instruments once played by artists such as Chuck Berry, Bob Dylan, Jimi Hendrix, John Lennon, Elvis Presley, Prince, and many others. This exhibition demonstrates that the value of musical relics comes not simply from their ownership history but from a unique kairotic dimension. These are the instruments that were used not only by famous artists but also at concrete historical points: during specific concerts, tours, shows and recordings, or other defining moments. For example, the exhibition "Play It Loud: Instruments of Rock & Roll" at the Met also included "a sculpture made from what was left of one of Pete Townshend's electric guitars after he smashed the instrument during a photo shoot with Annie Leibovitz, published in *Rolling Stone* as "How to Launch Your Guitar in 17 Steps".[3]

In June 2004, Eric Clapton's Fender Stratocaster "Blackie"—which had been his sole stage and studio guitar for around fifteen years—was sold by Christie's auction house for $959,500 to raise money for the Crossroads Centre Antigua, the drug and alcohol treatment centre founded by Clapton, at the time setting the record for the world's most expensive guitar. The identity of the buyer is rather revealing: "Blackie" was acquired by the US music equipment chain Guitar Center and can now be viewed in its Manhattan store on West 44th Street, displayed in a simple, unassuming glass cabinet in the Fender section (see Figure 4.3). This symbolically captures the entanglement of historical, cultural, spiritual, sentimental, artistic, commercial and many other webs in which relics

FIGURE 4.3 Eric Clapton's Fender Stratocaster "Blackie" on display in the Guitar Center in New York City, USA.
Photograph by the author

are suspended. The authentic relic, the "real Blackie", is not for sale (at least at the moment)—but thousands of other instruments like it, are.

Celebrity endorsement

This key element—"like it"—announces an undeniable translational potential. The desirability of instruments modelled on those used by famous musicians comes from the pursuit of an imagined connection. The commercial gospel is that if you have a guitar like Eric Clapton's, you can be like him in some way. Early on, instrument manufacturers and vendors realized that translationality is a formidable marketing mechanism, even though, of course, they did not frame it in these terms. By their own admission,

> Fender recognized decades ago that musical instruments can be infused with magic and meaning far beyond their utility. The continuing success of

vintage reissues says something not only about our appreciation of the craft and designs of the bygone era but also about the potency of nostalgia and our reverence for the lore of our instruments.

(Wheeler 2004: 241)

An important element of this lore, nostalgia, and magic is a translational link with iconic artists. It is not an accident that many of the guitarists mentioned in the previous section are so strongly associated with particular models and brands: these companies have worked hard on this association being made as instinctively as possible. There are obvious elements of sponsorship and advertisement—in the music industry usually labelled "endorsement"—broadly shared with other areas of commerce. We can all be like celebrities who are their sponsor's "brand ambassadors" or "faces" by using the same cosmetics, wearing the same clothes, and driving the same cars as they do. In those cases, though, the symbolic identification, "being like", is not translational in character. You may be drinking *the same* coffee as advertised by George Clooney or wear *the same* dress as Rihanna and feel good about it, but you would not normally think that you are drinking *his* coffee or wearing *her* dress. The feeling of satisfaction comes from an awareness of a shared source of the goods enjoyed, and the identification works both ways, creating a sense of imagined comradery: I am like Clooney, Clooney is like me. However, his coffee is not in any way more authentic than mine. There is no transfer; no relics are being carried across. With celebrity endorsement of this kind, you are not getting closer to a famous person by encountering or obtaining something that once belonged to him or her. Both you and them simply use the products that come from the same source and carry the same brand. Given the mass production of musical instruments, a sense of ownership of a standard model Fender Stratocaster—shared with millions of other players, some of whom may have been famous artists—is likely an expression of brand pride ("the experienced pleasure of being associated with a brand" [Taute et al. 2017: 240]) and could possibly signal brand tribalism (which usually involves "a sense of unity" and "emotionally charged hostility toward competing tribes" [242]) though probably not much else. Standard advertising and marketing mechanisms apply here, including the correlation of an object's monetary value to its new, unused and unmarked status (the "virginity" effect) and pristine condition: it is not an accident that the expression *brand new* has *brand* in it.

Originals and copies

Staying on the topic of brand, even though the most popular electric guitar body shapes may, in a diachronic perspective, be traced to specific manufacturers (mostly the two industry giants, Fender and Gibson), they have been so widely copied that, from a synchronic point of view, it is impossible to establish a source of the instrument based on body shape alone. This creates a peculiar situation in terms of authenticity. In 2009, after a five-year long litigation process, the Administrative Trademark judges of the United States Patent and Trademark Office (USPTO) ruled in favour of seventeen companies opposing the application by Fender Musical Instruments Corporation to register the Stratocaster, Telecaster and Precision Bass guitar body shapes as trademarks, "on the grounds that they are generic or, in the alternative, have not acquired distinctiveness in view of the widespread use of identical and substantially similar configurations by third parties over several decades" (USPTO 2009: 6). One of the witnesses in the proceedings testified as follows:

> Based on my years and years of looking at guitars and selling guitars and reading guitar magazines, I'm convinced this body shape here, Stratocaster, has absolutely no connection with any one manufacturer on this planet. The same with ... [Telecaster], this generic body shape has absolutely not one bit to do with any one manufacturer on the planet ... the Precision bass ... has absolutely nothing to do with any specific manufacturer on the planet. And you could look at these and have no clue whose guitar it would turn out to be. ... There is no way that these drawings have any degree of uniqueness that gives Fender some claim to the use of those body shapes. And if somebody said are there thousands of guitars that have body shapes that fall within the category of great similarity to these three shapes, I would say there are about as many of these as there are stars.
>
> *(USPTO 2009: 24–25)*

In other words, Fender seems to have fallen victim to its own commercial success. Its mass production of the three most popular body shapes made them iconic, which in turn led to their copying on a mass scale. Another witness in the case admitted:

> I've been making these body shapes for 30 years, unopposed, untrademarked, and have built a business on making these parts. There's a lot of demand for it. While I make other body shapes, the demand for them is pretty insignificant when compared to these three shapes.
>
> *(USPTO 2009: 40)*

Having reviewed some 20,000 pages of evidence, the Trademark Office concluded that

> these configurations are so common in the industry that they cannot identify source. In fact, in the case of the ... [Stratocaster] body outline, this configuration is so common that it is depicted as a generic electric guitar in a dictionary.
>
> *(USPTO 2009: 45)*

The judges pointed out that, over the decades, rather than try to stop others from producing instruments with the identical body shapes through legal action, Fender acknowledged the production by many other sources and instead centred its advertising on the concept of the original, as demonstrated by these advertisements in the industry magazines: "You can play an original or you can end up with one of the many copies"; "You're not taken in by look-alikes or by wild claims", and especially the following:

> Nothing can compare to the genius of an original. Because even the best copies are only imitations. The same is true in music. Eric Clapton and the Fender Stratocaster are probably the most imitated guitarist and guitar in the world. But there's no genius in imitation. Only confirmation of something we've known all along. There's only one Eric Clapton. And only one Fender.
>
> *(USPTO 2009: 44)*

In order to be able to present your product as "the original", you need the existence of copies, imitations and look-alikes, against which its genuineness can be demonstrated. Taking commercial pride from being imitated and at the same trying to stop this imitation as infringing the distinctiveness of the source has been shown to be logically incoherent and legally indefensible—but what is noteworthy here is Fender's appeal to the elusive translational effects: only an "original" Stratocaster has "the genius". Given that the production of instruments at an industrial scale is involved, this "genius" surely cannot directly correspond to Benjaminian aura—even "original" Stratocasters can be produced *ad infinitum*, like photo prints—but it is hard to shake the impression that it is some emotional inflection of this idea. Although "there is no genius in imitation", as Benjamin would insist, it is apparently not endangered by mass production, as long as it performed by a duly authorized source. But thus understood "originality" is rather weak in terms of its advertising power, as implicitly admitted by the manufacturer itself, and that is why the aura of the artist is invoked. Of course, there is "only one Eric Clapton", but in a very different sense than there is "only one Fender"—though by blending these two different concepts of uniqueness, all Fender Stratocasters become translationally authenticated. This effectively disqualifies any non-branded instruments and manufacturers who lack a powerful endorsement from the race for the holy grail.

As a result, we can now narrow our gaze to leading, "original" brands and their "genuine" products—though I must add that the inverted commas are not meant to signal sarcasm but rather the constructed nature of these categories. It is theoretically possible that if a certain small or otherwise niche manufacturer, a boutique guitar builder, creates a somehow distinctive instrument emulating a generic model, which then secures an influential endorser, it will earn the right to its own "originality". This possibility is largely theoretical because artist endorsement is a complex function of financial and promotional arrangements in which large corporations have an obvious advantage over small, independent businesses. Still, what is in strictly chronological terms a copy may, through a process of authentication, become an "original".

This phenomenon is well attested in textual translation: one only needs to think of the status held by the Authorized (King James) Version of the Bible in much of the English-speaking world (e.g. Israel 2011, 62–64; Blumczynski and Israel 2018: 213–214), for all intents and purposes functioning as an original. Some publishers go so far as to erase any difference between the original and translation; for example, the New International Version (NIV) is officially advertised as "a completely original translation of the Bible".[4] In short, originality and genuineness—and therefore, to some extent, authenticity—are largely pragmatic and contextual, rather than absolute categories.

Custom Shops and heavy relics

Even though standard models and, even more so, budget lines likely generate their main revenue streams, in a bid to monetize that powerful translational impulse we identified above, some guitar manufacturers are keen to offer aficionados and connoisseurs more than just a brand shared with their favourite artists. Industry leaders such as ESP, Fender, Gibson, Gretsch, or Jackson—incidentally (or not), all headquartered in the USA—run custom shops tasked with the job of crafting instruments to the exact specification of the customers: mostly artists but also collectors. Custom shop instruments normally carry price tags three to four times higher than standard series (which, in turn, are normally several times more expensive than entry-level or budget lines), and are meant to exude a sense of luxury and exclusivity, as illustrated by these opening lines of Fender's newest Custom Guitar Design Guide:

> A Fender Custom Shop instrument is extraordinary. You know it when you play one—it's definitely more than the sum of its parts. It's filled with intangible, electrifying elements that add a new dimension to your playing experience. It's as if the instrument itself is imbued with history, alive with the spirit of the place where it was built and the devotion of those who crafted it.
>
> *(Fender Custom Shop 2022: 1)*

Even this short description makes evident the sentiments the manufacturer seeks to stir in its target base, chief among which is a transcendental sense of a materially inscribed spatiotemporal connection. Standard line instruments may be top quality—insofar as it is achievable on what is effectively an assembly line (despite some portion of the manufacturing process still being done by hand)—but their only individuating element is the unique serial number. By contrast, when ordering a guitar from the Custom Shop, you get—or are promised to get—something much more. This "something", though, is not a matter of better materials, more advanced craftsmanship, extended durability, stricter quality control or any other verifiable characteristics. Marketing the Custom Shop in terms of higher quality would be damaging to the reputation of the brand, suggesting that its standard line up is actually substandard and one needs to pay extra for a level of attention guaranteeing a perfect instrument. That is why Custom Shop instruments are not usually advertised as materially or sonically better than standard series models—but as in some sense unique. Their uniqueness comes, in part, from a chance to build an instrument to your exact specifications in a process similar to completing the list of optional equipment when placing an order for a new car. However, that nod to personal preference—in effect, little different from being asked to select your pizza toppings—is only moderately satisfying to the egos of the target clientele. After all, with a finite number of customizing options, it is theoretically possible that your instrument might be exactly like someone else's, effectively putting you in a position of a standard series owner. Therefore, in addition to catering for your taste, the Custom Shop offers you not just a product but also an experience. The language of Fender's Design Guide is unashamedly emotive and unapologetically spiritual. Custom Shop instruments are supposed to be intuitively distinctive ("you know it when you play one"), experientially synergetic ("it's definitely more than the sum of its parts", "add a new dimension to your playing experience"), both elusive and exciting ("filled with intangible, electrifying elements"), and above all, to radiate some metaphysical energy (being "imbued with history, alive with the spirit" of its origins and the "devotion" of its originators). Cutting through the layers of glib marketing material, one gets to the core message: we can build you a relic.

This is not a hyperbolic use of the concept but its precise deployment in the prototypical sense. The guitar is a very anthropomorphic instrument—it has a *body*, a *neck* and a *head*[stock], often also a [tremolo] *arm*—and this corporeality readily lends itself to translationality typical of relics. Just like sacred relics, Custom Shop instruments promise to mediate a metaphysical connection with admired individuals. At the very least, there is a diachronic haptic link to the master builder or luthier personally tasked with the production of a specific instrument, confirmed by a unique certificate. Introducing its Custom Shop master builders, Fender is not shy to compare them to "the greatest artists in history gathered under one roof; Michelangelo, DaVinci, Picasso and Dali working next to each other, sharing pigments, knowledge and expertise" (Fender Custom Shop 2022: 8). However, none of the luthiers' names would ring a bell to anyone except the most devoted brand enthusiasts: their real claim to fame comes from their peculiar status of vicarious celebrities by virtue of the links to the artists they had built instruments for. Reading through this section of the Guide, one has a sense of the greatest guitarists being never more than two handshakes away. Even though you may not have heard of Todd Krause before, knowing that he "has built exquisitely crafted custom instruments for many of the world's greatest artists, including Jeff Beck, Eric Clapton, Bob Dylan, David Gilmour, Robbie Robertson, Kenny Wayne Shepherd, Robin Trower, Roger Waters and many others" (Fender Custom Shop 2022: 9) is likely to give you a sense of imagined connection with them when you find out that Todd is about to build your instrument. I grant that the link is relatively weak: you will not be playing David Gilmour's guitar—instead, both you and Gilmour will be playing Todd's. In Gell's theory of the art nexus which seeks to account for how "'objects' merge with 'people' by virtue of existence of social relations between persons and things and person *via* things … in 'art-like' situations" (1998: 12–13), this would be a case of two patients (you and Gilmour) who are also agents (by placing orders which initiated the manufacturing process)—though not in relation to each other but to the master builder who plays the role of the artist in crafting the two guitars (in Gell's model called indexes). Your guitar may have laid next to Bob Dylan's as Todd Krause was working on both, but there is no apparent energy flow from one instrument, and its owner, to the other.

Still, even in the absence of a direct link to a signature artist, Custom Shop guitars provide some translational pulsation in seeking to emulate the character of the instruments coming from particular historical periods. The series usually involve a designation of a specific decade or a year or are otherwise identifiable with a certain stage of technological development, sonic style and design. For example, Fender Custom Shop Vintage Custom series instruments are advertised as representing "early, almost prototypical, transitional and 'first rev' versions of classic Fender models before they were refined into their present-day form".[5] Many of them use materials and feature solutions that have since been modified or discontinued in the standard series, and thus carry with them a sense of parallel reality or alternative history (e.g., the Vintage Custom 1955 Stratocaster is described as "the legendary guitar you know and love with some rare 'what could have been' flair").[6] Gibson Acoustic Custom Shop offers a wide collection of models carrying largely self-explanatory designations, such as "1942 Banner Southern Jumbo" or "Pre-War SJ-200 Rosewood", the latter being advertised as follows: "No detail is left untouched: the bound fingerboard, *vintage* style script Gibson inlay, and *unique* pickguard add *custom* touches all over this *authentic recreation*" (added emphasis).[7] The haptic emphasis is unmissable—in one short sentence, there are two mentions of touch—and the selection of adjectives highlight exclusivity. Whereas in almost any other context it would have been an oxymoron, the phrase "authentic recreation" aptly illustrates Gibson's ambition and promise to give the customer what is effectively a time machine. Fender is even less shy about it, as it gives an entire series of its Custom Shop instruments precisely that label.

How does this time travel work? Sometimes it is achieved by using vintage designs, materials and technologies typical of the given epoch, though the instruments themselves are in visually perfect condition. In Schleiermacher's terms, it is the player who travels to the original era to discover a guitar as it would have been offered for sale then, brand new. Fender calls such instruments "New Old Stock": "Models from the past that have survived to the present day looking brand new. An all-lacquer finish that looks as if it hasn't aged at all—as if you went back in time and bought it."[8] For those who prefer less brazenly fictional scenarios, two kinds of "closet" models are available. "Closet Classic" plays to the stereotype of a guitar "kept in a case most of its life—perhaps even forgotten" which has "no real playing wear, but more subtle indications of the ages, such as a finish that has lost its sheen, mild discoloration of plastic parts, metal hardware showing slight oxidation, and minor surface scratches on the body and headstock"[9]. "DLX Closet Classic", on the other hand, epitomizes an instrument that has been

> well taken care of and religiously polished throughout the years. The owner of this guitar took pride in keeping it clean and shiny. Over time the finish started showing age and like a fine wine it evolved into something complex and refined. Moderate finish checking, oxidation of hardware, and mild discoloration of parts give this finish its distinct look and feel.[10]

By now, the player is being left in peace and the guitar completes the journey through time instead, collecting signs of wear and tear as is travels. The underlying conceptual framework in this case is particularly noteworthy. Gibson calls such instruments "heavily aged", and advertises one of them, the 1954 Les Paul Goldtop, thus: "the … Heavy Aged finish treatment, paired with heavily aged hardware, simulates decades of heavy play wear, giving it the unique character, vibe, and feel of an original example from the Gibson Golden Era".[11] Fender ventures straight into the religious domain as it calls its Time Machine series "our shrine to the heritage and legacy of those pioneers who made us what we are today", and the "meticulous replicas using the same techniques and tooling used to create the originals all those years ago"—"artfully 'relic-ed'". In the commercial pursuit of replicating a maximally authentic experience from the past, relic has just become a verb.

This latter scenario is especially relevant to our discussion because the evidence of the imaginary time travel is absorbed and displayed by the artefact and does not depend on the viewer's knowledge or experience. A non-expert would likely struggle to recognize Gibson's Pre-War SJ-200 as a recreation of an original 1930s instrument (though he or she might think that it looks somewhat old-fashioned); other classic models have changed so little in visual terms that the Historic and Modern ranges of Gibson's Acoustic Custom Shop are practically indistinguishable to a layperson, either by design or the price tag. By contrast, the Heavy Aged series, and—even to a greater extent—Fender's relic models, leave no such doubts. Three tiers are available in Fender's line; interestingly, the names of the all relic series are copyrighted. The catchphrase for the Journeyman Relic finish is "used but not abused", and the scenario is as follows:

> Handed down or changed hands through the years, but mostly played around the house, with the occasional jam session or weekend gig. Has been well taken care of over the years but has finish checking, some 'friendly' down-to-the-wood nicks and dings, dullish hardware, and moderate playing wear—a very lucky find.[12]

The mid-range Relic finish strikes rather Tolkienian notes ("There and back—and still here today") and is presented as "the authentic worn-in wear of a guitar that has experienced many years of regular use in clubs and bars. Marks that tell a story, finish checking all over the body, and scars, dings and dents from bridge to headstock".[13] Finally, on the extreme end of the time travel spectrum we find the Heavy Relic treatment, "designed to evoke decades of the most punishing play and touring. From serious dinging and wear to intensely discolored hardware and finish, the true battle-hardened workhorse of the Custom Shop collection".[14] The phrasing gives a clear clue as to the dominant market demand in this particular sector. In the broad logic of relics, less (beauty) is more (value).

Once again, the visual aspect is only one element. Relics are expected to not only look ancient but also work wonders. In this pursuit of creating a simulacrum, guitar manufacturers must straddle partially conflicting demands for historical authenticity with pragmatic requirements of playability, convenience, and top quality. If you thought that these heavy relics sound as scruffy as they look, you would be gravely mistaken. On the contrary: vintage models, despite their claim to authenticity, usually feature "a few subtle modifications for enhanced playability and tone"[15] in recognition that many modern-day players would not be prepared to put up with some aspects of the "truly authentic" experience. On the most obvious level, both right-hand and left-hand models are offered for much of the range: a clear case of anachronism. Think of Jimi Hendrix's iconic "flipped-over" and restrung Stratocaster—back in his day few manufacturers bothered to build guitars for left-handed players. But times and market expectations have changed. We cannot erase history and pretend that the civilisational and technological development never happened, especially if we count on mass appeal (if you are not particularly familiar with guitar ergonomic design, think of the typical tourist who enjoys his or her stay in "authentic" log cabins as long as they feature modern-style bathrooms and hotel-quality beds). If right-handed players were to get a reasonably authentic Jimi Hendrix experience, Fender should have simply built a mirror-image of his "flipped over" guitar, thereby replicating all the inconvenient features that Hendrix had to cope with (the controls and the tremolo bar on the top rather than bottom, the cable socket pointing up rather than down, the deeper cutaway on the wrong side of the neck, making access to higher frets difficult, etc.). But that is not the case; disbelief may be suspended, though not entirely and not for very long. The regular Jimi Hendrix model offered in the standard Fender Stratocaster range makes only superficial nods to Hendrix's unique instrument—including reversed headstock and reverse slant of the bridge pickup—but none of these features affect comfort or playability. The engraved neck plate with the artist's likeness and the inscription "Authentic Hendrix" completes the ironic picture of this contrived simulacrum, carefully controlled not to compromise comfort, in the service of commercial success. The Jimi Hendrix Stratocaster is (mass) produced in Fender's Mexican branch in Ensenada, which allows it to be offered at just under a thousand dollars—half the price of guitars made in the company's headquarters in Corona, California, which is also home to its Custom Shop.

This signals another aspect of authenticity, connected to the source or place of origin, which maps onto some geopolitical considerations. The two Fender factories are separated by less than 300 kilometres or 190 miles—but also by one of the most (in)famous country borders in the Western world. There is no question of originality: the materials and technological processes used in both plants are arguably the same, though of course the cost of labour is significantly lower in Mexico (which is why a large section of Fender's production was moved there in the first place). Given the geographical dispersion of many manufacturing plants in various industries in today's globalized economy, this fact in itself would not have to matter in terms of marketing strategy or customer perception (the sticker "Made in China" does not make Apple devices any less desirable or cheaper). But upper-end guitars have a translational potential, and the place of their origin, on either side of the border, translates into both monetary and symbolic value. As every Fender enthusiast knows, there is an undeniable difference in both prestige and price between Mexican-made and US-made instruments, immediately identifiable by their serial numbers. A "Made in Mexico" guitar may have the same logo on the headstock, sound exactly like its American cousin, and have been through just as strict quality control—but the difference in what can only be described as the level of authenticity never quite goes away. In fact, Fender deliberately fuels this distinction by highlighting the geographical designation of several series, including American Original, American Professional, or American Ultra. One can hardly resist the impression that this difference in "nationality" maps onto other important distinctions. Comparing the entry-level models made in Mexico and the US, perhaps more telling than the 20% difference in price is the fact that the former is called Player and the latter American Performer! Regardless of your actual skills as a musician, wielding a US-made guitar gives you a symbolic advantage in terms of professional and artistic status.

As we noted above, authenticity is a graded category, not a binary one. If historical authenticity were non-negotiable, the only fair game would be genuine period instruments actually discovered in closets, storage units, pawn and antique shops, typically in a less-than-perfect condition. But that kind of risky, inconvenient authenticity is not what most customers are after. Relics from the Custom Shop may not be pretty in the conventional sense (see Figure 4.4) but

FIGURE 4.4 A close-up view of a vintage heavy relic electric guitar.
© Semisatch | Dreamstime.com

they must sound top-notch and comply with the highest standards of modern playability. The Custom Shop clientele demand the best of both worlds—aged appearance and perfect performance—and are clearly happy to ignore the logical paradox at the heart of this carefully engineered sense of cosmetic imperfection. As with all relics, belief and adherence to a particular set of values are central. The mentions of classics, golden eras, legacies, vintage models, and so on, persistently invoked in the marketing materials, feed a nostalgic sense of a paradise lost but also a promise of its being somehow regained. Why else would one pick a beat-up, discoloured and scarred guitar for the price of several new, bright and shiny ones? Because, I suggest, it promises something that they cannot deliver to the same extent: translationality.

Signature models and limited editions

Translationality for sale offers different levels of authenticity, with different price tags. The stereotypical, anonymous and hypothetical busker who has played what is now your relic-grade guitar around pubs and clubs (note the scale: the imaginary scenarios described above do not mention any international venues or huge sports stadiums) offers only a generic touch of history. This is the bulk of Fender's Custom Shop output, as admitted by its marketing manager Mike Eldred: "The majority of what we do ... is vintage reproductions, for people who want an old Fender but don't want to spend $20,000 or $30,000 for an original" (Wheeler 2004: 242). But for those in pursuit of a something more specific than just "an old Fender", there are the signature models, replicating the specific instruments played by famous artists at particular times of their careers. Often, they are not merely visually distinctive but include modifications made by the players themselves or introduced by the manufacturers at their request. Let us look at several examples, differentiated with respect to their translationality effects.

Fender Custom shop sells several models of Eric Clapton Signature Stratocaster in various colours and finishes, advertising them as "built to Clapton's specs" or "mirroring Clapton's personal specs", and offering "the smooth feel and authentic sound of the original".[16] Robert Cray Signature Stratocaster is likewise presented in general terms as a "strong persuader" (a reference to one of Cray's best-known songs), "providing the sound, sustain and expression Cray is so well known for". In both cases, the descriptions are strikingly short but also vague, and the instruments themselves—apart from the signatures on the headstock—notably inconspicuous. This is the difference to the factory-produced Jimi Hendrix Stratocaster discussed above, whose main appeal is its visual quirkiness. Here, the emphasis is not on a mystical translational link but rather on the sonic qualities and technical aspects. The standard signature model allows you access to the specification and setup created by the artist—but otherwise communicates very little of his or her personal character or history. This line of signature models effectively sells recipes or blueprints received from the respective guitarists rather than their relics; they may be replicated *ad infinitum*. They are also being constantly updated, as the builders explain: "If we send Eric some new pickups that he likes better, and he puts them in his personal guitar, then we put the same ones in the Clapton Strat on the wall in the music store" (Wheeler 2004: 222). Some connection may perhaps be felt but only if you are "technically" inclined—the primary target of these models are professional musicians rather than collectors.

Other series, however, strike more recognizably translational notes as the flow of creative energy from the artist to the customer, via the Custom Shop, is envisioned. For example, a part of its permanent offer in its Artist Model line, Fender advertises Stevie Ray Vaughan (SRV) Signature Stratocaster Relic as "one of the most revered guitars in the world", which "Vaughan co-designed with us before his untimely passing".[17] The idea of reverence, additionally augmented by the mention of the artist's death, highlights the relic value of this model which SRV had "heavily modified to match his energetic, yet controlled, playing style". Fender stresses that they "cheerfully recreated" a modification connoting a further, second-order connection: "As an homage to his personal hero, Jimi Hendrix (who's also been known to pick up a Strat) SRV used a left-handed vintage-style synchronized tremolo bridge on his guitar, allowing him to work the tremolo arm with his elbow". As a result, your SRV signature Stratocaster channels not only Vaughan's but also Hendrix's creative spirit (for a discussion of textual translation as spirit-channelling, see Robinson 2001).

[Not quite] an authentic Hendrix experience

At the same time, at least in commercial terms, Hendrix appears too big of a spirit to be channelled exclusively by guitars of a single brand. Even though he is widely remembered for his flipped-over white Fender Stratocaster, the fiftieth anniversary of his death provided an opportunity for Gibson to remind the world that Hendrix also played two of its models—a Flying V and a SG—and issue their limited editions. Both were advertised drawing on strongly translational, kairotic links. Hendrix played his right right-handed SG (strung lefty) for a medley of songs during his TV appearance on *The Dick Cavett Show* on 9 September 1969; meanwhile, the left-handed Flying V was made famous thanks to Hendrix's performance at the Isle of Wight Festival on 31 August 1970, less than three weeks before his death. Gibson's promotional videos of the two guitars take the spiritual rhetoric to new heights in both visual and verbal terms. The limited-edition ivory SG is flanked by two black Flying Vs (a right and a left-hand version), in a clear reference to the holy trinity, all three displayed on stands in front of the altar of an imposing, completely empty Gothic cathedral. As the camera pans down to show the Gibson trinity from a low angle against backlit stained-glass windows, the image cuts to short fragments of Hendrix playing each of the two models on stage (looped multiple times over the course of the remaining four minutes of the video), and a female voice speaks in an inspired tone:

> For Jimi Hendrix, the electric guitar was a conduit to the human soul. A way to connect with audiences on a deeper, more spiritual level. And when he played the blues through these ethereal, humbucking pickups, he changed blues and rock music forever … Jimi was not monogamous when it came to guitars, and he didn't always play his SG or Flying V on stage. But in his more contemplative moments before a show, or when he really needed to channel his inner Clarksdale … he often turned to the weighty tone of his Gibsons.[18]

As the two limited edition models were being launched, Hendrix's step-sister, Janie, who is also the CEO of two limited liability companies Experience Hendrix and Authentic Hendrix (note the names!), issued the following statement:

> I don't know of a more perfect time than the present for the world to be inspired and electrified by the spirit of Jimi, embodied in these guitars. Jimi didn't play with just his hands, he played with his heart and really his soul, using his guitar to create positive energy. He wanted to awaken the world with it. Gibson has harnessed some of that energy, and beautifully! It's amazing to know that fans and those who love Jimi, and his music, will be able to plug into that power and keep his legacy alive.
>
> *(Shackleford 2020)*

What is notable in both these texts is the absence of any material or technical details (with the sole exception of humbucking pickups, a standard feature of

Gibson guitars) or description of any tonal qualities of these instruments. They carry no special modifications, custom specifications or otherwise distinctive features beside the standard hand-aged ebony and hardware finish—but even that is simply a generic period look, nothing uniquely Hendrixian. The instruments themselves are devoid of any meaningful links with the artist, which is best demonstrated by the fact that they come with custom-made hard cases which feature "interior linings inspired by the clothes Hendrix wore at Isle of Wight (for the Flying V) and the kimono he wore on *The Dick Cavett Show* (for the SG)" as well as "Certificates of Authenticity with photos of Hendrix playing the original guitars live" (Maxwell 2020). It is quite telling that the strongest connection with the artist that Gibson can offer for these models is between the clothes Hendrix wore for both performances and the hard case lining material!

In the absence of an imagined link, a reliquary alone—even if lavishly lined with period-feature fabrics—cannot turn a replica into a relic. Despite the best efforts by both Gibson and Hendrix estate companies to create an impression of translationality, the response from the community of players, both in specialist press and on social media, has been predominantly negative, perhaps even hostile. In the eyes of many commentators, the main stumbling block was the price. Retailing at $10,000 each, it was clear that "only serious collectors and corporate lawyers" would be able to afford them—in a sarcastic reference to one of Hendrix's classic lines, "wind cries expensive" (Laing 2020). In fact, the very short runs of just 150 instruments of each model make it obvious that they had been made with the collector market in mind. While the logic of limited-edition instruments is fundamentally kairotic, that each "is only available for a short time, which makes it eminently collectible and adds to its investment value" (to quote Fender's description of their Limited Edition), Jimi Hendrix's reissued Gibsons do not seem to have been particularly successful as "highly anticipated limited-edition models that go very quickly".[19] In fact, six months after the initial release, not only were both models still available directly from Gibson but they were also being resold by various online retailers as brand new, though at 70%–90% of the original price. Assuming that they had been acquired at full price, their resale noticeably below that threshold casts their "investment value" into doubt. If anything, they seem to be losing value as their price approximates the level typical of other, non-signature Custom Shop instruments—which they effectively are, lacking any sense of haptic connection with the actual guitars owned and played by Hendrix. The community of Hendrix's fans and collectors does not seem to have bought the myth of the two special edition models' embodying his spirit and channelling his powers; the mere rhetoric of energy flow unsupported by material substrate was quickly exposed as lacking credibility. Gibson's attempt to contrive Hendrixian translationality has largely fallen flat—probably because it was seen as a thinly veiled commercial ploy. A replica has failed to rise to the status of a relic.

"Blackie": a replica-turned-relic

By contrast, another attempt to manufacture a relic made only a decade and a half earlier was broadly applauded and enjoyed remarkable commercial success. The record-setting sale of Clapton's "Blackie" at Christie's auction in 2004 must have sparked the imagination of Fender managers who decided to recreate it in a short run of just 275 instruments. The limited edition "Blackie" guitars were to be exact replicas of what Gell (1998: 26) terms the prototype, the "true Blackie" (which distinguishes them from Gibson's Hendrix signature models for which no such prototypes appear to be known). In order to enable a maximally accurate reproduction, "Blackie" was loaned to Fender's Custom Shop in California, where it was painstakingly photographed, measured and taken apart. In the words of Michael Doyle, Director of Purchasing of Guitar Center (the current owner of "Blackie"), Fender builders, guided by the question: "Can you tell the difference between the most famous guitar in the world and a copy of it?", were tasked with making it into a replica "such that even Eric Clapton is happy with".[20] Unlike the ordinary signature models, available at the lower end of the Custom Shop line and manufactured on the basis of an artist's "blueprints", the limited edition "Blackie" replicas sought to recreate meticulously the tiniest details of Clapton's prototype: the cigarette-burned headstock with partially damaged decals, an odd-looking tuning machine for the E1 string, the rusty bridge, worn off frets and dirt stains on the fingerboard, and a pattern of numerous nicks, scratches and patches of scraped off paint, especially on the back of the body. Even though each of the 275 "Blackie" replicas were originally sold for an eye-watering $24,000, there was no outcry across the community as in the case of Gibson's Hendrix signature models, less than half their price. It was apparently understood that this pinnacle of the Fender Custom Shop offer, in the words of one re-seller, is "the holy grail for the ultimate Clapton fan".[21] A decade and a half on, at the time of writing this book in the summer of 2022, only a handful of these guitars were being offered for resale, with asking prices ranging from the original mark of around $26,000 to more than $41,000. In this case, the collectible desirability translating into investment value does not seem overstated. These are price tags more typical of works of art and luxury items than of musical instruments, and indeed any meaningful distinction between these categories is hardly possible in this case. With its limited edition "Blackie" reissue, Fender effectively succeeded in turning a replica—in fact, 275 of them!—into a relic.

What is the source of this success that would appear to defy the logic of authenticity? My suggestion is, once again: translationality. While in many other cases producing multiple copies of an authentic relic would likely qualify as a dual act of forgery and blasphemy, Fender demonstrated a stroke of genius in presenting "Blackie's" replication as an act of reverence and tribute, which is why this initiative struck a powerful chord with the community of guitar enthusiasts. From the name of the line—Tribute Series—to the rhetoric employed in the videos documenting the manufacturing process, there is a sense of debt to Eric Clapton who is the ultimate creator of this relic. Indeed, the whole endeavour is undertaken in his honour. Todd Krause, the senior master builder in charge of the project, made the following pledge on the part of the nine-strong team of luthiers: "We're gonna put out heads together and we're gonna replicate this guitar the best way that we know how ... I'm hoping that I can give Eric this guitar back that he's given".[22] A near-religious sense of devotion, commitment and adoration is evident. "Blackie" is received from a near-messianic figure as a prototype of perfection—to be studied, analysed, revered, and emulated. As the embodiment of the ultimate guitar craftsmanship and a material testimony of Eric Clapton's artistic expression, it is not just to be displayed as a precious artefact or a quasi-religious relic in a crystal box in the Guitar Center store in New York City (see Figure 4.3) but is also to be multiplied through devoted discipleship. There is no great exaggeration in viewing the Custom Shop team's effort to re-create and multiply his instrument and give it back to Eric Clapton as an offering of sorts, a proof that his musical "teaching" has been taken to heart and faithfully implemented. The commercial dimension is hidden so deeply that it never really comes to the surface. If anything, the exorbitant price beyond the reach of any but the most determined collectors has a further authenticating effect. True relics are priceless; surely getting the closest possible experience of the real "Blackie" at roughly 2.5% of its auction price must seem rather reasonable.

There are several reasons why I posit translationality as a concept which may help account for this complex dynamics between people, objects, ideas, and experiences. First, it appears to be the underlying principle of the several mutually sustaining processes of energy flow. The two instruments, the original artefact and its replica(s), are simultaneously Agents and Patients in that they channel the energy flowing both ways. The creative energy, the gospel of the perfect Stratocaster, flows from Eric Clapton to his fans; but the fans are also a source of energy following the opposite vector, conveying their adoration and veneration. If Clapton had no admirers, "Blackie" would not have been a relic but just an old, beat up, aesthetically unappealing instrument, with marginal if any market value, and nobody would ever think of replicating it. By seeking to emulate its original, a translation elevates it. Fender has been affirming this rather trivial truth in its pursuits to trademark its classic body shapes: the profuse copying or forging efforts confirm the desirability of the original. A similar insight is well-established in the theory of textual translation: "To class a source-text as worth translating is do dignify it immediately and to involve it in a dynamic of magnification ... The motion and transfer and paraphrase enlarges the stature of the original" (Steiner 1998: 317).

At the same time, "Blackie" replicas not only magnify its prototype but also multiply it in a promise to break its ubication and promote ubiquity instead. Through careful replication, its life is preserved and immortalized, as in Benjamin's famous formulation of translation proceeding from the original, though "not so much from its life as from its 'afterlife' or 'survival'" (2012 [1923]: 76). Indeed, survival is a very apposite framework: were the real "Blackie" to be lost, it would be possible to reconstruct it with a remarkable degree of precision based on its replicas using "back-translation" through a comparative funnel, as it were. The existence of multiple, meticulously detailed, if subtly different copies would enable multi-angulation: a synthesis of the existing versions, by definition more authentic than if it were to proceed from a single line of comparison. Obviously, thus re-created object would, in one sense, be just another replica rather than a miraculously regained original, though it could still be thought of as maximally authentic in offering the fullest composite image of the lost source.

Textual evidence is again reassuring in this regard. To point out the most obvious parallel: a vast majority of the modern translations of the Greek Bible (usually called the New Testament) are based on the so-called critical edition compiled in an extraordinarily complex process of comparative analysis of thousands of extant manuscripts (see Blumczynski 2020: 40–41). At this point, as with all parallels, it could perhaps be argued that significant differences are involved in addition to similarities. In the case of the Christian Scripture the idea of a single source text is problematic to begin with: at no point in time did the entire Greek New Testament ever exist as a singular, complete "proto-original"—it was only assembled into the form we know today over the course of many centuries. This marks a point of difference to "Blackie" which has existed as a single, concrete, completely functional object in time and space—though it is worth bearing in mind that it also has multiple sources, since Clapton had assembled it from components coming from three different guitars he had bought in Nashville: "with pickups from one, scratchplate from another and the neck from another".[23] But in a scenario that involves an absence or loss—real for the Greek Bible "originals" and hypothetical for "Blackie"—the differences would cease to be relevant, and in both cases reconstruction efforts would simply yield a "translated original": an ultimately imagined text or object, however strongly authenticated by multiangulation but without an extant prototype.

Parallels and analogies run deeper still. Maybe the several hundred of "Blackie" reissue replicas should be likened not so much to New Testament translations, abstract textual entities, but rather to the earlier material links in the chain of textual transmission, namely manuscripts copied from earlier manuscripts? There is no reason to suspect that the ancient and medieval scribes were working to any but the highest standards of diligence and accuracy, but since manual copying was an interpretive and not a mechanically reproductive process, there are inevitable, subtle differences between copies and their "originals", as well as between various copies. They also carry various individuating features, from the handwriting style, to the physical properties of the velum and the writing materials used, to the figurative and literal fingerprints of the copyists and any other agents in the process. This is exactly the case of all 275 "Blackie" clones: each of them was copied manually by a concrete luthier whose signature can be found by the serial number on the headstock, and fingerprints all over the instrument. Plus, none of the luthiers was working directly from the real "Blackie", the ultimate original, but from its detailed, colour fold-out photographs—some life-size, some enlarged—in short, from earlier copies and ones in a different medium! In both cases, despite the pursuit of accuracy, there was room for interpretive decisions, errors, idiosyncrasies, and so on—all the aspects that make every translation process and its outcome unique, if only subtly.

Finally, from a contemporary viewpoint, both sacred Scripture manuscripts and "Blackie" replicas have a different status and function than the one for which their originals had been intended—they are material witnesses rather than textual or musical instruments, respectively. The actual manuscripts are no longer used to be read, either in private or in liturgy; nor are they subjects of textual analysis or translation. For those purposes, they have been transcribed, photographed, digitalized and incorporated into critical editions; the manuscripts themselves are deposited in bank vaults, safe boxes and museum displays. Similarly, "Blackie" replicas are not really designed for use as musical instruments. The original "Blackie" itself was becoming unfit for that purpose, and that is why it was retired in the first place. In the summer of 1987 Eric Clapton said in an interview with Tom Wheeler:

> Blackie is simply worn out. It's unplayable. The problem is in the neck. The rest of the guitar is okay, the neck is worn out. The frets are almost down to the wood, and it's already refretted once and couldn't take another refret. I've played it so much that even the sides of the neck, running along the length of the fingerboard, are wearing down—the neck is actually thinner. It's not wide enough to support the six strings, so I simply had to go with something else.
>
> *(Wheeler 2004: 223)*

If "Blackie" replicas are as committed to authenticity and accuracy as Fender swears, they should likewise be practically unplayable. This is what brings them most closely to the status of religious relics which ordinarily have no utilitarian value. Religious relics serve no other purpose than mediating a metaphysical connection and channelling supernatural energy. Musical relics, authentic or manufactured, are similarly witnesses of the energy which once flowed from the artist through the instrument to his or her audience. This energy was at the same time artistically creative and materially destructive, leaving in its wake patterns of wear and tear as observable signs of a repeated, most intimate, physical, haptic engagement over a long period time. In a 1985 interview published in *Guitar Player*, Clapton described his relationship with "Blackie" thus:

> I feel that that guitar has become part of me. I get offered guitars and endorsements come along every now and then. [A guitar maker] tried to get

me interested in a fairly revolutionary guitar. I tried it, and liked it, and played it on stage – liked it a lot. But while I was doing that, I was thinking "Well, Blackie is back there. If I get into this guitar too deeply, it's tricky, because then I won't be able to go back to Blackie. And what will happen to that?" This all happens in my head while I'm actually playing [laughs]. I can be miles away thinking about this stuff, and suddenly I shut down and say, "This is enough. No more. Nice new guitar. Sorry. You're very nice, but ..." That's when I drag the old one back on, and suddenly it's just like jumping into a warm pool of water.[24]

If anything can be said to "embody the spirit" of Eric Clapton, "Blackie" is surely that thing—in a way that reissued Gibson signature models never "embodied the spirit" of Jimi Hendrix, despite the insistence of his estate companies.

Moreover, thinking of its quasi-religious value, the gospel communicated by "Blackie" and its replicas is quite strongly aligned with key spiritual lessons preached by the world's major religions. The fact that the relic guitar is a shabby-looking, worn off and definitely not a "pretty" artefact—rather than a diamond-stubbed, gold-incrusted instrument (picture Władziu Liberace's rhinestone piano, a pinnacle of stage extravagance)—carries the universal leitmotifs about the important difference between truth and appearances, richness and poverty, beauty and ugliness, power and weakness, and so on. It is the story of the Ugly Duckling, the Beauty and the Beast, David and Goliath, the Hobbit, Buddha, and Christ. This conflation of religious, literary, and commercial myths in the service of both spiritual edification and sheer entertainment brings to mind the climactic scene of *Indiana Jones and the Last Crusade* (1989). In the final trial of his discernment, Jones must identify the true Holy Grail among dozens of opulent golden cups encrusted with jewels, and in a flash of genius he "chooses wisely" by picking a simple, battered, clay cup—fit for a carpenter whose kingdom is "not of this world". If Indiana Jones were to choose the instrument used by the demigod of blues and rock from a range of guitars—some featuring gold tops, shiny lacquers, ivory linings, and mother-of pearl inlays—it would have to be "Blackie".

To push the analogy to its logical conclusion: there is no popular expectation that Fender should keep manufacturing further replicas of "Blackie" or make them more broadly accessible—either by pricing strategy or mass production—any more than is there a hope or expectation for new manuscripts of the Sacred Scripture to be discovered. The revelation is complete and closed, with just enough artefacts in circulation to uphold the belief in the genuineness of their origin.

Marketable translationality: concluding thoughts

The reflections presented in this chapter have their origins in my own material journeys: to the Vatican (including the Sistine Chapel, in 2015), to the caves of Altamira (also in 2015), and to the Guitar Center music store in New York City (in 2018). In all cases, these were my first and (so far) only visits to these sites. As I recall them today, in late 2022, between four and seven years after the actual experiences, for the first two locations, I am relying on my memory (no photographs were allowed or possible) and, for the last one, on one less-than-perfect picture snapped with a smartphone (see Figure 4.3). None of these trips were made with research or scholarly analysis in mind; my experiences and reactions described here were spontaneous and instinctive. In fact, it was not until much later that I began to group the memories of these visits together, realizing that both my disappointment and excitement could be explained by the anticipation and experience of translationality. At Altamira, I found how high my translational expectations had run only after they were not met: instead of Palaeolithic cave art relics, I was offered access to a replica. By contrast, my translational encounter with "Blackie" was entirely serendipitous: I stepped into the Guitar Center on West 44th Street in New York City without a clear purpose, simply to browse, and did not even know that Eric Clapton's legendary Stratocaster was on display there until I almost walked into the glass cabinet housing it.

This leads me to two concluding observations. First, that the experience of translationality may sometimes only become apparent in retrospect. Spontaneous psychosomatic reactions—amazement, excitement, shock, nostalgia, disappointment, and any mixture of these and many other emotions—may need time to register and conscious reflection to reveal themselves. It is only by considering our experience in relation to a range of expectations, hopes, gains and benefits, losses and absences, that we may become aware of its translational dimension. Many momentous events, watershed moments and iconic performances only receive these descriptions on the weight of evidence accumulated over time. Statements become prophecies only if they are fulfilled; if they do not, they remain hypotheses, speculations and acts of wishful thinking. That is one of the reasons why translationality, as understood in this book, sits so well with complexity thinking: seemingly small events and apparently unrelated factors may bring about powerful outcomes. The commercial success of one product or service over thousands of others is only partially explained by analysable data, and can only be predicted, let alone engineered, to a very limited extent; otherwise millionaires would far outnumber bankrupts.

The second concluding insight concerns precisely this commercial or more broadly economic aspect. In the previous chapters, we repeatedly referred to the economy of religious offices and the economy of relics—it is clear that this concept, however transcending strictly monetary questions, presupposes material as well as symbolic value. Economic concerns were among the chief reasons stimulating the translation of both bishops and relics. In fact, these practices would likely have not emerged in the first place, and certainly not have developed into patterns and traditions, had they not successfully addressed the twin threats of marginalization and impoverishment: the prospect of losing—or failing to gain— status and wealth. These are very down-to-earth origins of translations understood as material journeys. This is hardly surprising; "material", among other things, may relate to "physical objects or money rather than emotions or the spiritual world' (*Cambridge Dictionary* 2022).

As material transfers give way to metaphorical ones—both in religious shrines and their secular counterparts, such as museums and art galleries—the economic dimension does not become any less central. Neither sacred nor artistic relics are ever far removed from the practice of votive offerings and charitable donations (effectively, the trade of material benefits for symbolic ones), and from the material presence of collection boxes, ticket offices and auction houses. As we have just seen, one of the most iconic (and most expensive) musical relics in history is permanently displayed on the floor of a commercial outlet, in the centre of the richest borough of one of the world's financial capitals. Both a gift shop (at a museum/gallery) and a Custom Shop offer not just merchandise but also experience which must be paid for.

Gift shop-level translationality is usually fairly affordable. Souvenirs sold at museums are often identical to items that can be found at local bookstores or department stores; their higher price at a gift shop may be due to branding (a "Natural History Museum" sticker doubles the price of a plastic dinosaur made in China, compared to what its sticker-free lookalike retails at in a toy store) or simply to the "aura" of the place where they are sold. But that kind of translationality is non-transferrable because it is "target-heavy". The value of souvenirs is in the memories they have a power to evoke—but only to the person who had the experience in the first place. In short, souvenirs are usually not resalable as souvenirs, and that is reflected in their price.

By contrast, translationality communicated by signature series guitars built in the Custom Shop is "source-heavy". Their value comes from the connection to the artist whose instrument they replicate, and the master builder who made them. This is a link that they never lose: it is inscribed in them (and their accompanying certificates of authenticity) through their design and the production process. Consequently, over time, Custom Shop guitars keep their value (some even gain it) and may be resold without considerable loss—their translationality does not depend on ownership and is transferrable. But this is not the abstract value of works of art or religious relics whose function is purely aesthetic or symbolic. Custom Shop guitars are not simply judged by the criterion of authenticity reaching back to their origin. They are instruments in the strictest sense: to remain desirable and valuable, they must continue to perform their instrumental function perfectly, retain their outstanding tonal qualities, and offer exceptional playability. They are expected to open a portal enabling metaphorical transfer in both directions: to bring the player closer to experience of the original artist, and to allow the genius of the artist to be recreated in the present. This translationality is quantifiable inasmuch as aural, haptic and visual experience can be gauged and compared between individual instruments—and that is why it carries a specific, usually hefty, price tag.

Notes

1. Around 12:45 into this programme: https://www.youtube.com/watch?v=0pDE4VX_9Kk
2. https://www.metmuseum.org/press/exhibitions/2019/play-it-loud Accessed 31 October 2022.
3. https://www.metmuseum.org/press/exhibitions/2019/play-it-loud Accessed 31 October 2022.
4. https://www.biblegateway.com/versions/New-International-Version-NIV-Bible Accessed 31 October 2022.
5. http://www.fendercustomshop.com/series/vintage-custom/ Accessed 31 October 2022.
6. http://www.fendercustomshop.com/series/vintage-custom/vintage-custom-1955-stratocaster-nos-maple-fingerboard-wide-fade-2-color-sunburst/ Accessed 31 October 2022.
7. https://www.gibson.com/Guitar/ACC5RX962/Pre-War-SJ-200-Rosewood/Vintage-Sunburst Accessed 31 October 2022.
8. http://www.fendercustomshop.com/series/time-machine/ Accessed 31 October 2022.
9. http://www.fendercustomshop.com/series/time-machine/ Accessed 31 October 2022.
10. http://www.fendercustomshop.com/series/time-machine/ Accessed 31 October 2022.
11. https://www.gibson.com/Guitar/CUSJE3578/1954-Les-Paul-Goldtop-Heavy-Aged/Double-Gold Accessed 31 October 2022.
12. http://www.fendercustomshop.com/series/time-machine/ Accessed 31 October 2022.
13. http://www.fendercustomshop.com/series/time-machine/ Accessed 31 October 2022.
14. http://www.fendercustomshop.com/series/time-machine/ Accessed 31 October 2022.
15. http://www.fendercustomshop.com/series/ Accessed 31 October 2022.
16. http://www.fendercustomshop.com/series/artist/eric-clapton-signature-stratocaster-journeyman-relic-maple-fingerboard-2-color-sunburst/ Accessed 31 October 2022.
17. http://www.fendercustomshop.com/series/artist/stevie-ray-vaughan-signature-stratocaster-relic-rosewood-fingerboard-faded-3-color-sunburst/ Accessed 31 October 2022.
18. https://twitter.com/gibsonguitar/status/1329124778729496584 Accessed 31 October 2022.
19. http://www.fendercustomshop.com/series/limited-edition/ Accessed 31 October 2022.
20. https://www.youtube.com/watch?v=7d0Du6RqdTs Accessed 31 October 2022.
21. https://reverb.com/uk/item/37887543-fender-custom-shop-tribute-series-eric-clapton-blackie-stratocaster Accessed 31 October 2022.
22. https://www.youtube.com/watch?v=7d0Du6RqdTs Accessed 31 October 2022.
23. https://www.fender.com/articles/gear/iconic-mods-eric-claptons-blackie Accessed 31 October 2022.
24. https://www.christies.com/en/lot/lot-4303146 Accessed 31 October 2022.

5
THE EXPERIENCE OF TRANSLATIONALITY

In his essay "Translations: Words, Things, Going Native, and Staying True", the historian and rhetorical theorist Michael Wintroub notes:

> "Translation" is a common word. Its meaning, however, should not be reduced to common usage—to turn one language into another. Indeed, translation has always held materialist and commercial connotations—now usually overlooked—associated with the transport and movement of things as well as words.
>
> *(2015: 1186)*

If the main message of this book were to be distilled down to several lines, it would highlight similar points—but also press them further. Yes, the roots of the word *translation* (*trans* and *fero*), indicate a material, and often also commercial, practice of moving *things as well as words*. This order is meaningful. Moving physical things is a more fundamental, basic practice than moving words. In fact, inasmuch as things can be moved, words can only be "moved"—the former movement is (mostly) material and the latter (mostly) metaphorical. (If you want to argue that words can be rearranged, cut and pasted without much difficulty, you are likely thinking about their graphic representations, not words themselves—as soon as we remove the assumption of writing, any "movement" of spoken words quickly starts calling for inverted commas.) This dynamics largely dictates the direction of the flow of understanding. It is reasonable to expect that the insights from more concrete, embodied experiences will feed into our understanding of abstract, mental processes—this is generally how metaphors work—but not exactly the other way around. Yet, ironically, an opposite tendency may be observed. Even Wintroub, as he sets to explore this "transport and

DOI: 10.4324/9781003382201-6

movement of things as well as words" (2015: 1185–1186), puts words before things in the title of his essay!

Similarly, much of translation theory in the last several decades (especially if we follow the narrative of the various "turns") seems to have been proceeding on the conviction that textual translation—in some circles still called "translation proper"—is somehow the conceptual core of the discipline, capable of being "enlarged", "extended", and providing "correctives" to non-textual translational phenomena (often considered as unusual, atypical, peripheral, and so on). This view has been exposed and challenged in Chapter 1, so the argument does not need to be repeated here. Suffice it to say that—at least from a semasiological perspective following the historical trajectories of the word *translation*—metaphorical "transfers" involving languages, words and texts are conceptualized in relation to material transfers of people and things.

This is the second point on which I would press Wintroub's initial observation: the material transfers involve people, not only things. Again, the order matters: some lexicographic sources (including the *Oxford English Dictionary* 2022) mention human bodies, both living and dead, as objects of translation, before mentioning translated things. Chapters 2 and 3 have offered detailed studies of these kinds of translation involving religious officials and relics (both sacred and secular), arguing that translation as a cultural phenomenon and social practice involves a holistic, psychosomatic engagement traceable to corporeal transfers. The very title of this book carries a clue: this holistic engagement is framed as experience, and the transfers as journeys. This concluding chapter seeks to synthesize the insights offered so far and extrapolate them beyond their historical contexts. However, the main question is not necessarily: "what can we learn about translation by looking at these (largely) material journeys that we could not have inferred from studying (largely) metaphorical, textual transfers?" For one, there is no doubt that textual transfers have a material dimension: at the very least, our reading experience is inscribed in and mediated by pages, screens, surfaces, and textures traversed (metaphorically) by our gaze and perceived (physically) by our tactile receptors. Yet we should remember that not all looking is reading, and not all objects are texts. Given the richness and complexity of the semiotic experience available to us through all channels of sensory perception, narrowing it down to the domain of language ("linguistic landscapes"), or even more strictly, to textuality ("palimpsests"), is regrettably reductionist.

The irony is that materiality that in the last decade has been so keenly attributed or "restored" to translation—through, for example, the "material turn"—would never have been lost or ignored in the first place had we, instead of privileging textual phenomena and "translation proper", been cognisant of the full(er) spectrum of translationality. Removing a metaphorical layer from a practice that was unnecessarily metaphorized in the first place feels like a rather roundabout route (back) to materiality. Attention to material translations would have arguably yielded similar insights to those that were formulated after abandoning the exclusive focus on linguistic and textual transfers. Perhaps there was no other way, given the key role of writing, print, and textuality in the development of our civilisation.

Still, the main question guiding this chapter concerns not so much the WHAT as the HOW. I do not subscribe to the pragmatic belief that as long as the result is satisfactory, it does not really matter how exactly it has been achieved. Such a crude trial-and-error approach is disturbingly anti-ecological and un-economical, and it carries considerable ethical risks. I believe we should carefully manage our efforts and resources. Style matters, not just the final score. As we synthesize the key findings of this study of corporeal translations, it is worth asking ourselves whether these insights allow certain arguments to be made more immediately, directly, convincingly, and elegantly. Yet it is not an exercise in imagining an alternative past but rather an attempt to listen to views that have been voiced—and for which evidence exists—but that were often drowned by the dominant discourse. So, what do translations of bishops and relics tell us about the meaning of the word *translation*—but also about the conceptual scope of TRANSLATION? Let us briefly review the key themes.

Authority and power

Transfers of religious ministers from one post to another, as well as translations of sacred relics, highlight some of the oldest tropes in translation: influence, power, and authority. The practice of ecclesiastical translations emerged as a direct response to problems of governance and quickly became a vehicle of social mobility. With time, a more organic, bottom-up process of electing leaders in early Christian communities gave way to institutional appointments, with all their messy entanglements in various power plays, corporate benefits, and personal ambitions. New bishops were officially installed in office by bishops of the neighbouring dioceses in a haptic act of ordination by the laying on of hands. This evoked and reinforced a meshwork of crisscrossing links, both horizontal (with the leaders of other congregations) and vertical (with the church hierarchy, ultimately presided over by the pope, and through him, Christ). When a bishop was translated to another ecclesiastical post, that complex network was radically disturbed, as was the close relationship between a bishop and his local community (in the early period described in spousal terms). A translation could signal a range of different scenarios: resolving tensions between a bishop and his present church; a need for a disciplinary or doctrinal intervention in a new context; redeployment of managerial, organizational, financial, pastoral or evangelistic talent; broader power plays involving forging of alliances, removing opponents and awarding loyal friends; and many other combinations of economic, political, social and religious factors.

This implication of episcopal translations in the structures of authority highlights its ambivalent potential: it could bring enormous benefits but also cause considerable damage. That is why translations of bishops, at various historical periods, were prohibited in principle but often permitted in practice, as the gains were deemed to outweigh the risks. Translations reinforced structures of governance but also required skilful negotiations. Unpopular leaders could be resisted, rebelled against and even deposed; the support of the congregation at each end of the bishopric transfer had to be secured by persuasion, flattery, shame, guilt or whatever means necessary. A collective decision implies a difference of perspectives and opinions. Negotiated outcomes usually involve consensus which by definition leaves some interest groups only partially satisfied if not utterly disgruntled. This problematizes the idyllic, simplistic view of translation as always positive, beneficial, and received with open arms.

Distributed agency

Accounts surrounding episcopal translations bring evidence of powers of attraction as well as repulsion between both personalities and groups. These two perspectives—individual and collective—are inseparable. Translations are never autonomous acts of self-determining individuals; in fact, if anything is consistently condemned at all times and in all circumstances, it is precisely the initiative of a bishop seeking his own translation. It is worth stressing that the concept of episcopal translation does not specify the translator. It is clear who and where is being translated—a bishop from one diocese to another—but the translating agency is distributed between the two communities, the episcopal college, and the bishop himself. Translations are not redeployments of military servicemen whose personal opinions are irrelevant and who must obey their commanders. Not only are there no known accounts of transfers performed against the will of the bishops involved, but also any such act would be conceptually incongruous, unfeasible and simply impossible to carry out. This distributed sense of agency and authority is particularly prominent in the translations of relics: whether gifted, exchanged, sold, extorted or stolen, they are always implicated in multiple constituencies, both earthly and divine. Translations require elaborate negotiation of various interests (implying a system of favours, allowances, and concessions) and a fair amount of goodwill from each of the stakeholders.

Value

Indeed, the stakes are high for all individual and collective bodies involved in a translation and affected by it. Hardly anyone remains unaffected: a translation causes a powerful change to the entire structure within which it occurs, forging and reinforcing connections between people, communities and locations. The "donating" community loses a leader or a precious relic but receives validation as a showcase of success or blessing and as a generous benefactor or patron. The "receiving" group is recognized as a desirable destination: a site of promotion, a place of promise, opportunity and potential. The translated bishop or relic is elevated to a position of greater honour, significance, and influence. The transfer of value does not only follow the trajectory of the journey but flows in multiple directions. Translation does not just reassign value but multiplies it in various locations. This is especially evident in the translations of sacred relics which could be subdivided to be shared with other communities as a sign of friendship or patronage—but in this process were not perceived as fragmented or diminished. The privileges and benefits were perhaps most obvious to those being translated themselves, but they also extended to entire communities. Especially when a translation meant a foundation of a new church or establishing a new diocese (rather than just filling an existing vacancy), its effects for the material, symbolic, social and economic landscape were immense. In many cases, the histories of cities may be divided into two distinct epochs: Before and After Translation.

Significance

As occasions of enormous significance, often marking watershed moments in the life of a community, translations were performed and celebrated publicly. This gave them a special kairotic quality: a sense of momentousness which carried far beyond an original historical juncture. Solemn translations of relics were experienced as divine visitations, accompanied by miracles, indulgences, and various manifestations of divine, ecclesiastical, and feudal clemency. No wonder they were remembered, re-enacted, and memorialized—which gave rise to a separate hagiographic genre, also called translation. Many translations found their way into the ecclesiastical calendar, in some cases overshadowing the original feasts of particular saints. It was no longer a martyr's death but rather his or her translation that was viewed as a climactic point of their extended *vita*.

Materiality

This aspect is presupposed in each of the themes outlined above but deserves to be discussed explicitly. The translations of both church officials and sacred relics are public acts of material, corporeal transfer. A translation cannot simply occur in the mind or imagination, whether individual or collective. It is not like the Eucharistic transubstantiation of the bread and wine that unfolds mysteriously in the quiet sanctuary, imperceptible to the senses and only recognized by faith. On the contrary: translations are meant to be observed, witnessed, celebrated and experienced. Indeed, it is their materiality, exposure, and submission to public scrutiny that acts as an authenticating factor. Using Robinson's (2017) terminology, solemn translations of bishops and relics were not just performed but peri-performed: as public events, they were partially constituted by popular attention and mass participation, effectively creating the effect of a self-fulfilling prophecy ("something extraordinary must be happening since so many people have gathered to witness it"). In the case of relic translations, that shared, material experience was mediated by the senses: by the sumptuousness of reliquaries; by powerful choral chants (special hymns were composed for the occasion of relic translations); by the smell of incense (relics were often authenticated by their reportedly "sweet scent"); by the haptic contact with the sacred objects themselves—or at least, vicariously, with people who handled them. Translationality has its roots in an individual and collective sensory experience wrapped in thick layers of symbolic significance.

From (public) translation to (private) translationality

I hope that this brief overview of interlocking themes emerging from the material practices of translation demonstrates the worth of this semasiological project. What we have here is a solid framework for both a sociology and a semiotics of translation, though constructed using rather unconventional materials and methods. Their power, in my view, comes precisely from their materiality and concreteness. A traditional sociology of translation, especially that developed within the French intellectual tradition, tends to be highly abstract and conceptually dense; semiotic theorisation likewise relies on an elaborate conceptual apparatus that takes time and effort to master. By contrast, translations of living and dead bodies (discussed in Chapters 2 and 3, respectively) are observable, accessible, tangible, historical events, capable of offering similarly robust insights into translationality. One such major insight highlights its marketable power: a promise of translationality animates a range of artistic, cultural and commercial enterprises (as demonstrated in Chapter 4). But the image of translationality I wish to sketch in this book would be incomplete if our discussion stopped at museums, shops, and concert venues. My final contention is that translationality may also be found in much smaller, private, intimate settings, and that it may be experienced not only publically and collectively but also individually and personally.

I am going to discuss several examples of such private, idiosyncratic translationality effects. My inspiration comes from Bella Brodzki who devotes most of her book *Can These Bones Live?* to demonstrating that

> More than ever, translation is now understood to be a politics as well as a poetics, an ethics as well as an aesthetics. Translation is no longer seen to involve only narrowly circumscribed technical procedures of specialized or local interest, but rather to underwrite all cultural transactions, from the most benign to the most venal.
>
> (Brodzki 2007: 2)

I certainly share this conviction of translation's ubiquity and its ambivalence. Yet, the most powerful, memorable and moving part of Brodzki's book, in my reading, is the Epilogue, "The Home of the Photograph Is the Cemetery" (2007: 190–206), in which she reflects on her own experience as a second-generation

Holocaust survivor during a short family trip to Poland in 1987 to visit the birthplace of her parents, and the burial place of her father's young sister Guta, killed by the Gestapo over forty years earlier. It is Guta's photograph, "one of very few family relics that had mysteriously survived the devastation" (2007: 191), that her brother—Bella's father—takes with him on this poignant journey, to bring to a forgotten Jewish cemetery in central Poland, put on a tombstone over the collective grave of the thirteen murdered children, and say—with his wife, two grown daughters and a son accompanying him on this trip—*Kaddish*, a prayer for the dead. At that extraordinary, unbearable moment, Bella's husband Henry took another photograph of the Brodzki family: the parents and their three grown children, standing by a large, square gravestone, on which a small oval photograph of Guta is placed to complete this remarkable family portrait. Much of Bella Brodzki's closing essay is an extended reflection on these two photographs: a masterful, deeply touching narrative that is "irreducibly personal" yet "steeped in scholarly brew" and "composed within some sort of analytical framework" (2007: 198). Her profound, incisive insights about translation, survival, transgenerational transmission and cultural memory emerge in relation to personal, material journeys in space and metaphorical journeys through time, precisely "at the threshold of the literal and the metaphorical, in that strange mournful but generative space in which the living and the dead exchange ever-renewable meanings" (2007: 206). Without using this word, Brodzki describes her own experience of translationality.

In the remaining pages, I have a similar intention and follow a similar method by integrating elements of personal and family history into an analytical framework. I share Brodzki's recognition of the limitations of dispassionate analyses and purely theoretical deliberations, especially in relation to translationality which calls for experiential engagement. There is an obvious sense of proportion: my observations are necessarily of a different calibre than Bella Brodzki's reflections on transgenerational post-Holocaust trauma (not to mention her exceptional writerly refinement). At the same time, this focus on translationality in other than ultimately liminal spaces is a part of my broader argument. If translation is indeed ubiquitous, and translationality involves an experience of connecting—metaphorically, but through material, sensory mediation—with another reality across temporal and spatial distance, then we should be able to encounter it not only in the most dramatic circumstances but also in various aspects of everyday life. Here are several examples from mine.

A printer's tray

In our family room, slightly above a loveseat facing the fireplace, hangs a printer's tray (Figure 5.1). It is a standard size and shape (approximately 80 by 40 cm, or 32 by 15 inches), with three sections: smaller, narrow compartments on the left, mostly larger ones on the right, and a mixture of different sizes in the centre. It is

FIGURE 5.1 A printer's tray. Photograph by the author

filled with a colourful collection of small objects that invariably attract the attention of our visitors (especially children) but before we take a closer look at some of these artefacts, let us consider the tray itself. As far as I can tell, it is a vintage letterpress drawer—complete with a brass handle for easier sliding in and out—that one day may have served its original purpose, housing wooden and metal type blocks, large and small, for a printing press. A typical printer's cabinet would contain twenty or so such drawers; we only have one, but it is worth remembering that it was designed to function as part of a larger structure. Thinking about this original function brings to mind material aspects of pre-digital print technology: the shape, size, and weight of the individual types (it is such letterpress drawers that gave us the terms *uppercase* and *lowercase*), their mobility and tiniest individuating features, quirks and imperfections. It was a technology that literally (*litera* is Latin for "letter") allowed you to put words and sentences together, and carry them across a printer's bench in an act of material translation. This thoroughly translational artefact has since itself been translated in multiple ways: removed from its original context and structure, emptied of its initial content, refilled with new material, and reoriented from a horizontal to a vertical surface. In this process, a wholly utilitarian object has been transformed into an entirely decorative one. Printer's trays were not designed to be "cute"—it is their new *skopos* that gives them this perception.

This particular printer's tray has experienced a few more translational movements than many others. Purchased somewhere in New Jersey in the mid-1980s, twenty-some years later it crossed the Atlantic Ocean and arrived in Ireland, among surprisingly few possessions of a young woman who decided to leave the New World and make a life for herself in the Old. It has since moved several times across the island, following the adventures of its owner, to find a permanent display spot in the living room of our family home in Belfast.

The material journeys of this printer's tray are but one aspect of its translationality; its symbolic transfers are much more profound. It was a Christmas gift from a mother to her daughter. The girl—let's call her Lauren—who was only seven or eight at the time, opened the large, flat package not alongside some other presents on Christmas morning, but in the early afternoon, when the family came home from church. She knew it must have been something special, and wanted to savour the moment. Decades later, she still remembers the warm glow of the lights on the Christmas tree, the red wrapping paper, and her excitement when she realized what was in the package. A printer's tray—just like mom's and grandma's! This matrilineal link is one of the strongest translational effects of the tray. Lauren has a strong, affectionate relationship with her father, but the printer's tray powerfully connects her to her female ancestors.

On that Christmas Day in the 1980s, the tray came with only a few miniature figurines. Filling it with memories was to be a project of a lifetime. Nearly four decades later, there is not one empty compartment left: in fact, several objects (secured with blue tack) are crammed into some of the larger slots, while others have started spilling onto the outer frame. It is now home to over a hundred items, each one of which carries a unique story and evokes a translational connection with a special person, place, or time. Some come directly from other trays in the family: the red soldier, the miniature Big Ben, and a tiny Harrods shopping bag used to be displayed in Lauren's grandma's tray. You can see two thumbnail photographs in one of the central compartments: these are Grandma Regina and Grandpa Salvatore, both dead for many years, previously remembered in their daughter's tray, and now in their granddaughter's. Lauren's mother Diane, who enjoyed hand crafts, made a few further items especially for her, including a tiny festive wreath and a miniature Easter basket. Originally parts of a dollhouse that no longer exists, they carry memories of happy childhood moments mixed with the awareness of the inevitability of the passing time. The tray's translationality is wonderfully transgenerational. Young Lauren, to her mom's disbelief, could read the smallest print in the miniscule Bible sitting in one of the bottom compartments—she can no longer do it but now our ten-year-old son occasionally amazes us with this skill. Some memories concern very specific events: once, after a heated argument with her mom, a teenage Lauren stormed out and went for a drive to calm down; stepping into a small store to browse, still fuming, she saw two figurines of Alice and the Mad Hatter, and could not ignore the symbolic irony; she brought both home for a cathartic laugh, and the two Wonderland characters have since lived in the mother's and daughter's respective trays, tied with an invisible link of rage, forgiveness, love, and laughter.

The tray's translationality extends into other pasts. Several items come from mine, not Lauren's: a stained glass window I have had as long as I can remember, a painted mini-jar I got from a high-school friend I have not seen in thirty years.

Others are parts of our joint family history. The plaque with a cheesy quote came from my mother; the wooden cat from my grandmother (again, two women of previous generations). The little white oval rock was found by our then three-year old who insisted it was a "dinosaur eggie"; the tiny Harry Potter and Hermione Granger are gifts from our elder son, hinting at his cultural inspirations at the time. Some fragile items had to be carefully glued together more times than I can count—a testament to the irresistible attraction of mom's magical tray. We do not have a daughter, so the future of this tray is uncertain at the moment: but I am sure that it will continue to ooze translationality for our boys, connecting them to their own pasts and that of their family's, evoking memories as well as links with important people, some of whom they never had a chance to meet.

The material properties of this printer's tray—its small compartments can only fit tiny artefacts—makes it translational in itself. Unlike some bulky pieces of furniture or elements of décor that you remember from your family home but could never take with you when leaving, it is designed to be moved: originally, slide in and out; today, from one place to another. No wall is too small to display it. The miniscule dimensions of the objects carried by the tray additionally compound their translational density: full-size memories and relationships must squeeze into bits of matter no larger than a thumbnail. This is translationality at an atomic level, so to speak. These tiny objects are the smallest independent memory-building units. They cannot be subdivided without losing their translational power. They can only be translated on, given to someone else to be displayed in their tray. Following such a transfer, an empty compartment in one person's printer's tray is just as meaningful as a newly filled one in another's. This translates directly into their value: the most precious objects are those received from a person of special significance. They are effectively family relics. But the tray is not a sealed reliquary: every now and then, a new piece is added to the collection. There is even a degree of seasonal rotation: a few special Christmas and Easter pieces that normally live in a separate box are once a year solemnly translated to the tray for a festive display.

This tray's value, especially to Lauren, but also to all our family, is incalculable, even if its strictly commercial worth is negligible (similar trays, complete with "vintage and handmade curios", retail online for the price of a modest restaurant dinner for two). It is the kind of thing that you would instinctively try to take with you when evacuating your house in an emergency, right after you made sure that your loved ones are safe. If it were lost, some of its items could be replaced—our boys would find another rocky egg or buy one more Hogwarts character—but others could not, not least because their donors have since died. This kind of personal value inscribed in otherwise common objects is sometimes called "sentimental" but I do not think that this word—with some of its maudlin, schmaltzy connotations—adequately captures this translationality. This printer's tray makes you want to smile at your memories, not weep over a bygone past. It makes you stronger, not weaker; it acts as a visible, tangible repository of personal and family history, giving you calm confidence of who you are, a material memory of your roots. This, of course, makes it non-translational and untranslatable for strangers (who can only view it as a collection of cute curiosities) and only partially translatable for new family members (like me)—and that in direct proportion to the effort and commitment invested in becoming a part of someone's life, and making them a part of yours. The force of this kind of translationality becomes evident in the wake of life's dramatic turns and losses: translational objects may become unbearable and need to be borne out of view (often into a basement or an attic, to be put away but not disposed of). In this way, translation plays a therapeutic role.

Translationality in music

If translationality consists of an experiential sense of connection, some of its most immediate examples may be found in music. One dimension of musical translationality could be called diachronic. With a possible exception of improvisation (which also employs certain patterns), playing a familiar piece of music is an act of re-enactment, recreation, and remembering. All live performances of the same song are slightly different and yet recognisable as its instantiations or versions. In fact, this is how textual translation (in particular, the relationship between the source and the target text) is sometimes conceptualized:

> I think that translation is like a melody played on a different instrument or in a different key. Bach's *Air on a G-string* which was written for violin, will remain recognisable, even if played on a trombone and in the key of B flat. Some arrangements can be almost as good as Bach's. But they can never produce exactly the same sound.
>
> *(Davies 2003: 6)*

Importantly, this similarity or recognisability is gradable and listener-dependent, which highlights the hermeneutic character of experiencing music, and translationality in general. Each performance of a song—even by the same artist or band—somehow invokes and echoes previous presentations. That is why audiences at concerts burst into applause upon hearing the familiar opening chords: this is predictive applause, so to speak, expressing excitement at what is about to happen, rather than rewarding a completed performance. At the same time, one can imagine a series of arrangements progressively departing from the initial melody whose echoes get fainter and fainter to the point of becoming only discernible by some listeners as references, hints, or memories.

This system of relationships between artists, listeners, and musical compositions gets even more complex when we realize that pieces of music are not always performed by the original composers. It is especially true in classical and orchestral music: a composer cannot play all the instrumental parts himself or herself (and definitely not synchronously). In this sense, a premiere performance of a symphony is already a translation: it is a collective effort of multiple agents, carrying out the artistic vision of the composer.

And then there is the question of covers: pieces of music transferred—or shall we say, translated?—between artists. Generally speaking, copyright law regulates the issue of ownership in music rather strictly. Every now and then we hear of high-profile lawsuits to establish the degree of similarity between certain compositions competing for originality. The reliance of one piece on another is usually settled by demonstrating a chronological succession: an earlier composition obviously cannot be inspired by a later one.

However, this chronological and authorial logic does not always work, especially when some translationality effects emerge. Some songs become more strongly identified with the coverer than with the composer, and are perceived as "more authentic" in their iconic rather than the original version. For example, "With a Little Help from My Friends" was originally recorded by the Beatles in 1967 but became an anthem of the Woodstock era only when performed by Joe Cocker a year later. Many view the Beatles' version of this song not as the "original" but as a cover, despite its chronological primacy (a logical paradox notwithstanding). Similarly, the song "Hurt" was released by Nine Inch Nails in 1995 but only when covered by Johnny Cash in 2002, with a video featuring images from Cash's life, did it reach massive worldwide acclaim: in 2011, it was voted greatest video of all time by *New Musical Express*.[1] Trent Reznor, the composer of the song, described his reaction when he first received the recording of the cover thus:

> I listened to it and it was very strange. It was this other person inhabiting my most personal song. I'd known where I was when I wrote it. I know what I was thinking about. I know how I felt. Hearing it was like someone kissing your girlfriend. It felt invasive.
>
> *(Vinnicombe 2008)*

However, it was only when the aural experience was complemented by a visual narrative that the translational link to Cash became irresistible. Cash was seventy-one years old and had serious health problems at the time of making the video; his frailty is clearly visible and adds a new layer of poignancy to the lyrics ("What have I become/my sweetest friend/everyone I know/goes away in the end"). This is how Reznor recalls his own experience:

> Anyway, a few weeks later, a videotape shows up with Mark Romanek's video on it. ... I pop the video in, and ... wow. Tears welling, silence, goose-bumps ... Wow. I just lost my girlfriend, because that song isn't mine any more. Then it all made sense to me. It really made me think about how powerful music is as a medium and art form. I wrote some words and music

in my bedroom as a way of staying sane, about a bleak and desperate place I was in, totally isolated and alone. Some-fucking-how that winds up reinterpreted by a music legend from a radically different era/genre and still retains sincerity and meaning—different, but every bit as pure.

(Reznor and Rickly 2004)

It is noteworthy that Reznor recognizes the authenticity of his song's translation by Johnny Cash (aurally) and the makers of the video (visually) based on his psychosomatic reaction. His conscious reflection on losing his exclusive authorial connection with "Hurt" to Cash is experientially validated by "tears welling, silence, goosebumps"—though, as one journalist wryly remarked, "the royalty cheques presumably didn't hurt either" (Vinnicombe 2008). Our earlier discussion of authenticity as an experiential, pragmatically constructed notion (see Chapter 3) is relevant here: it may easily bypass considerations of origins, authorship, and chronology. For hundreds of millions of online viewers, "Hurt" is Johnny Cash's poignant swan song—which became even more powerful when he died only seven months after filming (his wife, June Carter, who also features in the video, four months before him) and the house that provided the main location, their home for 35 years, was destroyed in a fire four years later (BBC 2007). I have no doubt that the enormous success of this audiovisual experience is due to its translationality. At the time of writing, the video on youtube has attracted over 170,000,000 views and more than 70,000 comments, many of which highlight a sense of personal connection with the song's message: it carries them back to their own pasts, both remembered and imagined. I would suggest that describing an experience as "moving" is nothing else than recognizing its translationality, a power to carry you over.

Guitars all around

Meanwhile, powerful musical translationality is not just successfully harnessed in the show business. It may also be experienced individually, privately, and apart from any obvious economic considerations, as my own example illustrates. To prevent any misconceptions, I need to stress that I do not consider myself a musician, and definitely not a performer. The thought of playing in front of any audience fills me with dread, bringing to mind the memories of occasional compulsory performances that I had to endure during the brief period of my formal musical training. Brief, because the circumstances of my growing up were somewhat complicated. As a young child, and then a teenager, I had to spend extended periods of time in hospital, which made my regular schooling as well as any extracurricular activities rather patchy. I was able to take some piano and guitar lessons but they were so irregular that I effectively had to teach myself how to play both instruments. As a result, my technique leaves something to be desired, my musical education is full of gaps (many of which I probably do not even realize), and my playing is guided by intuition rather than knowledge.

Yet, my imperfect skills notwithstanding, playing music and experimenting with sounds give me one of the most immediate experiences of translationality. The connections extend in several directions. First and foremost, it is how I connect with myself. Various people have their ways of releasing tension, relaxing and regaining an internal sense of balance. For me, this often comes through a musical instrument, especially the guitar. Playing an instrument is a thoroughly psychosomatic experience: it involves the body as well as the mind. With time and practice, some elements of technique become instinctive and nearly automatic. Musicians sometimes speak about their fingers "remembering" certain scales, chord shapes and licks: this is exactly how it feels. In fact, some people with severe dementia and Alzheimer's disease are able to play musical compositions they had mastered in the past, even though they claim they do not know or remember them. This demonstrates that instrumental skills are internalized and encoded as holistic bodily operations. A large part of learning how to play an instrument is developing this sensory, haptic prowess and gradually detaching it from a conscious mental effort. You have only mastered a scale when you can play it perfectly amidst distractions, without actively paying attention to the progression of notes. This aspect of practicing an instrument is similar to meditation exercises: engaging in a repetitious physical activity that gives you that reassuring sense of routine, of following a familiar path, thereby encouraging mindfulness. Practicing scales, passages, and phrases can be a bit tedious, but it can also be meditative. However, I am not suggesting that all contemplative activities are necessarily translational. This one is to me—not only because it integrates the physical and the mental, the near-automatic and the aesthetic, the repetitive and the creative, but also because it fosters a sense of ontological continuity, a processual identity, a connection with myself from another time.

For reasons I cannot quite explain, I have always been drawn to the guitar. It is there in some of the earliest and happiest memories of my childhood: the bedtime routine of listening to stories read and songs sung to me and my sister by our father to the familiar sound of his beat-up nylon-string guitar. More than forty years later, I still remember some of these songs, complete with some improvised verses in which we tried to capture the adventures of the day. The music was not particularly refined—my father knew only a handful of basic chords—but it was an inseparable element of being together, safe, warm, and happy. And a little sleepy, too; a big part of the guitar's magic is that it can be played very softly (had my father played the trombone for us at bedtime, the experience would have been rather different). Today, reading stories and singing partially improvised songs is part of my own children's bedtime routine. I usually bring a guitar and play it gently as we chat, after the lights go out, about our favourite moments of the day. This is a wonderfully anchoring ritual for us as parents: no matter how stressful the day, we close it with a few minutes of calm with our kids, focusing on the important rather than urgent stuff. To me, the guitar is a prominent element of this ambience—so much so that when we travel and the suitcase space is precious, I still manage to pack a ukulele to keep our kids' bedtime routine away from home. This creates a translational loop, so to speak: the bedtime music carries with it a memory of home (when away), and memories of fun times elsewhere (when back home), experientially integrating the new and the familiar. Material and metaphorical journeys occur at the same time, though in opposite directions.

This mention of material considerations, including size and portability, signals some of the most powerful aspects of guitar-inspired translationality. The guitar, as far as I am concerned, is not only a musical instrument but also a fascinating artefact. Of course, this is true of many other instruments that regardless of their actual playability are often displayed in homes, hotels, pubs, restaurants, and similar venues simply for their aesthetic qualities (think of the Hard Rock Cafe chain and its collection of rock-and-roll memorabilia). Musical instruments, along with weapons and toys, must be among the oldest artefacts of any civilisation. Some part of the guitar's translationality has to do with its material history: the technology of production, availability of materials and tools, craftsmanship and artisanship, and so on. The fact that guitars are mostly made of wood highlights a strong connection to the natural environment—as well as some conservational concerns (for example, the trade of rosewood, historically used for fingerboards, is currently under some restrictions).[2] Crucially, their materiality is mediated by all channels of sensory perception. In addition to their tonal qualities, visual appeal is a major factor in guitar design and manufacturing. As we saw in Chapter 4, electric guitars in particular come in a broad spectrum of individuating shapes and colours, as well as with purely decorative elements such as body and neck binding, fingerboard inlays, headstock ornaments, and so on. Some guitars may become collectible items purely for their exquisite artisanship. They may embody different canons of beauty—defined by condition, wear, vintage features, and a host of other criteria.

Still, for many guitarists the most important question is how the instrument "feels". This composite experience, often conceptualized as "playability", obviously covers the sound (though this is determined largely by customisable electronic components and their adjustable settings) as well as the visual properties, but is chiefly determined by the haptic experience which includes the perception of weight and its distribution, body shape (including ergonomic contours, such as the "belly cut" on the back of the Stratocaster), neck profile and finish, fingerboard curvature, fret height and thickness, action (the distance between the strings and the fingerboard), and so on. In mass-produced guitars, most of these features are standardized—and designed to suit the most widespread preferences—and contemporary instruments are remarkably consistent, but even guitars of exactly the same model and specification will display subtle individuating features, their unique "aura". These are not attributable to differences in quality but rather to personal tastes and even more elusive factors, often described as a sense of connection with the instrument, or lack of such felt connection—a classic case of *je ne sais quoi*. To complete this brief overview of full sensory experience, we should note that guitars, especially newly crafted ones, may also appeal to smell, usually by a pleasant mixture of a woody scent with notes of paint and lacquer. Gustatory appeal is definitely the rarest, but it cannot be ruled out entirely. If the metaphorical image of "licks" (short improvised phrases) is not enough, think of Jimi Hendrix at the Monterey Pop Festival in 1967, playing the solo in "Hey Joe" with his teeth![3] There you have it: all five senses conspire to create a truly holistic material experience. On top of all this, the guitar is an extremely corporeal instrument—with a body, neck, head(stock), and a (tremolo) arm—that can be played in various positions: sitting down, standing up, and even walking around, carried by the player as an extension of his or her body. Given this material transferability, no wonder it is so thoroughly translational.

This generic translational potential of the guitar traceable to its material properties, in my experience branches out into two main strands of translationality. The first one is tied to the characteristics of particular models identifiable with specific artists and their distinctive tones (a cherry-red Gibson ES-335 brings to mind Chuck Berry, a white flipped-over Stratocaster is Jimi Hendrix's iconic instrument, and so on). This link is maximally exploited for commercial gain by Custom Shops through artists' signature models and limited editions, as was demonstrated it detail in Chapter 4. But even mass-produced standard models can give you a basic, reasonably approximated experience of how it feels to play—or simply hold—*a guitar like* Jimmy Page's or Carlos Santana's: how it sits in your lap, how much it weighs, how the neck feels, how you reach the controls. This is similar to sitting in a cockpit of an airplane, holding the rudder of a sailboat, or climbing into the cabin of a DeLorean—"Oh, so that's what it feels like!"—except that the experience mediated by a guitar is normally more private and available for free at the nearest music store that allows browsing. If you like it and are prepared to pay for it, you can take it home. With some practice, a few relatively inexpensive pieces of equipment, and willingness to experiment, you can recreate a sound that translationally evokes a particular artist, song or solo. Inseparable from the WHAT is the HOW: you want to emulate the iconic tone, not just the progression of notes. The electric guitar, when paired with a modulation amplifier and/or a pedal board, offers a dizzyingly broad tonal spectrum, allowing you to create a private simulacrum of a favourite artist.

Of course, by far the most important element of this emulation is the player's technique, not the equipment: great musicians can create magic using a few pieces of string attached to a cigar box.[4] In fact, this kind of "roots music" employing primitive, self-made instruments is often perceived as prompting immediate, irresistible translationality. One of the comments under Steve Arvey's mesmerizing YouTube video "Intense Blues Played on a Cigar Box Guitar from New Album Mississippi Diaries" reads: "Music that has local roots, will cross international barriers. These blues touched my soul. And I am a Brazilian! I am sure even Martians will enjoy this legit true soulful music".[5] This is the power of translationality capable of crossing not just international barriers but interplanetary distances.

This somewhat abstract, visual-haptic-tonal translational potential of the guitar is in my own experience complemented by a second strand of translationality, tied to specific instruments. Over the years, I have gathered a small collection of guitars. None of them come from the Custom Shop; in fact, most are budget versions of more expensive instruments. I select them as a player, not an investor. The precise number is fluid and there is some degree of rotation, but the underlying economy is so strongly translational that I can hardly think of a more fitting example for the concluding part of this chapter, and indeed the entire book. Let me unravel some of these threads.

The black electroacoustic Yamaha APX-4 (top left in Figure 5.2) holds a special place in my collection. It is the oldest of them all, and by a lot. I have had it since I was nineteen years old: the reason why I remember this so precisely is that it was a birthday present. I was spending the summer of 1995 in hospital, waiting for yet another surgery and then recovering from it. Meanwhile, my elder sister Marta found a summer job at a nursing home in Berlin, and on coming back decided to use nearly all of the money she earned to buy me a guitar. At the time, I owned a cheap guitar from the Polish state-owned manufacturer Defil whose quality was appalling: it was hardly playable at all, would not stay in tune

FIGURE 5.2 A collection of guitars.
A photograph by the author

for longer than two minutes, and produced discouragement rather than excitement—but nothing else was available (or accessible to my family). It is hard to describe my surprise, gratitude and elation when I realized that my sister's extraordinary gift could buy me a *real* guitar. After a few long weeks of waiting—first, for a maximally favourable exchange rate between the Deutsche Mark and the Polish zloty, and then, for a special discount at the Western-stocked music store in Wrocław—I was finally able to secure a beautiful, single cutaway Yamaha of the newly launched electroacoustic range. It was the most basic and cheapest model in the line—but it felt like an object from another planet. It was lovingly translated for me, the fullest sense of the word: at the time, I could only walk with crutches, so my sister had to carry the guitar for me from the store. For the next twenty years, it was my main and only guitar, played so much that the frets and the fingerboard are significantly worn out. Its story inscribes it with rich, powerful translationality: a link to an important person and her love for me, a time filled with both pain and excitement, a true dream-come-true moment. I do not play it very often anymore but would never let go of it.

The two-tone sunburst Squier Stratocaster (top centre in Figure 5.2) is the second oldest in the collection, and has a special story, too. One day in the spring of 2012, an absent-minded walk through the centre of Belfast brought me to the door of a music store. I did not intend to buy anything—money was tight anyway—but after I held this particular 50s Classic Vibe model for a few moments, I realized that I would be making a huge mistake should I walk out of the store without it. Even though it is a budget version of the Stratocaster ("designed and backed by Fender" but made in China and priced accordingly), I was only able to afford it because it was discounted (which allowed me to buy a cheap amp, too). I knew full well that buying it meant a diet of toast and baked beans for several weeks to come, but in some way these were the happiest weeks during the otherwise darkest time in my life. This guitar re-kindled my love of playing music; at that point, my Yamaha APX had been sitting in its case for several years and I was badly out of practice. My Squier Strat reminded me what music meant to me. I would play it for hours on end as I tried to keep my sanity and struggled to put myself back together again—today it feels like an old friend who stuck by my side when I needed them most. Over the years, I have made a few modifications and upgrades, both technical and aesthetic, which made it uniquely mine (I even learnt how to solder!). As a 1950s Classic Vibe model, it has the added translational connection to the early days of the electric guitar and some of the iconic players of that era (such as Buddy Holly); it is a Squier lookalike of Eric Clapton's second-most famous guitar, "Brownie" (a 1956 Fender Stratocaster, "the Layla guitar"), which in his own words served as a prototype for "Blackie".[6] It is the guitar with which I have the strongest connection. I often instinctively reach for it first. It has become my personal benchmark of effortless playability. Still, I realize that much of this guitar's magic is the untranslatable translatability I attribute to it: for anyone else, it is a relatively inexpensive instrument, a top-of-the-range Squier but not nearly as desirable as a Fender.

192 The experience of translationality

This brings me to the Fender (bottom row, second left in Figure 5.2): the New American Standard Stratocaster in Bordeaux Metallic. Likely the most valuable part of my collection in monetary terms, it was another present at a key milestone moment. My wife's aunt Vera masterminded it as a surprise "welcome-to-the-family" gift (a classic example of distributed agency) for me at our wedding: a most unexpected, generous present with a highly personal touch. In addition to being a superbly refined instrument, it brings memories of celebration, the joy of finding true love and friendship, and starting our new journey together.

The honey burst Gibson Les Paul Tribute (top right in Figure 5.2) I bought second-hand at an online auction a few weeks after the birth of our younger son—at that unforgettable time in the parents' life when sleep deprivation and utter exhaustion is mixed with excitement of getting to know your new baby. The orange flamed maple top PRS SE Santana (bottom left in Figure 5.2), even though I bought it in my early forties, takes me back to high school times and makes me think of Robert Frost's "the road not taken" (try a career in music or go to university? If I had chosen the former, I would likely never have come across Frost).

Most recently, the long isolation of the pandemic was sweetened by a few new acquisitions: the huge, opulent semi-hollow ebony black Epiphone Sheraton II PRO (bottom row, second from the right in Figure 5.2), bringing a translational link to B.B. King and John Lee Hooker (who used to call it "an out-did 335", suggesting that it surpasses its Gibson twin),[7] and a walnut Squier Starcaster Classic Vibe (bottom right in Figure 5.2)—a wonderfully effortless semi-hollow player with an unusual offset design, that I immediately bonded with and have since kept in my university office to enjoy on a daily basis.

This sense of "bonding", often mentioned by guitarists in reviews, is perhaps another dimension of the guitar's translationality. If you look closely at the photograph, you will see that each of my guitars has a plectrum stuck between the strings at one of the lower frets. They are all ready to be picked up and played at any moment; none is kept in a case or hung in an awkward spot. As I put up guitar hangers throughout the house, I was not primarily guided by display potential but by easy access.

A few guitars did not make it into the photograph. I am still unsure if I will keep them for good, or trade them in for others. A helpful way of thinking about this bond is to apply a hypothetical fire or flood test: if I could only take with me a few guitars when evacuating the house in an emergency, which ones would I pick up first? They are precious to me in various ways and for different reasons, but this mental experiment equalizes all differences. The order of preference is likely to reflect the depth and strength of translationality, however construed.

Other translationalities

As I have argued throughout this book, translationality is that aspect of material culture that experientially connects us to other people, places, times, and sensations. I have given two extended examples from my own immediate context—a printer tray's and a guitar collection—but I realize that despite my efforts to make them relatable, these may not seem relevant enough to you. In any event, I hope you will be encouraged to look for signs of translationality in various other domains and across practices in which this felt connection will manifest itself for you.

For some people, translationality will be evoked visually by photographs, either printed or displayed on their smartphones: material or digital witnesses of places visited, people encountered, and experiences had. For others, this effect will come through haptic contact with meaningful objects: souvenirs, gifts, cards or books. For many, translationality will likely be mediated aurally by music and poetry, or by various hybrid forms of artistic expression. The translational effects of food are getting increasingly more recognition these days (e.g. Chiaro and Rossato 2015; Cronin 2015; Vidal Claramonte and Faber 2017; Demirkol Ertürk 2022): among other things, researchers explore the power of gustatory stimuli and especially familiar flavours in evoking memories and fostering a sense of cultural identity and belonging. The idea of "comfort food" for those who have lost many other elements of not just their comfort but also safety zone—such as involuntary migrants and refugees—is especially poignant (e.g. Ciribuco 2020).

This multi-sensory translationality is by definition experiential; as such, it will always be tied to *someone's*—but not *everyone's*—experience. Precisely because of this highly individual, subjective, and personal perception, we need more research into all kinds of translationality effects so that we can understand them better. This quest dovetails with a broad range of studies conducted from philosophical, psychological, sociological, anthropological, historical, semiotic, cognitive, artistic, and many other perspectives—all asking questions about the material aspects of meaning making. I hope that this survey of corporeal translations and their echoes in a range of contemporary cultural practices will inspire further explorations into others kinds of translations and what they do.

Even if you are inclined to hold on to a more traditional view of translation as verbally mediated cross-cultural encounter, you may want to consider that good or successful translations are those that offer us precisely this sense of strong, meaningful link across time and space. Interestingly, within such a traditional, textual paradigm, that peculiar translational strength is still best accounted for in broadly psychosomatic rather than narrowly semantic terms. The poet and translator Stanisław Barańczak, in his "Small but maximalist translatological manifesto" (1990, 11), insists that good translations of poetry are those that bring "an unstoppable tear, an uncontrollable chuckle, or an ecstatic thrill felt down's one spine" (Blumczynski 2021: 227). I can see no reason why translationality inspired by a poetic or literary work should be regarded as qualitatively different from other similar psychosomatic experiences, or as somehow privileged among them. As far as I am concerned, there is no "translationality proper".

Notes

1 https://www.nme.com/list/100-greatest-music-videos-1097 Accessed 31 October 2022.
2 https://www.andertons.co.uk/cites-law-guitarists Accessed 31 October 2022.
3 https://www.youtube.com/watch?v=CiR36mDzqVI Accessed 31 October 2022. I am grateful to James Maxey for bringing this example to my attention.
4 An excellent example of Cigar Box Guitar mastery is Steve Arvey (https://www.youtube.com/c/SteveArvey).
5 https://www.youtube.com/watch?v=uNvDLfgWzNI Accessed 31 October 2022.
6 https://www.youtube.com/watch?v=BEBsDiuHF_A Accessed 31 October 2022.
7 https://richtonemusic.co.uk/epiphone-sheraton-ii-pro-ebony/ Accessed 31 October 2022.

REFERENCES

Ambrose. 1896. "Some of the Principal Works of St. Ambrose." Translated by R. De Romestin, E. de Romestin and H.T.F. Duckworth. *Nicene and Post-Nicene Fathers*, second series, vol. X, edited by Philip Schaff and Henry Wace. Edinburgh: T&T Clark.

Ambrosius. No date. "Epistola XXII." *Sancti Ambrosii Mediolanensis Episcopi Epistolae In Duas Classes Distributae*, vol. 1: 1019–1025. https://www.documentacatholicaomnia.eu/04z/z_0339-0397__Ambrosius__Epistolae_Prima_Classis__MLT.pdf.html.

Anonymous. 1980. "An Anonymous Greek Account of the Transfer of the Body of Saint Nicholas from Myra in Lycia to Bari in Italy." Translated by J. McGinley and H. Mursurillo. *Bolletino di S. Nicola*, N. 10, *Studi e testi*, Bari 3–17. https://sourcebooks.fordham.edu/basis/nicholas-bari.asp.

Armstrong, Guyda. 2016. "Response by Armstrong to 'Translation and the Materialities of Communication'." *Translation Studies* 9 (1): 102–106.

Arponen, Aki, Heli Maijanen, and Visa Immonen. 2018. "From Bones to Sacred Artefact: The Late Medieval Skull Relic of Turku Cathedral, Finland." *Temenos* 54 (2): 149–183.

Athanasius. 1892. "Select Writings and Letters of Athanasius, Bishop of Alexandria." Translated by Archibald Robertson. *Nicene and Post-Nicene Fathers of the Christian Church*, edited by Philip Schaff and Henry Wace, second series, vol. IV. Edinburgh: T&T Clark.

Aymard, Orianne. 2014. *When a Goddess Dies. Worshipping Ma Anandamayi after Her Death*. Oxford: Oxford University Press.

Bachmann-Medick, Doris. 2007. *Cultural Turns. Neuorientierungen in den Kulturwissenschaften*. 2nd edition. Reinbek: Rowohlt.

Bachmann-Medick, Doris. 2009. "Introduction: The Translational Turn." Translated by Kate Sturge. *Translation Studies* 2 (1): 2–16.

Bachmann-Medick, Doris. 2012. "Translation – A Concept and Model for the Study of Culture." In *Travelling Concepts for the Study of Culture*, edited by Neumann Birgit, and Ansgar Nünning, 23–43. Berlin: De Gruyter.

Bagnoli, Martina, Holger A. Klein, C. Griffith Mann, and James Robinson. 2011. *The Treasures of Heaven. Saints, Relics and Devotion in Medieval Europe*. London: The British Museum.
Baker, Mona. 2019. *Translation and Conflict. A Narrative Account*. London: Routledge.
Baker, Mona, and Gabriela Saldanha (eds). 2020. *The Routledge Encyclopedia of Translation Studies*. 3rd edition. London: Routledge.
Bal, Mieke. 2002. *Travelling Concepts in the Humanities: A Rough Guide*. Toronto: University of Toronto Press.
Barad, Karen. 2007. *Meeting the Universe Halfway: Quantum Physics and the Entanglement of Matter and Meaning*. Durham: Duke Unviersity Press.
Barańczak, Stanisław. 1990. "Mały, lecz maksymalistyczny manifest translatologiczny." *Teksty Drugie* 3: 7–66.
Baron, Arkadiusz and Henryk Pietras (eds). 2001. *Dokumenty Soborów Powszechnych*. Vol. I (325–737). Kraków: Wydawnictwo WAM.
Bartlett, Robert. 2013. *Why Can the Dead Do Such Great Things? Saints and Worshippers from the Martyrs to the Reformation*. Princeton: Princeton University Press.
Bartmiński, Jerzy. 2009. *Aspects of Cognitive Ethnolinguistics*. Edited by Jörg Zinken. Translated by Adam Głaz. London: Equinox.
Bassnett, Susan, and David Johnston. 2019. "The Outward Turn in Translation Studies." *The Translator* 25 (3): 181–188.
BBC. 2007. "Fire Destroys Johnny Cash House." 11 April.http://news.bbc.co.uk/1/hi/entertainment/6543503.stm (Accessed 16 October 2022).
BBC. 2012. "Dublin Patron Saint's Heart Stolen from Christ Church Cathedral." https://www.bbc.co.uk/news/world-europe-17248394 (Accessed 14 April 2021).
BBC. 2022. "The Queen's Funeral Watched by 28 Million Viewers in UK." https://www.bbc.co.uk/news/entertainment-arts-62966616 (Accessed 21 September 2022).
Beal, John, James Coriden, and Thomas Green (eds). 2000. *New Commentary on the Code of Canon Law*. Mahwah: Paulist Press.
Benjamin, Walter. 2012 [1923]. "The Translator's Task." Translated by Steven Rendall. In *The Translation Studies Reader*, 3rd edition, edited by Lawrence Venuti, 75–83. New York: Routledge.
Benjamin, Walter. 2019. "The Work of Art in the Age of Mechanical Reproduction." Translated by Harry Zohn. In Walter Benjamin, *Illumination: Essays and Reflections*, edited and with an introduction by Hannah Arendt, 166–195. Boston: Mariner Books.
Bennett, Karen. 2019. "Conclusion: The Veiled Guest: Translation, Hospitality and the Limits of Hybridisation." In *Hybrid Englishes and the Challenges of and for Translation: Identity, Mobility and Language*, edited by Karen Bennett and Rita Queiroz de Barros, 197–215. London: Routledge.
Berger, John. 1972. *Ways of Seeing*. London: BBC and Penguin Books.
Berman, Antoine. 1984. *L'Épreuve de l'étranger. Culture et traduction dans l'Allemagne romantique*. Paris: Gallimard.
Berman, Antoine. 2008. *L'âge de la traduction. "La tâche du traducteur" de Walter Benjamin, un commentaire*. Saint Denis: Presses Universitaires de Vincennes.
Bernard, Jean-Frédéric. 1731. The Religious Ceremonies and Customs of the Several Nations of the Known World. Volume II: *The Ceremonies of the Roman Catholicks*. London: Nicholas Prevost. https://play.google.com/books/reader?id=pGlZAAAAYAAJ&pg=GBS.PP1.
Berns, Ute. 2009. "The Concept of Performativity in Narratology. Mapping a Field of Investigation." *European Journal of English Studies* 13 (1): 93–108.

Blumczynski, Piotr, and Ghodrat Hassani. 2019. "Towards a Meta-Theoretical Model for Translation. A Multidimensional Approach." *Target* 31 (3): 328–351.
Blumczynski, Piotr, and Hephzibah Israel. 2018. "Translation and Religious Encounters." In *The Routledge Handbook of Translation and Culture*, edited by Sue-Ann Harding and Ovidi Carbonell Cortés, 207–222. London: Routledge.
Blumczynski, Piotr. 2016a. *Ubiquitous Translation*. London: Routledge.
Blumczynski, Piotr. 2016b. "Translation as an Evaluative Concept." In *Translating Values. Evaluative Concepts in Translation*, edited by Piotr Blumczynski and John Gillespie, 327–349. London: Palgrave Macmillan.
Blumczynski, Piotr. 2019. "Translational Roots of Western Essentialism." In *Languages – Cultures – Worldviews: Focus on Translation*, edited by Adam Głaz, 159–182. Basingstoke: Palgrave Macmillan.
Blumczynski, Piotr. 2020. "Bible, Jewish and Christian." In *Routledge Encyclopedia of Translation Studies*, edited by Mona Baker, and Gabriela Saldanha, 3rd edition, 40–46. London: Routledge.
Blumczynski, Piotr. 2021. "Polish. A Congenial Collaboration." In *Raids & Settlements. Seams Heaney as Translator*, edited by Marco Sonzogni and Marcella Zanetti, 206–228. Wellington: The Cuba Press.
Bostock, David (ed.) 1994. *Aristotle Metaphysics Books Z and H*. Oxford: Clarendon Press.
Braun, Joseph. 1911. "Pallium." In *The Catholic Encyclopedia*, edited by Charles G. Herbermann, Edward A. Pace, Condé B. Pallen, Thomas J. Shahan, and John J. Wynne. Vol. XI, 427–429. New York: The Encyclopedia Press.
Brazinski, Paul, and Allegra Fryxell. 2013. "The Smell of Relics: Authenticating Saintly Bones and the Role of Scent in the Sensory Experience of Medieval Christian Veneration." *Papers from the Institute of Archaeology* 1 (1) Article 11: 1–15. DOI: http://dx.doi.org/10.5334/pia.430.
Brodzki, Bella. 2007. *Can These Bones Live? Translation, Survival, and Cultural Memory*. Stanford: Stanford University Press.
Brown, Jeff. 2011. "Early Christian Decision-Making: And Now for the Vote." *Sharper Iron*. https://sharperiron.org/article/early-christian-decision-making-and-now-for-vote (Accessed 27 August 2022).
Brown, Peter. 1981. *The Cult of the Saints: Its Rise and Function in Latin Christianity*. Chicago: University of Chicago Press.
Bryant, Levi R. 2011. *The Democracy of Objects*. Ann Arbor: Open Humanities Press.
Burkette, Allison. 2016. "Response by Burkette to 'Translation and the Materialities of Communication'." *Translation Studies* 9 (3): 318–322.
Burns, James Patout Jr. 2001. *Cyprian the Bishop*. London: Routledge.
Calvin, John. 1989. *The Institutes of the Christian Religion*. Transl. Henry Beveridge. Grand Rapids: William B. Eerdmans.
Cambridge Dictionary. 2022. "Material." https://dictionary.cambridge.org/dictionary/english/material.
Camden, William. 1695. *Camden's Britannia Newly Translated into English, with Large Additions and Improvements*. Published by Edmund Gibson. London: F. Collins. http://name.umdl.umich.edu/B18452.0001.001.
Campbell, Emma, and Robert Mills (eds). 2012a. *Rethinking Medieval Translation. Ethics, Politics, Theory*. Cambridge: D. S. Brewer.

Campbell, Emma, and Robert Mills. 2012b. "Introduction. Rethinking Medieval Translation." In *Rethinking Medieval Translation. Ethics, Politics, Theory*, edited by Emma Campbell and Robert Mills, 1–20. Cambridge: D. S. Brewer.

Campbell, Madeleine, and Ricarda Vidal (eds). 2019a. *Translating across Sensory and Linguistic Borders: Intersemiotic Journeys between Media*. Cham: Palgrave Macmillan.

Campbell, Madeleine, and Ricarda Vidal (eds). 2019b. "Entangled Journeys—An Introduction." In *Translating across Sensory and Linguistic Borders: Intersemiotic Journeys between Media*, edited by Madeleine Campbell and Ricarda Vidal, xxv–xliv. Cham: Palgrave Macmillan.

Chesterman, Andrew. 1997. *Memes of Translation. The Spread of Ideas in Translation Theory*. Amsterdam: John Benjamins.

Chesterman, Andrew. 2020. "Transfer Troubles." In *Transfer Thinking in Translation Studies: Playing with the Black Box of Cultural Transfer*, edited by Maud Gonne, Klaartje Merrigan, Reine Meylaerts, and Heleen van Gerwen, 207–223. Leuven: Leuven University Press.

Chiaro, Delia, and Linda Rossato. 2015. "Food and Translation, Translation and Food." *The Translator* 21 (3): 237–243.

Chua, Liana, and Mark Elliott (eds). 2013. *Distributed Objects. Meaning and Mattering after Alfred Gell*. Oxford: Berghahn.

Church of Ireland. 2018. "New Home for the Heart of St Laurence O'Toole in Christ Church Cathedral, Dublin." https://www.ireland.anglican.org/news/8387/new-home-for-the-heart (Accessed 14 April 2021).

Ciribuco, Andrea. 2020. "How Do You Say Kélén-kélén in Italian? Migration, Landscape and Untranslatable Food." *Translation Studies* 13 (1): 99–115,

Classen, Constance, David Howes, and Anthony Synnott. 1994. *Aroma: The Cultural History of Smell*. London: Routledge.

Code of Canon Law. n.d. https://www.vatican.va/archive/cod-iuris-canonici/cic_index_en.html.

Coldiron, A. E. B. 2016. "Response by Coldiron to 'Translation and the Materialities of Communication'." *Translation Studies* 9 (1): 96–102.

Collinet, Annabelle, Sepideh Parsapajouh, and Michel Boivin. 2020. "Bodies & Artefacts. Relics and Other Devotional Supports in Shiʿa Societies in the Indic and Iranian Worlds: An Introduction." *Journal of Material Cultures in the Muslim World* 1: 191–198.

Cooke, Simon. 2009. "English as a Foreign Literature. Travelling Concepts in English Studies in Europe." *European Journal of English Studies* 13 (1): 25–41.

Corrington, Robert S. 1996. "A Web as Vast as Nature Itself." Review article. *Semiotica* 111 (1/2): 103–115.

Coughlan, Sean. 2017. "'Santa's Bone' Proved to Be Correct Age." https://www.bbc.co.uk/news/education-42239197 (Accessed 31 October 2022).

Cronin, Michael, and Sherry Simon. 2014. "Introduction: The City as Translation Zone." *Translation Studies* 7 (2): 119–132.

Cronin, Michael. 2015. "The Moveable Feast: Translation, Ecology and Food." *The Translator* 21 (3): 244–256.

Cronin, Michael. 2020. Review of *A (Bio)Semiotic Theory of Translation: The Emergence of Socio-Cultural Reality* by Kobus Marais. *Translation Studies* 13 (3): 371–374.

Cyprian. 1964. *The Fathers of the Early Church. St Cyprian, Letters 1–81*. Translated by Sister Rose Bernard Donna, C.S.J. Washington: The Catholic University of America Press.

Davies, Norman. 2003. "Foreword." In Elżbieta Tabakowska, *O przekładzie na przykładzie. Rozprawa tłumacza z EUROPĄ Normana Daviesa*, 6–15. Kraków: Znak.

Deely, John. 1994. *The Human Use of Signs or: Elements of Anthroposemiosis*. Lanham: Rowman and Littlefield.

Deely, John. 2009. *Purely Objective Reality*. Berlin and New York: De Gruyter.

Demirkol Ertürk, Şule. 2022. "Remembering the Multilingual: Translation, Memory and Food in *Amida's Table Fare*." *Perspectives* 30 (1): 57–70.

Duffy, Eamon. 2018. *Royal Books and Holy Bones: Essays in Medieval Christianity*. London: Bloomsbury Continuum.

Dziennik. 2016. "Nuncjusz apostolski odsłonił w warszawskim muzeum relikwię – kajak św. Jana Pawła II." https://wiadomosci.dziennik.pl/wydarzenia/artykuly/517834,nuncjusz-apostolski-odslonil-w-warszawskim-muzeum-relikwie-kajak-sw-jana-pawla-ii.html (Accessed 14 April 2021).

Eastman, David L. 2018. "The Cult of Saints." In *The Oxford Handbook of Early Christian Ritual*, edited by Risto Uro, Juliette J. Day, Rikard Roitto, and Richard E. DeMaris. DOI: doi:10.1093/oxfordhb/9780198747871.013.40.

Easton, Burton Scott. 2020 [1934]. *The Apostolic Tradition of Hyppolytus. Translated into English with Introduction and Notes*. Cambridge: Cambridge University Press. https://www.gutenberg.org/files/61614/61614-h/61614-h.htm.

Edwards, Kathleen. 1959. "The Social Origins and Provenance of the English Bishops during the Reign of Edward II." *Transactions of the Royal Historical Society* 9: 51–79. https://doi.org/10.2307/3678805.

Federici, Eleonora (ed.) (in collaboration with Manuela Coppola, Michael Cronin and Renata Oggero). 2011. *Translating Gender*. Berne: Peter Lang.

Fender Custom Shop. 2022. *Custom Guitar Design Guide*. https://www.fmicassets.com/sites/fender.com/themes/img/customshop/2022/2022_Custom_Shop_Design_Guide.pdf.

Fisher, Ian. 2004. "In a Gesture of Conciliation, the Pope Returns Orthodox Relics." *The New York Times*, 28 November 2004, national edition, 31.

Flanagan, Eimer. 2019. "Irish Cult of Relics a Case of the Head vs the Heart." https://www.bbc.co.uk/news/world-europe-47525605 (Accessed 14 April 2021).

Freeman, Charles. 2011. *Holy Bones, Holy Dust: How Relics Shaped the History of Medieval Europe*. New Haven: Yale University Press.

Gagov, Giuseppe M. 1948. "Uso e significato del terme corpus nell'antica agiografia cristiana." *Miscellanea Francescana* 48: 51–73.

Garceau, Ben. 2018. "The *Fidus Interpres* and the Fact of Slavery: Rethinking Classical and Patristic Models of Translation." *Translation Studies* 11 (3): 349–364.

Geary, Patrick J. 1978. *Furta Sacra: Thefts of Relics in the Central Middle Ages*. Princeton: Princeton University Press.

Geary, Patrick J. 1986. "Sacred Commodities. The Circulation of Medieval Relics." In *The Social Life of Things. Commodities in Cultural Perspective*, edited by Arjun Appadurai, 169–191. Cambridge: Cambridge University Press.

Gell, Alfred. 1998. *Art and Agency. An Anthropological Theory*. Oxford: Clarendon Press.

Glimm, Francis X., Joseph M.-F. Marique, and Gerald G. Walsh. 1947. *The Apostolic Fathers*. Washington: The Catholic University of America Press.

Gonne, Maud, Klaartje Merrigan, Reine Meylaerts, and Heleen van Gerwen (eds). 2020. *Transfer Thinking in Translation Studies: Playing with the Black Box of Cultural Transfer*. Leuven: Leuven University Press.

Goodspeed, Edgar J. 1950. *The Apostolic Fathers: An American Translation*. London: Independent Press Ltd.

Guldin, Rainer. 2010. "Metaphor as a Metaphor for Translation." In *Thinking through Translation with Metaphors*, edited by James St. André, 161–191. London: Routledge.
Harding, Sue-Ann. 2020. "Travelling Theory." In *The Routledge Encyclopedia of Translation Studies*, edited by Mona Baker and Gabriela Saldanha, 3rd edition, 611–615. London: Routledge.
Hartranft, Chester D. 1890. "Sozomenus: Church History from A.D. 232–425." *Nicene and Post-Nicene Fathers*, second series, vol. II, edited by Philip Schaff and Henry Wace. Edinburgh: T&T Clark.
Harvey, Sally Ashbrook. 2006. *Scenting Salvation: Ancient Christianity and the Olfactory Imagination*. Berkeley: University of California Press.
Hatch, Edwin. 1881. *The Organization of Early Christian Churches*. London: Rivingtons.
Hefele, Charles Joseph. 1883. *A History of the Christian Councils, from the Original Documents to the Close of the Council of Nicaea A.D. 325*. Trans. William R. Clark. Edinburgh: T&T Clark.
Hess, Hamilton. 2002. *The Early Development of Canon Law and the Council of Serdica*. Oxford: Oxford University Press.
Highfield, John Roger Loxdale. 1956. "The English Hierarchy in the Reign of Edward III." *Transactions of the Royal Historical Society* 6: 115–138. https://doi.org/10.2307/3678843.
Hoffman, Eva. 1998 [1989]. *Lost in Translation: A Life in a New Language*. London: Vintage.
Hołub, Jacek. 2014. "Krew Jana Pawła II wędruje po świecie." https://wyborcza.pl/1,87648,15845593,Krew_Jana_Pawla_II_wedruje_po_swiecie__CZ__3_CYKLU.html (Accessed 14 April 2021).
Hooper, Steven. 2014. "Bodies, Artefacts and Images. A Cross-cultural Theory of Relics." In *Matter of Faith. An Interdisciplinary Study of Relics and Relic Veneration*, edited by James Robinson, Lloyd de Beer, and Anna Harnden, 190–199. London: British Museum.
House, Juliane. 2006. "Text and Context in Translation." *Journal of Pragmatics* 38: 338–358.
House, Juliane. 2014. "Introduction." In *Translation: A Multidisciplinary Approach*, edited by Juliane House, 1–14. Basingstoke: Palgrave Macmillan.
Hsiung, Ann-Marie. 2022. "Mulan's Travel from Ballad to Movie: A Case Study of Intermodal Translation." *Translation Studies* 15 (1): 69–83.
Irish Examiner. 2018. "Saint's Heart Returned to Dublin Cathedral as Thieves Thought It 'Cursed.'" https://www.irishexaminer.com/news/arid-30839586.html (Accessed 14 April 2021).
Israel, Hephzibah. 2011. *Religious Transactions in Colonial South India: Language, Translation and the Making of Protestant Identity*. Basingstoke: Palgrave Macmillan.
Jakobson, Roman. 1959. "On Linguistic Aspects of Translation." In *On Translation*, edited by Reuben A. Brower, 232–239. New York: Oxford University Press.
Jerome. 1892. "The Principal Works of St. Jerome." Translated by W.H. Freemantle, G. Lewis and W.G. Martley. *Nicene and Post-Nicene Fathers of the Christian Church*, edited by Philip Schaff and Henry Wace, second series, vol. VI. Edinburgh: T&T Clark.
Jerome. 2012. "Letter to Pammachius." Translated by Kathleen Davis. In *The Translation Studies Reader*, edited by Lawrence Venuti, 2nd edition, 21–30. New York: Routledge.
Jones, Benjamin. 2001. "Travel Advisory; A Modern Copy of Ancient Masters." *The New York Times*. 4 November 2001, 3.
Jones, Charles W. 1978. *Saint Nicholas of Myra, Bari and Manhattan. Biography of a Legend*. Chicago: The University of Chicago Press.
Jurgens, William A. 1979. *The Faith of the Early Fathers*. Volume 3. Collegeville: The Liturgical Press.

References

Kazan, Georges. 2018. "Exploring the Past through Relics: The Oxford Relics Research Cluster." *Material Religion* 14 (4): 570–572.

King James Version [of the Bible]. 1987. https://www.biblegateway.com/versions/King-James-Version-KJV-Bible/.

Korzybski, Alfred. 1933. *Science and Sanity. An Introduction to Non-Aristotelian Systems and General Semantics*. Lancaster: Science Press Printing Company. https://archive.org/details/sciencesanityint00korz/page/n7/mode/2up.

Kosick, Rebecca. 2016. "Response by Kosick to 'Translation and the Materialities of Communication'." *Translation Studies* 9 (3): 314–318.

Kowalski, Waldemar. 2015. "Piłsudski pośród królów – droga marszałka na Wawel." https://dzieje.pl/artykulyhistoryczne/pilsudski-posrod-krolow-droga-marszalka-na-wawel (Accessed 21 April 2021).

Koziol, Geoffrey. 1992. "Monks, Feuds, and the Making of Peace in Eleventh-century Flanders." In *The Peace of God: Social Violence and Religious Response in France around the Year 1000*, edited by Thomas Head and Richard Landes, 239–253. Ithaca and London: Cornell University Press.

Kracik, Jan. 1994. "Przemiany jakościowe kultu relikwii w starożytności i wczesnym średniowieczu." *Saeculum Christianum: pismo historyczno-społeczne* 1/2: 95–107.

Lagarde, Roy. 2018. "Saint John Paul II's Blood Relic up for Veneration Anew." http://www.filcatholic.org/saint-john-paul-iis-blood-relic-up-for-veneration-anew/ (Accessed 14 April 2021).

Laing, Rob. 2020. "Gibson Releases $10k Custom Shop Jimi Hendrix Flying V and SG Custom Guitars." https://www.musicradar.com/news/gibson-releases-dollar10k-custom-shop-jimi-hendrix-flying-v-and-sg-custom-guitars.

Lakoff, George, and Mark Johnson. 1980. *Metaphors We Live by*. Chicago: University of Chicago Press.

Littau, Karin. 2016. "Translation and the Materialities of Communication." *Translation Studies* 9 (1): 82–96.

Litwin, Maciej. 2023. "The Jakobson Controversy: Toward an Understanding of the Glottocentric Drift in Translation Studies." *Translation Studies*.

Marais, Kobus. 2019. *A Bio(Semiotic) Theory of Translation. The Emergence of Social-Cultural Reality*. New York: Routledge.

Marais, Kobus (ed.) 2022. *Translation beyond Translation Studies*. London: Bloomsbury.

Marinetti, Cristina. 2022. "Doubly Invisible: Anna Larpent, Domestic Censorship, and the Translation of Performance Cultures in Georgian Britain." *Translation Studies*, doi:10.1080/14781700.2022.2120064.

Mason, Ian. 2014. "Discourse and Translation – A Social Perspective." In *Translation: A Multidisciplinary Approach*, edited by Juliane House, 36–55. Basingstoke: Palgrave Macmillan.

Massardier-Kenney, Françoise. 2010. "Antoine Berman's Way-making to Translation as a Creative and Critical Act." *Translation Studies* 3 (3): 259–271.

Maxwell, Jackson. 2020. "Gibson Announces Jimi Hendrix 1969 Flying V, 1967 SG Custom Guitars." *GuitarPlayer*. https://www.guitarplayer.com/news/gibson-announces-jimi-hendrix-1969-flying-v-jimi-hendrix-1967-sg-custom-guitars.

McAlhany, Joseph. 2014. "Crumbs, Thieves, and Relics: Translation and Alien Humanism." *Educational Theory* 64 (5): 439–461.

McGregor, Richard J.A. 2020. *Islam and the Devotional Object: Seeing Religion in Egypt and Syria*. Cambridge: Cambridge University Press.

McGuckin, John Anthony. 2001. *St. Gregory of Nazianzus: An Intellectual Biography*. Crestwood: St Vladimir's Seminary Press.

McLynn, Neil B. 1994. *Ambrose of Milan: Church and Court in a Christian Capital*. Berkeley: University of California Press.

Meri, Josef W. 2010. "Relics of Piety and Power in Medieval Islam." *Past and Present* 206: 97–120.

Michałowski, Roman. 1981. "Le don d'amitié dans la société carolingienne et les 'Translationes sanctorum'." In *Hagiographie, cultures et sociétés IVe-XIIe siècle*, 319–416. Paris: Etudes Augustiniennes.

Michałowski, Roman. 1983. "Przyjaźń i dar w społeczeństwie karolińskim w świetle translacji relikwii." *Studia Źródłoznawcze – Commentationes* XVIII: 1–39.

Montagna, Diane. 2017. "Stolen Relic of St. John Bosco Recovered." https://aleteia.org/2017/06/16/breaking-stolen-relic-of-st-john-bosco-recovered/ (Accessed 15 April 2021).

Morosini Codex https://engineeringhistoricalmemory.com/post/?p=7909.

Mościcki, Ignacy. 1935. "Przemówienie prezydenta podczas pogrzebu J. Piłsudskiego na Wawelu." https://pilsudski.org.uk/archiwa/dokument.php?nrar=709&nrzesp=1&sygn=17&handle=709.238/327 (Accessed 21 April 2021).

Nafte, Myriam. 2015. "Institutional Bodies: Spatial Agency and the Dead." *History and Anthropology* 26 (2): 206–233.

NBC News. 2004. "Vatican Returns Relics of Saints to Istanbul." https://www.nbcnews.com/id/wbna6588646 (Accessed 16 April 2021).

Neumann, Birgit, and Ansgar Nünning (eds). 2012. *Travelling Concepts for the Study of Culture*. Berlin: De Gruyter.

New Catholic Encyclopedia. 1967. *Volume X: Mos to Pat*. New York: McGraw-Hill Book Company.

New International Version [of the Bible]. 2011. https://www.biblegateway.com/versions/New-International-Version-NIV-Bible.

New Revised Standard Version [of the Bible]. 2021. Updated edition. https://www.biblegateway.com/versions/New-Revised-Standard-Version-Updated-Edition-NRSVue-Bible/.

Nicol, Donald M. 2008. *Byzantium and Venice. A Study in Diplomatic and Cultural Relations*. Cambridge: Cambridge University Press.

O'Connor, Anne. 2021. "Translation and Religion: Issues of Materiality." *Translation Studies*. doi:10.1080/14781700.2021.1893805.

Oder, Sławomir and Saverio Gaeta. 2014. *Zostałem z Wami. Kulisy procesu kanonizacyjnego Jana Pawła III*. Bytom: Wydawnictwo Niecałe.

Owens, Joseph. 1963. *The Doctrine of Being in the Aristotelian Metaphysics: A Study in the Greek Background of Mediaeval Thought*. Toronto: Pontifical Institute of Mediaeval Studies.

Oxford English Dictionary. 2022. "Translate, v[erb]." https://www.oed.com/view/Entry/204841 (Accessed 30 October 2022).

Pas, Justine M. 2013. "Language and Belonging in the Polish Translation of Eva Hoffman's *Lost in Translation*." *Translation Studies* 6 (1): 64–77.

Peng-Keller, Simon. 2019. "Genealogies of Spirituality: An Historical Analysis of a Travelling Term." *Journal for the Study of Spirituality* 9 (2): 86–98.

Percival, Henry R. 1886. "The Seven Ecumenical Councils of the Undivided Church." *Nicene and Post-Nicene Fathers of the Christian Church*, edited by Philip Schaff and Henry Wace, second series, vol. XIV. Edinburgh: T&T Clark.

References

Piłsudski, Józef. 1935. "Na wypadek nagłej śmierci." https://pilsudski.org.uk/archiwa/dokument.php?nonav=1&nrar=709&nrzesp=1&sygn=2&handle=709.238/25 (Accessed 21 April 2021).

Pym, Anthony. 2010[1992]. *Translation and Text Transfer.* https://www.google.com/url?sa=t&rct=j&q=&esrc=s&source=web&cd=&ved=2ahUKEwjJxpDq0Ij7AhWOY8AKHWqjBNgQFnoECBEQAQ&url=https%3A%2F%2Fusuaris.tinet.cat%2Fapym%2Fpublications%2FTTT_2010.pdf&usg=AOvVaw2bwPkJ-IC09u_wr0c6r-Hd (Accessed 30 October 2022).

Pym, Anthony. 2014. *Exploring Translation Theories.* 2nd edition. London: Routledge.

Reuters. 2020. "Relic of Pope John Paul II's Blood Stolen from Italian Cathedral." https://www.reuters.com/article/us-italy-pope-relic-idUSKCN26F2W1 (Accessed 14 April 2021).

Reynolds, Matthew (ed.) 2019a. *Prismatic Translation.* Cambridge: Legenda.

Reynolds, Matthew. 2019b. "Introduction." In *Prismatic Translation,* edited by Matthew Reynolds, 1–18. Cambridge: Legenda.

Reznor, Trent, and Geoff Rickly. 2004. "Geoff Rickly Interviews Trent Reznor." *Alternative Press,* 26 June. https://www.theninhotline.com/archives/articles/manager/display_article.php?id=11 (Accessed 31 October 2022).

Ricoeur, Paul. 1990. *Time and Narrative.* Vol. 3. Translated by Kathleen Blamey and David Pallauer. Chicago: University of Chicago Press.

Roberts, Alexander, James Donaldson and A. Cleveland Coxe. 1885. *Fathers of the Third and Fourth Centuries: Lactantius, Venantius, Asterius, Victorinus, Dionysius, Apostolic Teaching and Constitutions, Homily, and Liturgies.* Ante-Nicene Fathers, Vol. VII, edited by Philip Schaff. Grand Rapids: Eerdmans.

Robinson, Douglas. 1991. *The Translator's Turn.* Baltimore: The Johns Hopkins University Press.

Robinson, Douglas. 2001. *Who Translates? Translator Subjectivities beyond Reason.* Albany: State University of New York Press.

Robinson, Douglas. 2017. *Translationality. Essays in the Translational-Medical Humanities.* London: Routledge.

Rushdie, Salman. 1982. "Imaginary Homelands." *London Review of Books* 4 (18), 7 October. https://www.lrb.co.uk/the-paper/v04/n18/salman-rushdie/imaginary-homelands.

Santoro, Gene. 1986. "The Mojo Man Rocks Out." *Guitar World,* March 1986, reprinted (2006) in *Guitar Legends: The Rolling Stones.*

Schleiermacher, Friedrich. 1813/2012. "On the Different Methods of Translating." Translated by Susan Bernofsky. In *The Translation Studies Reader,* edited by Lawrence Venuti, 3rd edition, 43–63. London: Routledge.

Sender, Ron, Yinon M. Bar-On, Shmuel Gleizer, Biana Bernshtein, Avi Flamholz, Rob Phillips, and Ron Milo. 2021. "The Total Number and Mass of SARS-CoV-2 Virions." *Proceedings of the National Academy of Science USA* 118 (25): e2024815118. doi:10.1073/pnas.2024815118.

Shackleford, Tom. 2020. "*Gibson Recreates Jimi Hendrix's 1969 Flying V & 1967 SG Custom Guitars.*" https://liveforlivemusic.com/news/jimi-hendrix-guitar-auction/ (Accessed 31 October 2022).

Shuler, Eric. 2010. "The Saxons within Carolingian Christendom: Post-conquest Identity in the Translationes of Vitus, Pusinna and Liborius." *Journal of Medieval History* 36 (1): 39–54.

Sinha, Chris, and Kristine Jensen de López. 2001. "Language, Culture, and the Embodiment of Spatial Cognition." *Cognitive Linguistics* 11 (1–2): 17–41.

Smith, Julia M. H. 1990. "Oral and Written: Saints, Miracles, and Relics in Brittany, c. 850–1250." *Speculum* 65 (2): 309–343. https://www.jstor.org/stable/2864295.

Smykla, Dagmara. 2020. "*To była krew Jana Pawła II. Nie do wiary, co się stało.*" https://www.o2.pl/informacje/to-byla-krew-jana-pawla-ii-nie-do-wiary-co-sie-stalo-6575224947346400a (Accessed 14 April 2021).

Sommar, Mary Ellen. 1998. "The Changing Role of the Bishop in Society: Episcopal Translation in the Middle Ages." Unpublished PhD disseration. Syracuse University. *History – Dissertations* 27. https://surface.syr.edu/hst_etd/27.

Spring, Michael. 2015. *Sacred Bones: Confessions of a Medieval Grave Robber*. San Francisco: Four Winds Press.

Stahuljak, Zrinka. 2012. "Medieval Fixers: Politics of Interpreting in Western Historiography." In *Rethinking Medieval Translation: Ethics, Politics, Theory*, edited by Emma Campbell and Robert Mills, 147–163. Cambridge: D. S. Brewer.

Steiner, George. 1998. *After Babel: Aspects of Language and Translation*. 3rd edition. Oxford: Oxford University Press.

Strathern, Marilyn. 1988. *The Gender of the Gift*. Berkeley: University of California Press.

Strong, John S. 2007. *Relics of the Buddha*. Delhi: Motilal Banarsidass.

Super Express. 2011. "Ksiądz z Legionowa wypożycza wiernym relikwiarz z zębem Jana Pawła II. Przyjmij do domu relikwię papieża." https://www.se.pl/wiadomosci/polska/ksiadz-legionowa-wypozycza-wiernym-relikwiarz-z-zebem-jana-pawla-ii-przyjmij-do-domu-relikwie-papiez-aa-j5mC-rRnQ-dP6s.html (Accessed 20 September 2022).

Sywenky, Irene. 2014. "(Re)constructing the Urban Palimpsest of Lemberg/Lwów/Lviv: A Case Study in the Politics of Cultural Translation in East Central Europe." *Translation Studies* 7 (2): 152–169.

Taute, Harry A., Jeremy J.Sierra, Larry L.Carter, and Amro A.Maher. 2017. "A Sequential Process of Brand Tribalism, Brand Pride and Brand Attitude to Explain Purchase Intention: A Cross-continent Replication Study." *Journal of Product & Brand Management* 26 (3): 239–250. doi:10.1108/JPBM-08-2016-1289.

The Independent. 2005. "Millions Mourn Pope at History's Largest Funeral." https://web.archive.org/web/20081201121502/http://www.independent.co.uk/news/world/europe/millions-mourn-pope-at-historys-largest-funeral-757246.html (Accessed 14 April 2021).

Thomas, Nicholas. 1998. "Foreword." In Alfred Gell, *Art and Agency. An Anthropological Theory*, vii–xiii. Oxford: Clarendon Press.

Toury, Gideon. 2012. *Descriptive Translation Studies – and beyond*. Revised edition. Amsterdam: John Benjamins.

Ugé, Karine. 1999. "Relics as Tools of Power: The Eleventh-century Inventio of St Bertin's Relics and the Assertion of Abbot Bovo's Authority." In *Negotiating Secular and Ecclesiastical Power: Western Europe in the Central Middle Ages*, edited by Arnoud-Jan A. Bijsterveld, Hendrik Teunis and Andrew Wareham, 51–71. Turnhout: Brepols.

Underhill, James W., and Mariarosaria Gianninoto. 2019. *Migrating Meanings: Sharing Keywords in a Global World*. Edinburgh: Edinburgh University Press.

United States Patent and Trademark Office (USPTO). 2009. *Trademark Trial and Appeal Board Inquiry System*. "Opposition nos. 91161403 et al." https://ttabvue.uspto.gov/ttabvue/v?pno=91161403&pty=OPP&eno=246.

Vanderputten, Steven. 2011. "Itinerant Lordship. Relic Translations and Social Chance in Eleventh- and Twelfth-century Flanders." *French History* 25 (2): 143–163.

Venuti, Lawrence. 2019. *Contra Instrumentalism: A Translation Polemic*. Lincoln: University of Nebraska Press.

Vidal Claramonte, MªCarmen África, and Pamela Faber. 2017. "Translation and Food: The Case of *Mestizo* Writers." *Journal of Multicultural Discourses* 12 (3): 189–204.

Vidal Claramonte, MªCarmen África. 2022. *Translation and Contemporary Art. Transdisciplinary Encounters*. London: Routledge.

Vinnicombe, Chris. 2008. "Trent Reznor Talks Johnny Cash." *MusicRadar*, 5 August. https://www.musicradar.com/news/guitars/trent-reznor-talks-johnny-cash-168199 (Accessed 16 October 2022).

Wagner, Roy. 1991. "The Fractal Person." In *Big Men and Great Men: Personifications of Power in Melanesia*, edited by Maurice Godelier and Marilyn Strathern, 159–173. Cambridge: Cambridge University Press.

Wallace, Daniel B. 1996. *Greek Grammar beyond the Basics*. Grand Rapids: Zondervan.

Ward, Perceval. 1837. *Isle of Mann. And Diocese of Sodor and Mann. Antient and Authentic Records and Documents Relating to the History and Constitution of That Island*. London: Rivington. http://www.isle-of-man.com/manxnotebook/fulltext/wd1837/index.htm.

Watson, Nicholas. 2008. "Theories of Translation." In *Oxford History of Literary Translation in English*, Vol. 1, edited by Roger Ellis, 73–90. Oxford: Oxford University Press.

Watt, Jeffrey R. 2020. *The Consistory and Social Discipline in Calvin's Geneva*. Rochester: The University of Rochester Press.

Weckwerth, Andreas. 2021. "The Twenty Canons of the Council of Nicaea." In *The Cambridge Companion to the Council of Nicaea*, edited by Young Richard Kim, 158–176. Cambridge: Cambridge University Press.

Wheeler, Brannon. 2006. *Mecca and Eden: Ritual, Relics, and Territory in Islam*. Chicago: University of Chicago Press.

Wheeler, Tom. 2004. *The Stratocaster Chronicles. Celebrating 50 Years of the Fender Strat*. Milwaukee: Hal Leonard Collection.

Wilson, Stephen. 1983a. "Introduction." In *Saints and Their Cults: Studies in Religious Sociology, Folklore, and History*, edited by Stephen Wilson, 1–53. Cambridge: Cambridge University Press.

Wilson, Stephen. 1983b. "Annotated Bibliography." In *Saints and Their Cults: Studies in Religious Sociology, Folklore, and History*, edited by Stephen Wilson, 309–419. Cambridge: Cambridge University Press.

Wintroub, Michael. 2015. "Translations: Words, Things, Going Native, and Staying True." *American Historical Review* 120 (4): 1185–1217.

Wycherley, Niamh. 2015. *The Cult of Relics in Early Medieval Ireland*. Turnhout: Brepols.

Zlatev, Jordan, Timothy P. Racine, Chris Sinha, and Esa Itkonen (eds). 2008. *The Shared Mind: Perspectives on Intersubjectivity*. Amsterdam: John Benjamins.

Złożenie zwłok Adama Mickiewicza na Wawelu dnia 4go Lipca 1890 roku. Książka pamiątkowa z 22 ilustracyami. 1890. Kraków: Drukarnia Związkowa. https://sbc.org.pl/dlibra/publication/11165/edition/10416.

Zwischenberger, Cornelia. 2023. "On Turns and Fashions in Translation Studies and beyond." *Translation Studies* 16 (1): 1–16.

INDEX

AC/DC 150
agency 1, 16, 40–41, 43, 56, 62–63, 68, 70, 77–78, 84, 86, 89, 91, 129, 177–178, 192
Alexandria 45, 55, 57, 93, 111
Altamira caves 147–148, 170–171
Ambrose 83–87, 116, 119
Anthropocene 1
anthropology of art 40–41,146
Antioch 48, 55–57, 59, 61, 63, 65, 92–93
Antiochan Synod 56–57, 60–61
Arianism 45–46, 83, 86
Aristotle 22, 46
Arvey, Steve 189
Athanasius 57–58
auditory/aural sensations *see* hearing
aura 148–149, 155, 172, 188
authenticity 4, 6, 28, 76, 77, 80, 92, 100, 103, 105–113, 146–147, 149, 152–156, 158–169, 172, 178–179, 185–186
authority 4, 5, 16, 47–54, 61, 63–65, 68–71, 79–81, 88–91, 94, 106, 112, 114, 120, 136, 143, 176–177

Bachmann-Medick, Doris 16–19
Bal, Mieke 23
Barad, Karen 38–39
Barańczak, Stanisław 193
Bari 92–103, 108, 116–117
Barnabas, apostle 48
Bartholomew I, Ecumenical Patriarch 130, 132

Bartholomew, St 108–109
Bassnett, Susan 8, 10, 15, 31
Beatles 185
Beck, Jeff 150, 158
Beijing 141
Belfast 123, 182, 191
Benedict, St 96–97, 119
Beneventum 90
Benjamin, Walter 6, 148–149, 155, 167–168
Bennett, Karen 14
Berger, John 6, 145–146
Berry, Chuck 151, 189
Bible 156, 168–169, 182
bishops; deposition of 51–52, 65; succession of 50–54, 77; *see* translation of
"Blackie" (Eric Clapton's Fender Stratocaster) 6, 151–152, 166–171, 191
Blumczynski, L. 181–183
Blumczynski, Piotr 9, 31, 47
Brodzki, Bella 141–143, 179–180
Brown, Peter 90, 113–115, 117–118
Bryant, Levi 38–39

Calvin, John 68–71
Camden, William 67
Canterbury 65, 73, 119
Carthage 48, 51, 92
Cash, Johnny 185–186
celebration 111, 116, 119, 123, 125, 130–131, 137–139, 178, 192
celebrity endorsement 152–153

ceremony 50–51, 76–77, 79–81, 85, 88, 100, 112, 117, 125–126, 130–132, 135–136, 138, 143
Charles the Great (Charlemagne) 92, 120
Chaucer, Geoffrey 12, 105, 116
cheirotonia (laying on of hands) 47–50
Chesterman, Andrew 23–25, 27–28, 31
Chichester 67
Clapton, Eric 6, 150–152, 155, 158, 163, 166–171, 191
Clement 52, 53
Clooney, George 153
Cocker, Joe 185
Collins, Albert 150
complexity 34–35, 65, 78, 115, 171, 175
Constantine the Great 45–46
Constantinople (Istanbul) 59, 63, 65, 88, 103, 120, 129–132, 137
Corona 161
Counter-Reformation 5, 67, 71
COVID-19 pandemic 5, 39, 50, 75–77
Cray, Robert 163
Cronin, Michael 1, 5, 32–33
Cyprian 48, 51, 53, 54, 92

Dali, Salvador 157
Dawkins, Richard 27
Deely, John 37–38
DeLorean 189
distributed person 40, 102–103, 177
Drogheda 123
Dublin 123–126
Dylan, Bob 151, 158
Dziwisz, Cardinal Stanisław 126

Elizabeth II, Queen 134–135
energy 3, 12–13, 23, 25, 35, 39, 135, 157–158, 163–165, 167, 169
Ensenada 161
entanglement 5–6, 29, 34, 38–40, 64, 99, 142, 151, 176
Epiphone 192
Eucharist 47, 80, 88, 178
Evermarus, St 89
experience 4–7, 14, 18, 24, 26, 31, 34, 37–38, 41, 43–44, 79, 82, 107–108, 117–119, 135, 143–144, 146–149, 153, 156–157, 159–160, 163–164, 167, 171–172, 174–175, 178–180, 185–190, 193

Fender (guitar brand) 6, 150–164, 166–167, 169–170, 191–192

First Crusade 99–100
Flying V (Gibson) 164–165
Fourth Crusade 132–133
Fourth Lateran Council 109
Foy, St 109
Freeman, Charles 109, 120
Frost, Robert 192

Geary, Patrick 42, 106–107, 111, 113, 115, 122, 127
Gell, Alfred 6, 40–42, 146, 158, 166
Geneva 68, 69
Germain, St 90, 108, 120
Gibson (guitar brand) 149–150, 153, 156, 158–159, 164–166, 170, 189, 192
gift shop 146, 148–149, 172
Gilmour, David 150, 158
Glasgow and Galloway 75–77
Greek 9–10, 43, 45–48, 56, 92–93, 116, 129–130, 168
Gregory of Nazianzus, St 58–59, 102, 127, 129–133
guitar(s) 5, 19, 149–172, 186–193
gustatory sensations *see* taste

haptic sensations *see* touch
hearing (auditory/aural sensations) 5, 7, 34, 111–112, 130–131, 134–135, 140, 150–151, 160–165, 172, 179, 185–190, 193
Hendrix, Jimi 150–151, 160–161, 163–166, 170, 189
Hilary of Poitiers, St 91
Hoffman, Eva 79
Holly, Buddy 191
Holocaust 180
Hooker, John Lee 192

invariance 2, 23–24, 27, 142
Ireland 67, 123–125, 181

Jakobson, Roman 3, 4, 15–16, 22, 33
Januarius, St 90, 108, 111–112, 123
Jerome, St 87, 91
Jerusalem 55, 65
John Bosco, St 127
John Chrysostom, St 129–133
John Paul II, pope 126–130, 132, 135
Johnston, David 8, 10, 15, 31

Kaczyńska, Maria 136–137, 143n10
Kaczyński, Lech 136–138, 143n10

kairos/kairotic 6, 77, 116–119, 127, 151, 164–165, 178
King, B.B. 149, 192
King, Kaki 150
Knopfler, Mark 151
Korzybski, Alfred 8, 31
Kracik, Jan 102–103
Kraków 126, 136–140
Krause, Todd 157–158, 167

Latin 2, 5, 10–11, 34, 43, 46–48, 56, 62, 67–68, 79–80, 85, 87, 89, 92, 100, 129, 181
Latour, Bruno 38
Laurence O'Toole, St 123–126
Led Zeppelin 150
Lenin, Vladimir 141
Lennon, John 151
Leonardo da Vinci 145, 151, 157
Les Paul (Gibson) 150, 159, 192
Liberace 170
linguistic bias 4–5, 32
Littau, Karin 30
Litwin, Maciej 33
London 73, 134–135, 145

Madrid 147
Mammes, St 120
Manila 127–128
Mao Zedong 141
Marais, Kobus 3, 4, 32–37
Mark, St 93, 111
Martin of Tours, St 119
martyr(s) 37, 83–90, 97–98, 102, 110, 116, 119, 123, 133, 136
material turn 3, 30, 175
materiality 1–3, 5–7, 12–14, 17, 19–25, 29–30, 32, 36–40, 47, 57, 61, 64, 67, 78–82, 87–88, 107, 113, 123, 131–132, 135, 142, 144, 146, 149, 151, 156–158, 161–162, 164–165, 167–172, 175–175, 178–184, 188–189, 192–193
May, Brian 150
Mediolanum (Milan) 83–86, 90, 98, 116
memes 27–28
metaphor 8, 11–13, 16–30, 36–37, 40, 44, 91, 133, 149, 172, 174–175, 180, 188–189
Metheny, Pat 149
Mexico 128, 161
Michałowski, Roman 88, 112–114
Michelangelo 145, 157
Mickiewicz, Adam 137–138

miracle 42–43, 84–87, 90, 94–97, 106–108, 111–112, 119, 120, 123, 126, 128, 138, 145, 178
Mona Lisa 145, 151
Moore, Gary 151
Moscow 141
museum 5–6, 123–124, 126–127, 144–149, 151, 169, 172, 179
Myra (Demre) 66, 92–97, 99–101, 103, 108

Naples (Napoli) 90, 111–112, 123
New York 151–152, 167, 170–171
Nicaea 45, 47, 53–57, 59–62, 90
Nicene Canons 54–57, 59, 60–61, 62, 70
Nicene Council 45–47, 49, 53–57, 59, 61–62
Nicene Creed 45–47, 83
Nicephorus 92–93, 98
Nicholas, St 92–104, 108, 116
Nine Inch Nails 185
Norwich 73–74

O'Connor, Anne 14
Oder, Sławomir 128
olfactory sensations *see* smell
Oliver Plunkett, St 123
onomasiology 8–9, 28
ousia 45–46
outward turn 8
Oxford 73–74, 104

Page, Jimmy 150, 189
palimpsest 31, 175
pallium 79–82
Paris 68, 90, 137–139
Paschal I, pope 88
Patrick, St 123–124
Paul, apostle 48, 49, 53, 58, 59
Pearson, Kevin (bishop) 75–77
Peirce, Charles Sanders 32–36
Pepin the Short 120
periperforming 36, 40, 179, 189
Petty, Tom 150
Philibert, St 122
Picasso, Pablo 157
pilgrimage(s) 87, 90–91, 108–109, 114, 123–128, 141
Piłsudski, Józef 139–140, 143n
Pius XI, pope 140
Poitiers 91, 120
Poland 89, 97, 123, 126–127, 136–137, 139, 180
Polycarp 86–87

Popovič, Anton 35
Presley, Elvis 151
Prince 151
Princess of Wales 153
printer's tray 6, 180–183, 193
prismatic view of translation 28–29
procession 85, 107, 109, 111–112, 117, 129–131, 134–135, 140
prototype 11, 15, 27, 31, 35, 38, 116–117, 157–158, 166–168, 191
Pusinna, St 98
Pym, Anthony 24
Pyongyang 141

Queen (band) 150

Reformation 5, 67–69
relic 4, 6, 12, 14, 37, 40–43, 63, 72–73, 77–78, 83, 85–93, 96–133, 137–140, 142–143, 145–149, 151–153, 156–157, 159–163, 165–167, 169–172, 175–180, 183
reliquary 88–89, 105–106, 108–111, 117, 123–124, 127–130, 145, 148, 165, 179, 183
replica 6, 147–149, 159–160, 162–163, 165–172
representation 5, 9, 41, 102, 106–107, 109, 174
reproduction 24, 30, 148–149, 162, 166
respect 41–42
Reynolds, Matthew 28–29
Reznor, Trent 185–186
Rictrudis, St 121
Richards, Keith 151
Robertson, Robbie 158
Robinson, Douglas 4, 13–14, 35–36
Rolling Stones 151
Roman Empire 45, 51, 64–65, 83, 88, 92, 113–114
Rome 50–51, 55, 38, 79–80, 83, 87–88, 94, 102, 114–116, 123, 129–133, 145
Rushdie, Salman 27–28, 79

Santana, Carlos 150, 189, 192
Schleiermacher, Friedrich 91
Schrödinger, Erwin 38
semasiology 8–10, 12, 14, 21, 27–28, 36
semiotics 3, 5, 31–37, 40–41, 179
sensory perception 4–7, 11, 29–31, 34, 43, 107–108, 175, 179–180, 187–189, 193
Serdican Council 61
SG (Gibson) 150, 164–165

Shakespeare, William 27
Shepherd, Kenny Wayne 158
Shrewsbury 74
sight (visual sensations) 5, 7, 31, 106, 109, 125, 129, 148, 150–151, 159–160, 162–164, 172, 185–186, 188, 190, 193
Sistine Chapel 145, 157, 170
Słowacki, J. 138–139
smell (olfactory sensations) 4, 7, 11, 31, 99, 107–109, 130, 179, 189
Sommar, Mary 53, 57, 64
souvenir 146–147, 149, 172, 193
Springsteen, Bruce 150
Stalowa Wola 127
Starcaster 192
Steiner, George 13, 111, 133, 167
Stratocaster 6, 150–155, 158, 160–161, 163–164, 167, 171, 188–189, 191–192

tactile sensations *see* touch
taste (gustatory sensations) 7, 189, 193
Tedeschi, Susan 150
Telecaster 150, 154
Theodoret of Cyr 102
Thomas of Canterbury, St 119
Thomassin, Louis 64–65
touch (haptic/tactile sensations) 5, 42, 47–50, 77, 85, 87–88, 94, 108–109, 129, 157–158, 162, 165, 169, 172, 176, 179, 187–188, 190, 193
Tournus 122
Toury, Gideon 144
Townshend, Pete 151
transdisciplinarity 41
translatio studii et imperii 20–21, 43
translation proper 3–5, 10, 14–16, 18–21, 25–27, 29, 31, 35–36, 44, 142, 175, 193
translational turn 16–17
translation: of bishops 4–5, 12, 14, 41, 43, 55–67, 70–81, 171, 176–178; as elevation 6, 61–62, 79, 88, 90, 108, 120, 126, 136, 143n, 167, 178; as material transfer 2–5, 11–14, 17, 21–22, 24–25, 27, 36–37, 39, 43, 56–57, 60–61, 74–75, 78, 80–81, 85, 89, 91, 101, 113, 115, 117–119, 121, 131, 133, 135–136, 140, 142, 144, 149, 172, 175–178, 182, 189; as metaphorical transfer 2–3, 11–13, 21–24, 26–28, 43, 81, 142, 149, 167, 172, 175–176, 178, 182, 185; of relics 6, 13–14, 41, 85–122, 125–133, 177–178; of texts 3, 5, 10–14, 16–17, 19–20, 26–32, 35, 61, 78, 91, 105, 112–113,

122, 142, 156, 163, 167, 168–169, 175–176, 184, 193
translationality 4–10, 13–14, 32, 34–37, 41, 78–82, 135, 141, 143–144, 146–147, 149, 152, 157, 162–163, 165–167, 170–172, 174–175, 179–180, 182–193
transubstantiation 47, 88, 178
Trower, Robin 158
Turin Shroud 104–105

Urban II, pope 100

value 11, 16, 61, 81, 98–99, 105–107, 109, 111, 115, 125, 145–146, 149, 151, 153, 160, 161–163, 165–167, 169–172, 177–178, 183
Vanderputten, Steven 119–121
Vatican 80, 126–127, 132–133, 145, 170

Vaughan, Stevie Ray (SRV) 150, 163
Velázquez 147
Venice 93, 99–103, 111
Venuti, Lawrence 19–21, 26–27, 29
Vidal Claramonte, MªCarmen África 41
Vincent, St 115
visual sensations *see* sight
Vivian, St 108

Warsaw 126, 128, 136, 139–140
Waters, R. 158
Wawel Royal Castle, 136–140
Wintroub, Michael 174
World Trade Center 103
Wrocław 191

Young, Angus 150

Zwischenberger, Cornelia 18, 23

Printed in the United States
by Baker & Taylor Publisher Services